# Praise for *Warmed by the Fires*

A rare and sensitively written collection of writings inspired by the uniquely gifted psychoanalyst, Allan Frosch, a North American analytic clinician, teacher, thinker and writer of the highest caliber. Frosch's own papers demonstrate remarkable breadth and depth while carrying a humble brilliance that embodies the soul and wisdom of an authentic psychoanalytic genius. The essays by Frosch's colleagues, each bringing both a personal and scholarly perspective to the generous work of their late colleague, serve to illuminate his curious, independent-minded thinking across a wide range of analytic issues and ideas. What comes through, both in Frosch's writings and those of his interlocutors, is a love of psychoanalysis and learning. *Love* is the operative term for Allan Frosch's legacy – one that conveys intelligence, wit, an open-minded yet hard-headed pursuit of knowledge, and considerable integrity throughout his notable contribution in his writings – for his patients, and on behalf of his colleagues and students at IPTAR. I enthusiastically recommend this book for beginning and experienced analysts alike, and in particular for those who have yet to be acquainted with the treasures and warmth of Allan Frosch's unique fires.

**Michael J. Diamond, PhD,** is a training and supervising analyst, Los Angeles Institute and Society for Psychoanalytic Studies and author of several books including *My Father Before Me: How Fathers and Sons Influence Each Other Throughout Their Lives* and *The Second Century of Psychoanalysis: Evolving Perspectives on Therapeutic Action* (with Christopher Christian, PhD).

~

This memorial collection of 20 years of the writings and legacy of the late Allan Frosch has been lovingly compiled, with deep gratitude and appreciation, by Cancelmo, Monder, and Myers, his long time peer supervision group. Each of the chapters is prefaced by the "reflections" of colleagues who convey their deep respect for Frosch's teachings as well as for him as a leader and innovator. Frosch's thinking is deeply Freudian, intellectually brilliant, resonating with character and integrity. This is indeed a gift for the entire psychoanalytic community.

**Janice S. Lieberman, PhD**, is a training and supervising analyst and faculty at IPTAR, the author of *Body Talk: Looking and Being Looked at in Psychotherapy* and *Clinical Evolutions on the Superego, Body and Gender in Psychoanalysis*.

~

This is a brilliant and moving book about one man's engagement with the unique psychic world of each of his patients. It is clinically exciting, and the theory that informs each analytic encounter with the clinical is never stodgy or dogmatic but always "evenly hovering" between experience and the wish to grasp it. Each chapter is introduced by experienced colleagues who engage with Dr Frosch's ideas with great respect, but also with their own originality enriching the engagement. The result is a book full of brilliant ideas about the complexity of the psychoanalytic situation. There will be no readers of this remarkable book who will not be challenged to review all of their own psycho-analytic experience and learn from the courage of Dr. Frosch's work with the complexities of the human condition as we all encounter it hour by psycho-analytic hour. It is a book to cherish and be challenged by, which is surely what every great book hopes to achieve.

**Eugene Mahon, MD,** is a training and supervising analyst at the Columbia Psychoanalytic Center for Training and Research. He is the author of *A Psycho-analytic Odyssey, Rensal the Redbit,* and *Boneshop of the Heart.* He practices psychoanalysis in New York City.

~

In compiling this wonderful book, the editors have given us an invaluable gift. Allan Frosch's remarkable essays, innovative, insightful and rich with clinical wisdom, make an enduring contribution to analytic theory and practice. The book's original format with its use of scholarly introductions to the papers by a group of Frosch's peers, many themselves notable authors, only adds to its value. This is a book to be treasured by anyone seriously interested in analytic therapy.

**Theodore Jacobs, MD,** is a training and supervising analyst at the New York and IPE Psychoanalytic Institutes and author of *The Use of the Self: Counter-transference and Communication in the Analytic Situation* and *The Possible Profession: The Analytic Process of Change.*

# WARMED

## BY THE FIRES

*Selected Papers of*
## Allan Frosch

**IPBOOKS**.net
International Psychoanalytic Books

International Psychoanalytic Books (IPBooks),
Queens, NY
Online at: www.IPBooks.net

Frosch, A. (1995). The preconceptual organization of emotion. *Journal of the American Psychoanalytic Association,* 43:423–447.

Frosch, A. (1998). Narcissistic injury and sadomasochistic compensation in a latency-age boy. In P. Beren (Ed.), *Narcissistic disorders in children and adolescents: Diagnosis and treatment* (pp. 263-280). Northvale, NJ: Jason Aronson.

Frosch, A. (1999). The effectiveness of psychoanalytic therapy: The role of treatment duration, frequency of sessions and the therapeutic relationship (with J. Hoffenberg, N. Vorus & N. Freedman). *Journal of the American Psychoanalytic Association,* 47:741–772.

Frosch, A. (2002). Survival, symbolization and psychic space. In R. Lasky (Ed.), *Symbolization and desymbolization: Essays in honor of Norbert Freedman* (pp. 366-386). New York: Other Press.

Frosch, A. (2002). Transference, psychic reality and material reality. *Psychoanalytic Review,* 19:603–633.

Frosch, A. (2003). Psychic reality and the analytic relationship. *Psychoanalytic Review,* 90:599–614.

Frosch, A. (2003). Psychoanalytic treatment and patients' lives. In J. A. Dryer & M. A. Simmons (Eds.), *IPTAR at the dawn of the 21st century* (pp. 68-73). New York: IPTAR Press.

Frosch, A. (2006). Control cases and institutional responsibility: A creative or coercive process? *The Round Robin,* XXI, Winter.

Frosch, A. (2006). The culture of psychoanalysis and the concept of analyzability. *Psychoanalytic Psychology,* 23:43–55.

Frosch, A. (2006). Analyzability. *Psychoanalytic Review,* 93:835–843.

Frosch, A. (2012). The effect of frequency and duration on psychoanalytic outcome: A moment in time. *Psychoanalytic Review,* 98:11–38.

Frosch, A. (2012). Introduction. In A. Frosch (Ed.), *Absolute truth and unbearable psychic pain* (pp. xix-xxxi). London: Karnac.

Frosch, A. (2014). Psychoanalysis: The sacred and the profane. *The American Journal of Psychoanalysis,* 74:133–146.

Frosch, A. (2016). Warmed by the fires of the unconscious or burned to a crisp. *The American Journal of Psychoanalysis,* 76:111–121.

Cover photograph by Samantha Hale
Cover design by Kathy Kovacic
Interior book design by Maureen Cutajar, gopublished.com

ISBN: 978-1-949093-04-9

# TABLE OF CONTENTS

# Acknowledgements

We would like to acknowledge Allan's many colleagues, supervisees, and patients whose names do not appear in these pages but without their impact on his life, this book would not exist.

We would like to thank Allan for the final gift he gave us, his "study group pals." His decision to continue meeting in the face of imminent death allowed us to deepen beyond measure our understanding of the analytic process and the power of the analytic relationship.

Lastly, we would like to express our deep gratitude to Ruth Oscharoff for the keen intelligence and gentle spirit she provided us. Ruth was Allan's unwavering support throughout his life and through these many papers; this year she became ours.

# Editors and Contributors

## Editors

**Joseph A. Cancelmo, MSED, PsyD,** is Past President, Training and Supervising Analyst and Faculty of the Institute for Psychoanalytic Training and Research (IPTAR) and a Fellow of the International Psychoanalytical Association (IPA). He is a graduate of IPTAR's Socio-Psychoanalytic Organizational Training Program and currently serves as Co-Chair of *The Gould Center for Psychoanalytic Organizational Study and Consultation.* He maintains a private practice in New York City with adolescents, adults, couples, and in consultancy with executives and organizations.

**Batya R. Monder, MSW, BCD,** is a Training and Supervising Analyst at the Contemporary Freudian Society (CFS), a member of IPTAR and a Fellow of the IPA. From 2002 to 2007, she was Editor of *The Round Robin,* a psychoanalytic newsletter of Section I of Division 39 of the APA, and is currently a Curator of the online *Virtual Psychoanalytic Museum,* www.thevirtualpsychoanalyticmuseum.org, with IP Books. She maintains a private practice in New York City.

**Hattie B. Myers, PhD,** is Past Director of IPTAR's Clinical Center (ICC), Training and Supervising Analyst and Faculty of IPTAR, a Fellow of the IPA, and a graduate and participating member of the Washington Psychoanalytic Program, New Directions in Writing and Psychoanalysis. She is the Founder and Editor in Chief of the online magazine *Room: A Sketchbook for Analytic Action,* www.analytic-room.com. She maintains a private practice in New York City.

## Contributors

**Tessa Addison, LCSW**, is a practicing psychoanalyst in New York City, a graduate of IPTAR and a Fellow of the IPA.

**Sheldon Bach, PhD,** is Adjunct Clinical Professor of Psychology at the NYU Postdoctoral Program for Psychoanalysis, a Training and Supervising Analyst at CFS and IPTAR and a Fellow of the IPA. He is the author of several books on psychoanalysis and of many papers, some of which have been collected in *Chimeras and Other Writings: Selected Papers of Sheldon Bach*. He is in private practice and teaches in New York City.

**Phyllis Beren, PhD,** is a Training and Supervising Analyst, Faculty and the Director of the Child and Adolescent Training Program (CAP) of IPTAR. She is a Training and Supervising Analyst at CFS and a Fellow of the IPA. She maintains a private practice in psychoanalysis and psycho-therapy with children, adolescents, and adults in New York City. Publications include *Narcissistic Disorders in Children and Adolescents: Diagnosis and Treatment* (Ed.).

**MaryBeth M. Cresci, PhD, ABPP**, is the Director of the Postgraduate Programs in Psychoanalysis and Psychotherapy at the Gordon F. Derner School of Psychology at Adelphi University, Garden City, NY. She is a former President of the Division of Psychoanalysis (39) of the American Psychological Association (APA) and a Representative from that division to APA Council. She maintains a private practice in Brooklyn, NY.

**Elizabeth Cutter Evert, LCSW**, is in private practice in New York City. She is on the Faculty at IPTAR, a Fellow of the IPA and a Supervisor and Director of the ICC. She has published papers on female sexuality and on psychoanalysis, politics, and religion.

**Janet Fisher, PhD**, is a Training and Supervising Analyst and Faculty at IPTAR and a Fellow of the IPA. She has a private practice in psychoanalysis and psychotherapy in New York City, is on the editorial board of *Room:*

*A Sketchbook for Analytic Action*, www.analytic-room.com and is a member of the voluntary faculty of Mt. Sinai School of Medicine, Department of Psychiatry, Division of Psychotherapy.

**Richard B. Grose, PhD, LP**, after obtaining a Doctorate in Russian Studies from the University of Chicago, found his way to IPTAR, where he received his psychoanalytic training. He is a member of IPTAR, a Fellow of the IPA and has a practice in adult psychotherapy and psychoanalysis in New York City.

**Nancy R. Goodman, PhD**, is a Training and Supervising Analyst at CFS in Bethesda, MD. Many publications reflect her interest in trauma and symbolizing processes as well as female development and enactments: *Finding Unconscious Fantasy in Narrative, Trauma, and Body Pain: A Clinical Guide* and *The Courage to Fight Violence against Women* (both with Paula Ellman); *Battling the Life and Death Forces of Sadomasochism: Clinical Perspectives* (with Harriet Basseches & Paula Ellman); and *The Power of Witnessing: Reflections, Reverberations, and Traces of the Holocaust* (with Marilyn Meyers). She is Director of the online *Virtual Psychoanalytic Museum*, www.thevirtualpsychoanalyticmuseum.org, with IPBooks.

**Joan D. Hoffenberg, PhD,** is a Past President and former Dean of Training at IPTAR, where she is a Training and Supervising Analyst, and a Fellow of the IPA. She has also served as Director of the ICC. She is a psychologist and psychoanalyst in private practice in Brooklyn, NY.

**Phyllis F. Hopkins, PhD,** is past Dean of Training, Faculty and Training and Supervising Analyst at IPTAR and a Fellow of the IPA. She is in private practice in Stratford, CT.

**Richard Lasky, PhD, ABPP,** is a Training and Supervising Analyst and Faculty at IPTAR, a Clinical Professor of Psychology and a Training and Supervising Analyst at the NYU Postdoctoral Program, and a member of the Supervising Faculty of the Doctoral Program in Clinical Psychology at the City University of New York.

**Anthony Mazzella, PhD,** is a member of IPTAR, a past Director of the ICC and a Fellow of the IPA. He is on the faculty and is a supervisor at the Metropolitan Institute for Training in Psychoanalytic Psychotherapy (MITPP). He is a certified continuing education provider who has run close to forty workshops and has lectured to thousands of health care professionals on various topics that are related to working with the more challenging patient. He has taught at NYU and Fordham University.

**Michael Moskowitz, PhD,** is President and Training and Supervising Analyst at IPTAR and a Fellow of the IPA. He has written about psychoanalytic theory, race, ethnicity, and neuroscience. A recipient of the Gradiva Award for his contributions to psychoanalytic publishing, he was an associate producer of the film *Black Psychoanalysts Speak.*

**Ruth Oscharoff, LCSW,** is a member of IPTAR and a supervisor and instructor in the CAP Program. She is also a Training and Supervising Analyst at the National Psychological Association for Psychoanalysis (NPAP) where she was Director of the Clinical Center and twice President of the Training Institute. She is a Fellow of the IPA and has written and presented on transference. She is a psychoanalyst in private practice with adults and adolescents in New York City.

**Arnold Rothstein, MD,** is Faculty and was past Director at the Institute for Psychoanalytic Education (IPE) affiliated with NYU School of Medicine. He is the author of *The Narcissistic Pursuit of Perfection; The Structural Hypothesis: An Evolutionary Perspective; Psychoanalytic Technique and the Creation of Analytic Patients;* and *Making Freud More Freudian.*

**Jane Tucker, PhD,** is a member of IPTAR and a Fellow of the IPA. She is a Clinical Assistant Professor and Clinical Consultant at the NYU Postdoctoral Program in Psychotherapy and Psychoanalysis and is in private practice in New York City.

**Neal Vorus, PhD,** is a Training and Supervising Analyst and Faculty at IPTAR, a Fellow of the IPA and an Adjunct Clinical Assistant Professor in the NYU Postdoctoral Program in Psychotherapy and Psychoanalysis. He is also a Book Review Editor of *Psychoanalytic Psychology*. Dr. Vorus has written a number of papers on the integration of Contemporary Freudian and Modern Kleinian approaches on therapeutic action and technique. He has a private practice in New York City where he treats adults, adolescents and children.

# Memorial for Allan Frosch

## SHELDON BACH

In this age of totally strident narcissism, when some people live in golden penthouses and spend their days glorifying their own image, Allan Frosch was a humble man. Humble but not weak, for I have seen him fending off a room full of people while fighting for an idea of which he was the only proponent. He believed in good causes and he believed in people, and anyone who met him, even for the first time, knew that they had encountered a good man.

Allan and I worked together on cases for a few years, and it was a true collaboration in which each of us learned a lot. Apart from his empathy, his intuition, his interest in new ideas and his enormous desire to help, the one thing about him that stood out most of all for me was his dependability. You could count on him and you knew without having to worry about it that if Allan was seeing a patient, that patient was in good hands. Since so many of the people we see today have been fragmented by discontinuity and trauma, Allan's dependability was therapeutic and his presence was healing.

Allan was twice President of IPTAR, and he was one of the founding fathers of the IPTAR Clinical Center, both daunting tasks that he sustained with his usual calm resolve. For years he was always available to sit on a committee or to perform some other task that needed doing. Later in his professional life he became more interested in finding his own unique voice, and he published almost a dozen cogent, lovingly written papers. Many of these papers seem to me to have a moral or ethical quality that one finds only in the best writing in our field, and they all seem to point to a widening vision for psychoanalysis and a plea for open-mindedness in our analytic community.

In one of his last papers, "The Sacred and the Profane," Allan uses the concept of quantum entanglement as a metaphor for the relationship between patient and analyst. In quantum entanglement, two particles that have interacted or been intimately connected will continue to influence one another even long after they have separated. Allan compared this to many situations where, long after an analysis has been completed, the analysand may no longer be thinking much about the analyst, but she will still continue to feel that he is always with her. And I think that this is how many of us feel about Allan. We knew him and we grew to love him and we became intimately involved with him, and now, although we are separated by a great distance, we remain entangled with him forever.

# Commemorating Allan Frosch

### JANE TUCKER

Allan Frosch, who died on October 28, 2016, at the age of 78, was esteemed as a psychoanalyst, teacher, mentor and writer; he also was treasured as a friend and colleague. The qualities that brought him such high regard were evident: a keen intelligence, integrity, thoughtfulness, careful scholarship; he had a serious demeanor but was kind, warm, engaging and without self-importance. He also had a merry disposition and could be fun to be with.

It was apparent that psychoanalysis was the perfect field for Allan, and that he was deeply involved in and loved the work. I knew him best as a member of a small group in which we met together for nineteen years. Our mission was to read our way through the twenty-three volumes of the *Standard Edition of the Complete Psychological Works of Sigmund Freud.* We sought to question, clarify, explicate and appreciate what we read, and Allan excelled at the task. Our own experiences as clinicians contextualized our understanding, and as we went along we often brought up vignettes from treatments we each were conducting to provide illustrations or pose conundrums. Such instances offered a good sense of what Allan was like as a therapist, and how sensitive and astute an analyst he was. He'd had an early career as an actor, and that proclivity to capture the essence of another was carried forth into his analytic work, where it funded the empathic disposition that so well informed his clinical understanding.

As such long-enduring congenial collaborations can and must, ours came to go beyond the task at hand; we shared concerns that were personal and concerns that were political, and some particular topics came to be central to our discussions: What is the relationship between emotional development and the development of symbolic thought? What is the nature of unconscious communication? How do we come to know what we know in the treatment situation? What contributes to the emotional reactions that may arise in transference-countertransference constellations, and how may they ultimately enable understanding?

You will see in the papers collected here that Allan was intrigued by such questions and thought deeply about them. He made some very important points. Chief among them are that retranscriptions of meaning are essential to progress in psychoanalytic treatments, and that such transformations are unlikely to occur without the abiding affectionate concern of the analyst. He specified the steps that need to take place in order for the psychoanalytic process to build missing psychic structures, structures that allow for differentiation between self and object, thought and action, past and present, when the structures for such functions have been compromised. Those are assertions that speak to issues beyond the psychotherapeutic endeavor, they are fundamental to the understanding of cognitive and psychic development. Allan has offered clinical observations that support the concept that an object relational component is essential to the creation of mind and meaning: relationship is a catalyst that potentiates thought.

You will find in these papers also an appreciation of how we can use ourselves as instruments to locate meaning, and descriptions of clinical encounters that bring such phenomena into focus. Allan fully recognized the extent to which therapeutic action involves a mutual living through of the patient's experience, and how necessary it is to be open to that. He further wrote about the kinds of clinical interactions that can rile, torment, despair and dismay us, and reminded us how we could use what we register to move treatments forward. Additionally represented are Allan's thoughts on the parameters of the treatment situation and ideas on issues relevant to psychoanalytic education; those were abiding concerns as well.

Allan's intellectual and professional abilities were of the highest caliber, so too the moral and ethical sensibilities that characterized him. These papers convey much about what he had to offer. They are an impressive, important contribution to the literature, and they are a fine legacy; but Allan's smile, his wit, his intelligent conversation and the sweet pleasure of his company will always be missed.

# Introduction

JOSEPH A. CANCELMO, BATYA R. MONDER
AND HATTIE B. MYERS, CO-EDITORS

Like the analytic process, this project has been a labor of love, loss and internalization. It began when we compiled a spiral-bound compendium of Allan's writings on the occasion of his birthday, October 16, 2016. It was a moment of celebration, of honoring Allan and his work. But it was also the moment we faced our worst fears. A letting go of the hope he would be well again. The hope we could return to *before*.

When we presented Allan with the "published" volume from what we dubbed the *By Hook or by Crook Press,* he smiled broadly and teared up. First, he expressed his surprise and heartfelt appreciation— gave a big thanks to his study group pals. Then he turned to the Table of Contents. He counted the number of entries. He counted *twice*, his eyes wide with astonishment and delight. He clearly loved the gesture, proud but also embarrassed by his own riches, all at once. So Allan.

While we had read many of his papers over the past two decades, this project put us in touch with how closely our experience with him in our group tracked his theoretical understanding and developmental perspective. His quiet, keen listening style, his sensitive and unique conceptualization of the analytic relationship and process, his honest and open sharing of struggles and points of confusion and impasse were honed over the course of his writing. So it was in our study group: the clinical and pedagogical went hand in hand.

Allan treated us as analysts on our own unique developmental trajectory, and our group process was a mutual and collegial exchange of ideas and feedback. He always gave and received with a sensitivity, warmth and generosity of spirit. But Allan could also be direct and honest as well, delivering his thoughts with an empathic but firm hand that underscored the authenticity of his comments.

It was impossible to have been at The Institute for Psychoanalytic Training and Research (IPTAR) between 1977 and 2016 and not have crossed paths with Allan Frosch as a candidate, teacher, analyst, supervisor, or a leader. Allan was brilliant, modest, loyal, ironic and very funny. Above all, he was a man of integrity. Future generations of IPTAR candidates and members will not know Allan, but they will, unknowingly, be the recipients of the formative organizational impact Allan had on IPTAR's analytic culture. Here again, we see him thinking outside the box—his willingness to question existing structure both in analytic training and in the organizational structure of IPTAR, the place he trained as a psychoanalyst and made his professional home.

A few examples: Allan chaired and was the lead author on the grant project that enabled IPTAR to found its clinical center (the ICC), which he co-directed for six years. For the last quarter century, the ICC has treated over 4,000 patients, developed school-based therapy programs in more than half a dozen schools, published research on therapeutic outcomes, and has been the training ground for analytic candidates and doctoral students. It was under Allan's leadership, first as Dean of the Institute and then twice as President of the Society, that IPTAR moved into a new psychoanalytic era best defined by the words "transparency" and "relevance." Allan's presidency opened the doors for candidates to take part on committees and boards; he developed the Diversity Committee and established the Enrico Jones Fellowship to support the psychoanalytic training of under-represented groups. Under his tenure, the Arts and Psychoanalysis Program, highlighting the interrelationship between psychoanalysis and other disciplines, was launched. Allan was convinced that the presence of students from other countries would enrich psychoanalysis, and in the final year of Allan's presidency, IPTAR was granted permission by the United States Government to train non-immigrant foreign students. Since then IPTAR has opened its doors to candidates from Argentina, Canada, China, England, France, Israel, Italy, Korea,

Mexico, Peru, Serbia, Switzerland, Taiwan, Turkey, and Venezuela; and the clinical center has been able to offer treatment to patients in more than nine different languages.

Allan's belief that, in his words, "psychoanalysis was for everyone" was the overarching philosophy that connected his clinical and supervisory work, his political agenda and his analytic scholarship. Allan was a shy man; but as Joan Hoffenberg, a colleague and close friend, said of him, each person Allan came in contact with felt a level of intimacy and intention that made the relationship special and unique.

The book begins with heartfelt introductions by Sheldon Bach and Jane Tucker, two dear friends and colleagues who worked closely with Allan for over three decades. It culminates with a loving Postscript by Ruth Oscharoff, Allan's wife.

We intended that this collection of papers would honor, illustrate and preserve the extraordinary scope of Allan's analytic scholarship. In keeping with the essence of who Allan was, we also wanted this book to recollect and honor the intellectual and analytic community Allan built around him.

Toward this end, each paper is preceded by a short introductory essay by a colleague who worked closely with Allan or had a particular interest in the subject of the paper. We would like to acknowledge the essayists whose responses to Allan's papers brought new insight to Allan's work, challenged us to keep thinking and showed remarkable synergy. We imagine Allan would have been deeply touched by their care and intelligence. In order of appearance, they are Michael Moskowitz, Phyllis Beren, Tessa Addison, Neal Vorus, Richard Lasky, MaryBeth M. Cresci, Janet Fisher, Richard B. Grose, Joan D. Hoffenberg, Anthony Mazzella, Phyllis F. Hopkins, Arnold Rothstein, Elizabeth Cutter Evert, and Nancy R. Goodman. The papers, presented more or less in chronological order, are divided into five sections that reflect both the trajectory and deepening of Allan's thought: Developmental Roots, Psychoanalytic Realities, Deconstructing Analyzability, Empirical Psychoanalytic Inquiry and From the Frame to the Field. Each section is preceded by an editorial comment. Taken together, the comments serve to integrate the multifaceted trajectory of Allan's work.

The title, *Warmed by the Fires*, emerged in an uncanny moment of mutuality after we finished reading the marvelous essays that annotate and reflect on the individual papers. And so, with Allan's impish smile in mind (and with just a touch of the *profane),* we invite you to read the development of Allan's ideas, not as *sacred* texts to reify, but as touchstones that fire future exploration into the warm essence of psychoanalysis.

# Developmental Roots

Like the best of jazz improvisationists, Allan Frosch knew his classical scales—cognitive, developmental and psychoanalytic. Allan's orientation to psychoanalysis was rooted in his training and experience as a cognitive and developmental psychologist: these first two papers reflect this pedagogic base. As an analyst, he immersed himself in Freud and in neo and contemporary Freudian extensions and elaborations in the literature. Along the way, in the course of his explorations of vexing clinical problems that began in earnest with this first paper, he also parlayed his broad interests in philosophy and science, and borrowed from these in true interdisciplinary style. This was the beginning of a dialogue he would sustain and develop over the course of his writings.

In his first paper, "The Preconceptual Organization of Emotion," Allan mined Piaget's theory to deepen our psychoanalytic understanding of the nature of patients' emotional difficulties with the as-if quality of the transference. As Michael Moskowitz notes, here Allan anticipated later writings of Fonagy and Target on psychic equivalence and the difficulties that this preconceptional organization of emotion presents in clinical process.

Allan's next paper, "Narcissistic Injury and Sadomasochistic Compensation in a Latency-Age Boy," was primarily a clinical exemplar of these ideas, but with a movement toward the subtle and not so subtle dance in the analytic relationship between psychic and material reality.

1

Here Phyllis Beren describes Allan's deep immersion in the analytic process and his view of the necessity of that immersion as well as the emotional challenges that present in the countertransference.

CHAPTER 1

# The Preconceptual Organization of Emotion

## Reflections on "The Preconceptual Organization of Emotion"

*Michael Moskowitz*

Varieties of knowing, such as knowing not being enough, knowing but not believing, accurate interpretations failing, are some of the central issues Allan Frosch addresses in this paper. Finished in 1994, seventeen years after Allan received his doctorate, and three years after his graduation from IPTAR, this paper gives the impression of a creative psychoanalyst working hard to bring a new cognitive perspective to haunting psychoanalytic questions, especially questions about what it means to know.

Allan was a 1977 graduate of the City University of New York's (CCNY) doctoral program in cognition. The cognition program was located at City College of CCNY, coterminous with the clinical psychology program. Some faculty taught in both programs, and some classes were joined. The time that Frosch was at City College was a time of great excitement and hope. Among the faculty were scholars of psychoanalysis, Piagetian theory, neuroscience, sleep and dream studies, separation-individuation and attachment theory. Thinking about theoretical integration was in the air.

Students were encouraged to understand and integrate various perspectives. Allan's thesis, chaired by Steven Ellman, "Neuroelectric Correlates of

Children at High Risk to Manifest Schizophrenia," is an example of such an integration, as is this paper. Within a few years after graduation from City College, Frosch began analytic training at IPTAR. Graduating in 1991, he began his full-time practice of psychoanalysis.

This is Frosch's first published paper. By this point he is an experienced analyst working primarily in the transference. He describes a patient who is frustrated in her desire to have a satisfactory romantic relationship, and is unhappy about work. During the first two years of treatment the transference "was organized around a sense of danger and feelings of panic." She feared Frosch would do something to her. Most prominent was her near conviction that he would get excited by her sexual feelings and seduce her. It felt like it really could happen, and she often thought of how it would happen and what would be its consequences. She was stuck in fantasy, and transference interpretations–which seemed correct and were often accepted by the patient–did not reduce her fear. Reality meant little in comparison to her intense feelings about her analyst. Using aspects of Piaget's theory, which he had earlier outlined, Frosch concluded that his patient's emotions were constructed in a qualitatively different way than most other patients. In the sphere of emotions, she was thinking like a preoperational child. Her emotions were organized preconceptually. "Preconceptually organized emotions are action-oriented, perceptually driven mental representations that can overpower abstract thinking," wrote Frosch. For this patient, if she felt something powerfully, it was real. Her relationship to her analyst must be as she intensely wanted it to be. Without naming it here, Frosch anticipates Fonagy's and Target's idea of psychic equivalence.

Frosch goes on to discuss some of the difficulties and subtleties of interpretation when working with patients whose emotions are organized preconceptually. What does it mean when a patient acknowledges the truth of an interpretation, but does not fully know it is true? How do you help the patient take perspective and gradually come to know that emotions do not have to lead to action? In the course of this discussion he touches on the importance of enactment, the role of play, and the perennial question: how to keep the analysis real but not too frighteningly real.

# The Preconceptual Organization of Emotion

*Allan Frosch*[1]

## Abstract

*The suggestion is made that emotions organized on a preconceptual level are psychic constructs different in kind, as well as degree, from emotions organized on a more abstract conceptual level. For many people the regressive alteration in ego functioning that gives rise to these emotional constructions represents a characterological way of handling conflict. Emotions organized on a preconceptual level and rigidly maintained through primitive defenses ward off a host of fears ranging from castration to dedifferentiation. The shift from the preconceptual world of sensation to the conceptual world of abstraction complements the resolution of oedipal themes and is essential for free and easy movement between reality-based interactions and the imaginary experience of both self- and object representations in the transference. Structural and dynamic aspects of these emotional constructions are discussed and their relation to a person's experience of reality is explored through transference material taken from different points in an analysis. The problem of the analyst's use of concepts to refer to preconcepts is also discussed, as is the issue of enactments.*

My aim in this paper is to show how a preconceptual organization of emotion interferes with the sense of reality in the transference. Preconceptually organized emotions are action-oriented, perceptually driven mental representations that can overpower abstract thinking. Reality appraisal is interfered with in a particular way which I describe as a reversal between fantasy and reality. It is not that the person cannot

---

[1] The author wishes to acknowledge his gratitude for the thoughtful comments of Dr. Joseph Cancelmo, Betsy Distler, Laura Kleinerman, Dr. Richard Lasky, Roda Neugebauer, Ruth Oscharoff and Dr. Irving Steingart during the preparation of this paper.

formally test reality, but that he or she cannot take reality very seriously when it conflicts with libidinal and aggressive wishes.

## Pertinent Aspects of Piaget's Theory

The paper begins with a short discussion of pertinent aspects of Piaget's theory and moves on to clinical material highlighting the dynamic and structural aspects of preconceptually organized emotions. This is followed by a discussion of relevant theoretical and developmental issues and a section that integrates these issues with clinical material taken from different points in an analysis. For the purpose of this paper emotion is considered to be the association between sensations of pleasure and/or unpleasure and ideas (Freud, 1926; Brenner, 1974, 1982, 1991).

Piaget's theory emphasizes the increasingly rational and abstract nature of thought (Piaget, 1951; Flavell, 1963; Beilin, 1992; Sinclair, 1992). Cognitive development proceeds from the reflexive sensorimotor stage to the preoperational period, where early forms of mental representation (preconcepts) begin, to the increasingly abstract and complex functioning associated with concrete and formal operations.

The preoperational phase covers the period from about age two to seven. The preoperational child centers on a single striking aspect of an event so that "things are as they appear to be" (Flavell, 1963, p. 159). Piaget characterized this period as falling somewhere between socialized adult thought and the egocentric thought of the unconscious (Piaget, 1951).[2]

Early in the preoperational period (age two to four) rudimentary concepts are called *preconcepts* (Piaget, 1951, pp. 221–230). A child at this level of intellectual development does not have "good thought relative to the conceptual forms into which it eventually evolves"

---

[2] Both Rappaport (1951) and Wolff (1960) view Piaget's ideas as complementing the psychoanalytic conceptualization of the shift from primary to secondary process organization. It is in this sense that the term *preconceptual thought* is used here. The more a person is rooted to a world of sensation and action, the less able he or she is to establish or use abstract concepts that by definition lead to the world of logic characteristic of secondary process organization.

(Flavell, 1963, p. 156). For Piaget (1951) preconcepts were the initial manifestations of representational intelligence through their possession of the symbolic function (see Flavell, p. 151). From about age four to seven, what Piaget (1951) referred to as the intuitive phase of the pre-operational period, representations move from the sensorimotor orientation of the previous period to the more abstract, reality-oriented thought characteristic of the concrete operational period. Representations become more flexible, and the child is better able to decenter from an event and form an accurate picture of reality.

How and when representations (abstract thought) are formed has been questioned in recent years. Meltzoff (1985), for example, believes that infants possess the capacity to represent "adult behavior in an abstract (supramodal) form that not only encodes the event, but also serves as the basis of self-perception and action. In this view perception and motor production are closely linked and mediated by a common representational system from birth" (p. 28). Meltzoff's position stands in opposition to that of Piaget, for whom the development of a representational world evolves out of action during the sensorimotor period. Beilin (1992), in a recent article entitled "Piaget's New Theory," points out that toward the end of his life Piaget's work evolved to a point where the standard theory of his earlier writings moved in a new direction. In his last publication (Piaget and Garcia, 1989), Piaget took the position that early forms of operations are in evidence even in the sensorimotor period. Many contemporary Piagetians hold to the view expressed in a recent paper by Sinclair (1992) that abstract thought is apparent at all levels of intellectual development "and progresses in spiral-like fashion, reorganizing coordinations of actions or of operations into structural fragments or subsystems and, at higher levels, by abstractions of abstractions into ever more coherent and powerful systems" (pp. 221–222; see Furth, 1992, for a different point of view). Some of these differences may hinge on how we think of an "abstraction" (see Greenspan, 1979, pp. 73–74, for a discussion of the difference between simple and reflective abstraction, and Piaget, 1951, p. 67, for a relevant discussion).

As important as these questions are for an overall theory of cognition, the crucial issue in the present context is the difference between preconcepts and representations organized on a more abstract, logical, and reality-oriented level. The recent work of Flavell (1992), in which the focus of inquiry is on increments in representational development between early (preconceptual) and late (intuitive) preoperational children, is particularly relevant here.

Flavell argues that while three-year-old children have an impressive array of cognitive accomplishments, they possess only a limited understanding of mental representations. Children of this age believe that things are as they appear to be at any given moment; three-year-olds shown a white stimulus that is then put behind a blue filter cannot correctly distinguish between the object's real and apparent color. This is so even when they are given pretraining in the discrimination between appearance and reality. Flavell finds that a marked improvement on such tasks occurs with age; five-year-olds perform quite well, while three-year-olds are unable to understand that "people may for one reason or another 'seriously' represent [a] thing very differently from the way it is (seems to the child), that is, describe it very differently other than when pretending, joking, dreaming, lying, or the like" (p. 128). Thus, the preconceptually organized child cannot take representations of experience and look at them from a variety of perspectives. This inability has important implications for the psychoanalytic concepts of splitting and denial. It is to these issues that I turn in the discussion of Ms. A.

## Dynamic and Structural Considerations

Ms. A, a forty-year-old single woman, came to New York when she was eighteen and took a job as a file clerk for a large financial institution. Over the next twenty years she rose to a middle-management position and earned undergraduate and graduate degrees in economics. She entered analysis because, as she put it, "a good life is wasted on me. I'm attractive and smart and I can't find a man and I don't feel good about my work."

Ms. A, tall, blond, blue-eyed, and freckle-faced, grew up "deep in the heart of Dixie." She speaks with just a hint of a southern accent and when upset can insert, much to her chagrin, a "y'all" into the conversation. Ms. A grew up as the only child in a middle-class family. She felt that she had had a very close and exciting relationship with her father for the first three years of her life, after which he withdrew from her. She recalls feeling hurt and confused by her father's behavior. In many ways he seemed to fill the void created by an emotionally unavailable mother. Ms. A came to believe that one of the reasons her father withdrew was his discomfort with sexual feelings aroused by his daughter's sexuality. Over time she came to see him as self-involved and emotionally distant.

Growing up in a small agricultural community, Ms. A had plenty of time to engage in her favorite pastime—daydreaming. She recalls having spent most of her childhood in endless fantasies of having a boyfriend. As an adult she feels that her life has no meaning unless she can find a man she can love and who loves her. At the same time, she does not believe there is a man "out there" with whom she can have such a relationship. This fills her with a sense of hopelessness and despair.

In the third year of Ms. A's four-times-a-week analysis, she was scheduled to make a presentation for her firm in an area in which she was an expert. "This is not a big thing. ... It doesn't represent a move up or anything like that. People do this kind of thing in my company all the time; I've done it a lot. But this time I feel terrified. I'm convinced something terrible will happen. ... I feel like I did when I was in kindergarten and had to get up in front of the class. I'm terrified. I remember the first time I had to do that in school . . . how my mother calmed me down. She walked me to school and kept telling me I would be all right. It felt good . . . she was so comforting. I want you to make me feel better too." For days before the talk her sessions were filled with intense longings for me to take care of her. She wondered would I extend the session if she cried and became upset. Uncomfortable with her fleeting thoughts that she wanted me to attend the meeting, she recalled how wonderful she felt when her mother stayed outside the classroom when she got up to speak: "I looked at her through the little glass window. It's one of the few times I felt my mother really understood what I was going through."

As Ms. A described her thoughts that she would be humiliated and disgraced during the presentation, I had the distinct impression that she was happy and excited. I asked her about this. "That's right," she replied. "This is all good analytic material. I'm sure you love it. I know that I

9

want to be mothered, but as soon as I say that I think I'd rather just be by myself. I want to be mothered and I don't want to be mothered. I want to be alone but then I will feel all alone." I said that she wanted *me* to mother her, to come to the talk and extend the session if she became upset. "It's true. I really do know that, but I still feel I have to take care of you. As you were talking I kept thinking of this guy at work that I'd like to go out with. And I don't even like the guy. He's self-centered, emotionally unavailable. This is the kind of guy I've always gone out with." I said that it was hard for her to experience the longing for me to care for her—to mother her—and she moved to a sexually exciting theme with a disappointing man. Ms. A said that she had been going through her adolescent journals and remembered an incident that occurred when she was getting ready to come to New York. Nervous about the move away from home, she went to see Tom, a neighbor who was a year or two older. She had always had a crush on him and hoped he would listen to her concerns and give her "some brotherly advice." She went on: "Of course I wanted him to say, 'Don't leave; stay with me forever.' He talked about himself and when he was finished he fondled my breasts. I never did say anything about going to New York. I wanted him to help me, but I wound up giving him what he wanted—a good listen and a quick feel. He was too self-involved to give a damn about me one way or the other."

Ms. A's recollection of the story is the enactment of wishes for me to understand and nurture her, and to please and excite me. The displacement of her wishes to be mothered onto emotionally unavailable (and sadistic) men represents a shift from the emotionally unavailable preoedipal mother to the sexually exciting, emotionally distant, and self-involved father. It is the nucleus of a transference paradigm that has appeared in different forms at each stage of the treatment.

For the first two years of treatment, Ms. A's experience in the transference had a relatively static quality and was organized around a sense of danger and feelings of panic. Often she was very frightened that she might find something out about me that would be terrible: "Suppose I turn the TV on and see that you're a member of some ultra-right wing antifeminist group? Now, I don't really believe that, but who knows?" Her most pronounced fear, however, was that I would do something to her. A very clear example, one that occurred with a fair amount of frequency, was Ms. A's fear that I would become so excited by her sexual feelings that I would lose control and seduce her. I found that interpretive work emphasizing projection, for example, or the confusion between thoughts, feelings, and action, was not particularly helpful. The same was true when I was able to make a transference interpretation outlining the shift from the wish for a nurturing mother to the sexually exciting, emotionally unavailable, and sexually aroused father. The patient understood these interpretations and often produced associations that supported them. She felt, however, that I was missing the point, that I did not really understand her. She felt hurt, disappointed, and terribly alone when I was unable, as she put it, to reflect or resonate her internal state in a particular way. I felt that my interpretations were accurate, but that Ms. A was also right in saying that I did not understand her. As I tried to find a way into her world, to see things as she did, I began to think more and more about her emotions. In particular, I wanted to understand why these psychological configurations were so intransigent. Part of the answer seemed clear. Like any other complex psychic construct, Ms. A's emotions were compromise formations that served to defend against unpleasant affect (e.g., anxiety, depression, guilt) associated with sexual and aggressive wishes. At the same time, these compromise formations provided a measure of gratification. For Ms. A both of these functions were extremely resistant to change because of the intensity of her drives, the anticipation of the expected unpleasant emotion, and a relative inability to obtain satisfaction through reality-oriented means. In addition, Ms. A's emotions seemed different from those of most other patients, and the difference was not simply one of degree. There seemed to be a qualitative difference in the way her emotions were constructed.

In the transference, Ms. A's belief that some untoward action would occur is part of an infantile world in which meaning is organized around action. In this context the word *action* can refer to a discrete event or, in a broader sense, to what many authors call an *enactment* (see Panel, 1992). For McLaughlin (1991) an enactment "strongly suggests an action ... whose purpose and force were raised to high impact and influence upon the implicit other in the field of action ..." (p. 597). Enactments may therefore be seen to involve a two-party interactional system (Johan, in Panel, 1992, p. 841) in which each of the participants tries to persuade or force the other into a reciprocal action (McLaughlin, in Panel, 1992, p. 827). Enactments have also been described as a form of play in which ideas and wishes are transformed into a performance, dramatization, or happening (Roughton, 1993, pp. 457–458). They can be initiated by patient or analyst (Chused, 1991) and highlight the importance of the analyst's attempt to understand his or her role in the psychoanalytic situation (Goldberg, 1994).

With this in mind, let us return for a moment to the session in which Ms. A talked about her fears of making a presentation. There I called her recollection and presentation of the story of Tom an enactment. From the two-person perspective (Skolnikoff, 1993), however, the entire session might more adequately be described as a performance in which I participated. My initial intervention moved away from Ms. A's attempt to tell me about her fear and led eventually to the recollection of Tom, who like me wanted something else. Ms. A talked about what Tom wanted, not what she wanted, and allowed him a quick feel. In what appeared to be a response to my intervention, Ms. A talked about the transference (which is what I wanted) and, through her presentation of the Tom story, allowed me the analytic equivalent of a quick feel.

These issues are important with all patients but particularly so with patients whose words cannot adequately convey their inner experience. With these patients, enactments can provide an immediacy to the analytic experience by expressing what words cannot: "As nonverbal conveyors of rising memories, concealed resistances, and fantasies waiting to see the light of day, they are avant-garde messengers that anticipate and signal what is to come. . . . As messengers, enactments play a vital part in clinical work" (Jacobs, in Panel, 1992, p. 836). I will return to this point after discussing relevant theoretical and developmental themes, beginning with the transition from the phallic/oedipal phase to latency or, as Piaget (1951) would put it, the transition from the preoperational period to the period of concrete operations.

## Theoretical and Developmental Considerations

It is through the development of abstract concepts that the discontinuous nature of perceptually bound experience is converted into the coordinated system of conceptual categories that characterizes an objective view of the world. It is the shift from the preoperational period to the period of concrete operations that allows perception to come under the control of the intellect (Greenspan, 1979; Mahon, 1991; Sarnoff, 1976). The transition from thought bound to the world of sensation and action, to thought organized around abstractions that go beyond immediate experience, is part of a developmental process that reaches its highest level of organization, at least in early childhood, around the resolution of the Oedipus complex. Mahon (1991) argues that the Piagetian perspective complements that of psychoanalysis and that the repressions and identifications associated with a successful resolution of the Oedipus complex apply to the cognitive domain as well: "By diminishing the power of the perceptual in favor of the conceptual, the child has repressed one way of thinking and has identified with a more abstract, or more mature confederacy of thought not unlike his parents" (p. 631).

On the one hand, a diminution of preconceptual thinking is necessary for a successful resolution of the Oedipus complex; on the other, this diminution is seen as a *consequence* of oedipal resolution. This is the cognitive revolution that complements the psychological changes associated with the resolution of the oedipal complex (Mahon, 1991). Movement away from a perceptually bound affect motor existence allows for the development of a more pluralistic view of the world (e.g., increased differentiation of self and object representations). This is essential to free and easy movement between reality-based interaction and the imaginary experience of both self- and object representations in the transference.

In the psychoanalytic situation the patient reconstructs the past in the present. For the patient whose world is organized on the basis of preconceptual thinking, two issues are of particular importance. First, the meaning of an event is organized to a significant extent by the emotional intensity of the experience. While to some degree this is true for all people, it is particularly so when meaning is determined by perceptually driven (i.e., nonconceptual) aspects of the situation. The second issue concerns the interface between what is actually going on in the room and what the patient is emotionally convinced is going on. Steingart (1983) points out that for a child the "image representation continues to participate in the existence of the referent" (p. 30). He gives as an example the child who puts on a cowboy hat, plays at being a cowboy, and in effect becomes one. In a similar vein, in the transference a patient who is in love with the analyst, or is otherwise emotionally involved, can participate in the charged image of the situation with as much excitement and as great a sense of conviction as the young child playing cowboy. For Ms. A, reality pales in comparison to the eye-catching and emotionally charged representation of the analyst, who is on the verge of doing something to her.

We would expect the relatively well-structured person to be able to identify an association of sensations (of pleasure and/or unpleasure) and ideas as an instance of a category labeled *emotion*. This act of categorization is a way of ordering the world and allows the person to make inferences about an event that goes beyond the immediately observable experience (Bruner et al., 1956). Once a person has achieved a mature level of conceptualization regarding emotions, he can in effect say: "This sensation/idea configuration is something I know about. It is identified as anger, love, anxiety—in short, it is an emotion. I know that this emotion is an internal experience that has a temporal duration and is not necessarily linked to action. I control the emotion; it does not control me. I may feel great love or great anger, but this does not mean I will act on it. I am not transparent, and you will not necessarily know that I love you because I feel this way." Within certain parameters the emotion is a private experience. There are, of course, exceptions to this, even with relatively healthy people. Sometimes, for example, a person can feel that his affective state will never end, is totally transparent, and must lead to action. These highly charged states are usually short-lived and are not syntonic. With some people, however, the emotional configuration can be characterological and syntonic. Eissler (1953) discussed a schizophrenic patient who experienced her emotions as omnipotent forces that were transparent and would always lead to action. She was certain that if she felt love for someone, this would be immediately apparent to the other, who would humiliate her. Other emotions would then be called into play to guard against the first emotion. Like Eissler's patient, some people experience their emotions as all-powerful, irreversible, and dangerous. Unlike that patient, however, these people are neither schiz-ophrenic nor delusional. They may believe that their emotions are all-powerful, but they simultaneously know that they are not.

In his paper on the loss of reality in neurosis and psychosis, Freud (1924) discussed the role of fantasy in a person's construction of reality. In the psychoses, fantasy replaces reality; this we refer to as delusion. In the neuroses, by contrast, the fantasy does not replace reality but instead, "like the play of children attaches itself to a piece of reality and lends that piece a secret meaning ... which we (*not always quite appropriately*) call a symbolic one" (p. 187; italics added). What Freud may be referring to here is that for some people there is a *disturbance* in the symbolic function of fantasy. He had addressed this issue nearly ten years earlier, when he referred to some patients as being amenable only to the "logic of soup, with dumplings for arguments" (Freud, 1915a, p. 167).

It is this not quite symbolic type of fantasy to which I will refer throughout this paper. These intermediate constructs, neither delusional nor typically neurotic, play a crucial role in the construction of emotion for certain patients. These constructions date to a preconceptual world dominated by "static configurations" (Piaget, 1973, p. 57) that are rigid and irreversible. A child at this stage cannot treat his thoughts as an object of thought (Flavell, 1963); instead they are treated as external sensations, and momentary impressions reign supreme.[3] Similarly, for the prelatency child the highly charged images that characterize emotional experience can lend a sense of conviction regarding the omnipotence of the emotion. At this stage emotions, like thoughts, bear a peremptory quality. The young child is indeed drawn to the emotion, which defines the reality of the situation.[4] If

---

[3] Schafer (1968) believes that some primary process presences are prototypical configurations that are "structuralized"; i.e., they do not have to be created anew each time they appear: "They are ideas that recur or persist under specific intrapsychic or situational conditions ..." (p. 131). They are, in short, fixations, or relatively static configurations, that can be brought up in situations of conflict. Schafer's ideas have a "good fit" with the preconceptual orientation presented in this paper and are discussed more fully below.
[4] These ideas are similar to those presented by Horowitz et al. (1991), for whom emotion is considered an integral part of the meaning structure and determines future meaning (pp. 204-205).

the child feels frightened, then this fear must have a concrete referent. For the prelatency child anxious at bedtime, the sensorily imbued prototypical image of a monster in the closet, ready to strike, is the concrete representation of the emotion.

In the following vignette, emotion is organized around just such a representation, a monster poised for action in the guise of the analyst: Ms. A says that she often feels very excited before and after a session, but never during the session. This is explored, and over time it becomes clear that indeed Ms. A does feel sexually excited during sessions. These feelings, however, lead immediately to a feeling of panic accompanied by the following thoughts: "If I tell you my fantasies, you'll become as excited by them as I am. I have this picture in my head of you squirming with excitement, and then you touch yourself. You know what I mean; you'll begin to masturbate. At some point you'll get on the couch with me. That would be sexually abusive behavior, and I know I'd have to leave. I don't want to stop my analysis." As the patient says all of this, she quickly adds that she does not believe it; she has faith that the analyst is an ethical person. Yet she cannot feel excitement in the session, but only panic. She has split the representation of the analyst, and both images, however contradictory, are available to consciousness. Each version is a prototypical object representation, either idealized or devalued, and has a corresponding self-representation. These self- and object constructions are imbued with positive or negative affect (Kernberg, 1967) and are perceptually compelling events.

In this situation incestuous sexual wishes are denied or projected, and excitement and passion lead to danger and panic. There is a regression to a preoedipal position that can be characterized as a sadomasochistic anal world where thoughts and feelings are organized as preconcepts. This leads to an experience defined not by logic but by the focus on a compelling aspect of the event, here the prototypical image of the masturbating analyst and associated feelings of danger and panic. That image, of the sexually excited analyst on the verge of losing control, becomes the counterpart of the monster in the closet, and Ms. A suffers a relative loss in her capacity to move freely between different perspectives.

Bach (1991) considers the capacity to appreciate multiple perspectives "a basic prerequisite for transference interpretation" (p. 89). It allows the person to move freely between reality and fantasy, and this is the essence of psychoanalytic work. Freud (1912, 1914) addressed this directly in his paper on technique. He highlighted the dilemma for both patient and analyst by arguing that for treatment to be successful the transference has to be real but, in effect, not too real. Nonetheless, he quipped (Freud, 1912), the enemy cannot be killed in absentia. Feelings and beliefs from the past must be displaced onto the person of the analyst so that the patient can work through these issues in the transference (Freud, 1914). To do this, the patient must be able to see that these reactions to the analyst are illusions or fantasies. This is what Freud (1914) meant when he referred to the analytic work as a playground.

Just as in healthy play the child is able to stop and move back into the world that adults define as reality (Winnicott, 1958, 1971), the patient must do the same in analyzing transference reactions. This is what Ms. A has difficulty doing. When emotion prevails, it is hard for her to move from the thought based on a sexual wish, and organized around preconceptual imagery, to one based on an objectification of reality. It should be emphasized that Ms. A understands (but denies) that she is producing the thought of the sexually abusive analyst, and that she understands (but denies) the concept of transference. She would have no difficulty saying that her thought about the analyst seducing her comes from her own sexual wishes toward the analyst and, before that, toward her father. In this sense it is fair to say that her ability to test reality is intact but lacks emotional conviction. Her sense of reality, however, is not based on an intellectual appraisal of the situation. In his review of the concept of reality testing, Hurvich (1970) makes the point that emotional factors influence a person's reality appraisal beyond accuracy of perception and the ability to differentiate inner and outer. The emotional component in this situation, the feeling of panic, is so powerful that it outweighs any objective or logical understanding.

A number of contemporary analysts have addressed this variable interface between reality and fantasy. Bach's notion of "state constancy" (1985) refers to a person's ability to move along a continuum of alternate states and still be able to return to a point of consensual reality: "I believe that the function in question is the capacity to move freely, voluntarily, and consciously between the realm of illusion and reality, or playing and reality (Winnicott, 1971), or subjectivity and objectivity, or not-real and real experiences (Steingart, 1983), or, in general, between the realms of the inner and outer world" (p. 178). Schafer (1968) uses the term *primary process presence* (p. 131) to refer to a form of mental activity in which the person suffers a loss in the capacity to identify thoughts as thoughts and not as concrete realities. A primary process presence falls somewhere between fantasy and hallucination. Schafer conceives of such presences as a special case of unconscious object representations, a kind of solitary play in which the past is alive in the present. Schafer's discussion is of course directly related to Freud's paper on the unconscious (1915b). There Freud argued that a hypercathexis of the unconscious thing (or object) presentation was necessary to "bring about a higher psychical organization and make it possible for the primary process to be succeeded by the secondary process" (p. 202). Lasky (1993) makes the important point that it is this hypercathexis (or linkage) that transforms "representations that were exclusively perceptual, motoric, and sensational [i.e., unconscious object or thing presentations] into mental representations that are also conceptual [word presentations]." It represents a shift from "experience-bound mental representations to mental representations that stand for experience" (p. 260n).

Loewald (1978) has emphasized an optimal linkage between word and thing presentations so that a new meaning or understanding can be attributed to conscious ideas. For Loewald meaning is a function of the differentiation and linkage of words and unconscious objects. For example: Ms. A's words are imbued with powerful emotion that is fueled by unconscious determinants so that they are treated as concrete things or actions. At the other extreme they can be so far from the unconscious determinants (thing presentations) that they have acquired a "lifeless nimbleness"; they "are void of or deficient in experiential meaning" and "have deteriorated to more or less hollow echoes of secondary process presentations" (Loewald, 1978, p. 188). Steingart (1983) too is concerned with how a person attributes meaning to the world and postulates a "meaning disturbance" in borderline and narcissistic patients; this is described as a "(mis)use of cognition as pathological play which a young child uses to deny certain actualities, or an adult uses to deny certain realities, and which have become attached to intolerable psychodynamic conflicts" (p. 41). The negative form of this disturbance is denial. The positive is illusion: "it is the presence of illusion vs. gratifying but productive play which discriminates clinical health and pathology" (p. 41). These meaning disturbances are conceptualized as "preconceptual thought structures, which are symbolized as prototype-images saturated with perceptual-like quality, and now used defensively for the purpose of denial and splitting" (p. 53). As belief structures, they alter the interface between what the person experiences as real and as not real. All of the ideas discussed here refer to a person's ability, or inability, to move between the world of imagination and the world of "objective" reality, between inside and outside, or psychical reality and material reality (Freud, 1900). In this sense the ideas are functionally equivalent, however different their theoretical contexts and emphases.

In the vignette in which Ms. A fantasizes her analyst as sexually aroused, the play feels too real to her. It threatens to lead to what Winnicott (1958) referred to as an id orgasm in the session, as distinguished from an ego orgasm. The patient believes something will really happen if she gets excited, a belief energized by her feeling of panic. The emotion, a consequence of the patient's construction of the situation, in turn lends conviction to this construction. The regressive alteration in ego functioning leads to a situation in which a kind of feedback loop is created so that the reciprocal relation between wish and preconceptual imagery becomes more emotionally charged for Ms. A and therefore more meaningful to her than objective reality.

In this situation we could indeed say that a picture is worth a thousand words. The image of the unethical analyst carries far more weight for the patient than does her intellectual appraisal of the situation. Ms. A withdraws interest from the more objective view of reality and raises the cathectic level of the fantasy construction. In economic terms (Freud, 1926), a disavowal or denial of reality occurs, together with a hypercathexis of fantasy. From another perspective, this break with reality can be thought of as a fantasy construction that is not symbolic in the usual sense.

Here Steingart's notion of pathological playful illusion is helpful, in that it places the difficulty in the realm of cognition and refers specifically to a preconceptual organization of the world. Prototypical imagery holds more meaning for this patient than do words or thought mediated by language. Her own language cannot fully convey or contain the power of her emotions, which are linked to such imagery. In this sense Ms. A's words are deceptive. In pathological play, according to Steingart, the emphasis is on the child's investment in play rather than on the ability to objectify reality. For the prelatency child it is not a question of whether the play is real or not; it is simply exciting and far more meaningful than the actualities of the situation. Only after successful passage through the phallic/oedipal period and entrance into latency can the child invest more fully in reality and move freely between the world of make-believe and the world of reality (Sarnoff, 1976; see Piaget, 1951, p. 168n). Ms. A's relationship to reality is more like that of a child who has not yet resolved the oedipal conflict and who remains bound to a preconceptual world. For her the treatment is a game she can play with the analyst, and the play (e.g., her belief in the unethical analyst) becomes reality. Ms. A "understands" that the belief is not real, but *she cannot take this understanding seriously*. In this situation the construction of the unethical analyst is not a delusion, in that it does not replace reality. But neither is it a fantasy, in that it does not endow a piece of reality with some secret meaning that could appropriately be called symbolic.

Ms. A's construction of the unethical analyst is a conflict-induced pathological playful illusion that serves many functions. The defensive aspect of this compromise formation wards off the emotionally charged experience of libidinal wishes toward the analyst. The sense of omnipotence surrounding Ms. A's sexual wishes, and their culmination in the image of the analyst losing control and seducing her, lead to a feeling of panic and represents a perverse gratification, as well as serving a defensive function. It is a conscious reflection of the second phase of the unconscious beating fantasy described by Freud (1919) in his study of the perversions. To paraphrase Freud, this patient's idea that the analyst will abuse her is a "regressive debasement" (p. 189) of the wish that her analyst love her in a genital sense. What Freud called "the essence of masochism" (p. 189) is the libidinal excitation that attaches to the sado-masochistic relationship. For Ms. A the excitement is not only, or even primarily, in the genital realm. While Ms. A's conflicts are played out on the stage of the Oedipus complex, many of the players come from an earlier time. Thus, the feelings of excitement, danger, and panic that are part of the perception of the unethical analyst can be thought of as a turning around of the longed-for excitement and love in the mirroring gaze of the preoedipal mother; this is now displaced to the overly sexualized (but negatively cathected) oedipal father.

## *Technical Considerations*

In Ms. A's "fantasy" of the masturbating analyst, which occurred in the first year of treatment, the preconceptual images and incestuous longings have not been repressed, and an interference is seen in the capacity to move freely between real and not-real experience. Interventions at this early stage of the analysis were designed to stay as close as possible to the patient's experience. I emphasized the central role of omnipotent emotional configurations organized around action: "You say that I will not do these things, but you are frightened that your sexual feelings will so excite me that I will lose all control here." Interventions that moved away from the concrete, action-oriented configuration and more toward concepts organized on an abstract level (e.g., "You become anxious when you have sexual thoughts or feelings toward me") were not helpful. The difficulty was that concepts were being used to refer to preconcepts. Ms. A, whose emotions are organized on a preconceptual level, nonetheless knows very well what emotions are. She also could understand the meaning of my interventions. What she does not understand is what her emotions are, and in this sense the interventions were meaningless. We were not speaking the same language.

I found that by staying close to Ms. A's immediate experience a more complete picture of emotion began to unfold. At times her emotions were likened to "incredibly powerful forces" that invaded the patient and over which she had no control. Intense feeling led always to danger. As the emotional constructions became clearer, it was possible to take the interpretive work a bit further: "Your sexual feelings lead to panic and confirm your belief that I will seduce you. I know that you value the analysis, so I can well understand why you cannot have sexual thoughts and feelings here that might lead to your feeling excited. Then I would get excited, and that feels dangerous to you." Here the intervention was directed toward Ms. A's wish to see the analyst as an ethical person and to preserve the analytic relationship. What might have been added to the interpretation is some indication of the narcissistic enhancement provided by the sense of danger and panic adhering to the belief in the unethical analyst; e.g., "If you did not believe that I would get so excited, you would feel that your sexual feelings did not exist and, ultimately, that you did not exist." As treatment continued, I could more readily address my comments to the patient's observing ego and help her to see that her ideas about her feelings were very different from what one would ordinarily think of as feelings: "You are talking about your feelings, and I know that you are aware that feelings are not all-powerful external forces that you must struggle against or some disastrous action will occur. Yet this is what you believe when you feel excited here."

This kind of intervention carries a certain danger. "You are telling me that my thoughts and feelings are not real," the patient can protest, "and that I should not have them." Alternatively, the patient can become compliant and a therapeutically induced false self can develop. Yet another danger is that the patient will feel totally misunderstood: "I know my feelings are not real, but they feel real and your telling me they aren't doesn't help. It only makes things worse." It was this last type of response that was brought into the session when my timing, my impatience to move more quickly, did not find a good fit with the patient's receptivity.

By the second year of treatment the locus of the danger had been reversed. Ms. A was concerned less about what I would do than about her own propensities. She felt that she wanted to be sexually aggressive with me, and for her this was tantamount to action. It filled her with a sense of danger and panic. These feelings reinforced her belief that her wishes would lead to action and simultaneously served as a defense against this eventuality by inhibiting the fuller expression of her wishes: "Sometimes I feel so excited here it terrifies me. I don't feel the dam will break. The dam is an illusion—there is no dam. I use the danger to control things. The danger is what controls me. You wouldn't lose control; I could. The danger comes from me." This sexualized sadomasochistic construction is a version of missing psychic structure (Tolpin, 1978, p. 174) that allows the person to maintain differentiation between self and object (or thought and action) when the structuralization necessary for such differentiation has been compromised (Bach, 1991).

As Ms. A's libidinal excitement began to dominate the sessions, a change occurred in her sense of danger. If I did something she considered a mistake, then I was deficient in her estimation, just as she was. How could she possibly allow herself to become emotionally involved with such a person? At these times she became enraged at me and acknowledged how exciting and pleasurable the anger was—how, in effect, she loved to beat me up: "I want to believe that you can be empathic, but maybe you can't. Maybe you're an emotional cripple just like me. I have this voracious hunger for you to understand me, to resonate how I feel. When you don't I feel I'm not getting my dues and I want to go for the jugular. I want to get you, and that's exciting to me. You're a jerk, just like me. That feels real. Don't tell me it's transference—the good feelings are transference. They're just a fantasy. I feel excited and connected to you when I'm mad at you."

This construction represents another variation of a perversion of reality (Steingart, 1983; Arlow, 1991; Grossman, 1993). The belief that I am an emotional cripple or a jerk has become reality, and the reality of Ms. A's exciting feelings has become a fantasy. The all consuming emotional configuration of anger has drowned out the libidinal feelings. The perversion is created and maintained through splitting and denial: "I can't put the two together: I feel you're really all these terrible things and sometimes I feel that you're just wonderful—my ally. Right now I don't know who you are."

This vignette calls to mind an example Piaget (1951) once gave of preconceptual thinking. His two-and-a-half-year-old daughter could not recognize a picture of her sister in a bathing suit but recognized her immediately when she was wearing a familiar dress. It was, to quote Piaget, "as if her sister had changed identity in changing her clothes" (p. 224). When Ms. A is very angry at me, it can feel to her that I have changed into another person. Ms. A was able to say in the midst of this that she was aware that her reaction was an exaggeration that fit well with her expectation of being disappointed by me, but this understanding had little impact on her sense of reality. Her emotional conviction was determined by the intensity of her anger, and the libidinal feelings temporarily faded into the background.

Here the second phase of the beating fantasy, a masochistic one, is replaced by a fantasy whose form, like Freud's third-phase beating fantasy, is sadistic. Ms. A is beating me. I am the child, but we are also the same—emotional cripples or jerks. There is a masochistic satisfaction to the fantasy that is an extension of the earlier fantasy of being abused by me. The current fantasy, as in Freud's third phase, has a conscious sexual excitement attached to it. Ms. A says that the fantasy is exciting and that it maintains a connection to me. It is a way of having an exciting and passionate relationship without the anxiety of feeling that she will lose control and not want to leave the office, or that she will suffer humiliation and despair. These "fantasies," of course, were indexed by a sense of conviction more consistent with pathological playful illusion than with fantasy in the symbolic sense.

These angry and exciting fantasies (i.e., pathological playful illusions) were only temporary stopgaps in the flow of Ms. A's positive feelings. As these loving feelings intensified, so did her fear of becoming depressed and nonfunctional. She felt that no matter how accepting I was of her longing, or her excitement, it would never be enough. Unless there was an element of danger, the excitement felt unreal. Ms. A's wish/belief that something would happen, some action occur, was part of the action-oriented, preconceptual organization of her experience. The analyst's love, appropriately expressed as attentive listening, empathy, and interpretation (Pine, 1985), is a symbolic representation of Ms. A's deepest desires. Unfortunately, however, for Ms. A, who has difficulty experiencing emotions on a symbolic level, only the "real thing," represented by something untoward happening in the session, has any emotional meaning. "You never say how much this means to you. You don't mirror my excitement. The panic mirrors my excitement and keeps me from feeling disappointed. I remember when I was growing up and the carnival came to town. Where I grew up that was probably one of the major events of the year. It certainly was for me. I didn't care much for the rides, but I loved the fun house mirror that distorted things. That's how it is here. It's like a fun house mirror that turns excitement into panic."

## Summary and Discussion

In any complex system such as the psychoanalytic model of the mind, or the psychoanalytic situation, input and output variables can be interchangeable (Moran, 1991). Emotions organized on a preconceptual level are an integral part of conflict-induced belief structures that interfere with free and easy movement between fantasy and reality. These emotional constructions also become input variables that fuel these beliefs with a conviction of reality. It is the intensity of these emotional constructions that is the crucial variable in a person's sense of reality, as differentiated from the ability to test reality. In oversimplified but nonetheless accurate terms, this fact could be expressed thus: "If it feels this good (or bad), it must be true." The cognitive psychologist Jerome Bruner has called this phenomenon "affective congruence" (Bruner et al., 1956, p. 20).

It is my impression that emotions organized as preconcepts are both qualitatively and quantitatively different from emotions categorized in a more conceptual, abstract way. These latter constructions yield information that goes beyond the immediate experience; the former do not. Emotions organized preconceptually tend to be all-consuming because their parameters cannot be inferred. They are compelling representations that cannot be referenced to a body of concepts providing information about such variables as duration and relation to action.

These belief structures, or pathological playful illusions, provide meaning to the person about self- and object representations that is at odds with objective or consensual reality. This way of organizing the world is an integral part of pathological compromise formations that ward off the expectation of intolerable emotion and provide gratification to the person at the expense of growth and development. The person lives in a world that can be tolerated emotionally, but little or no maturation or differentiation occurs in the areas affected by these compromise formations. This is particularly clear in the transference.

During the early part of her analysis, Ms. A believed that the analyst would become so excited by her sexual feelings that he would lose control and seduce her. This belief was her characterological way of handling conflict. In Ms. A's construction of reality, the self-representation is seen as an all-powerful way of coping with the feeling that if the analyst was not excited by her sexuality, then her sexual feelings, and ultimately Ms. A herself, would cease to exist. The image of a fun house mirror that turns excitement into danger and panic is a condensation of the mirroring function of the preoedipal mother in the guise of the perversely exciting oedipal father.

The danger and panic that adhere to this image is also a defense against these infantile longings. To acknowledge wishes to be loved, comforted, and affirmed as a human being, without the intervening step of a "perverse" reversal (i.e., a regression to an anal-sadistic organization), is associated with a sense of annihilation.

The shift from preconceptual thought to a more abstract world complements the resolution of oedipal themes and is necessary if emotion is to be experienced as instantiating categories that can be referenced to a larger conceptual network. Since emotion can index a situation as real or not real, a failure to categorize the configuration of sensation and idea on an abstract level makes it difficult, if not impossible, for a person to engage in the cognitive equivalent of healthy play during the analytic hour.

At various points in this paper I have mentioned the defensive and gratifying functions of Ms. A's emotions. I will conclude with a few comments about their adaptive value and their impact on the analyst. In "Remembering, Repeating and Working-Through," Freud (1914) used the term "repetitive reactions" to describe the patient's acting out in the transference (p. 154). The editors of the Standard Edition point out that the phrase "repetitive actions" was used in the first version of this paper (p. 154n). That Freud changed this phrase indicates his awareness of the importance of the analyst in relation to these repetitions. That the original phrase omitted any recognition of the person of the analyst was probably a reflection more of Freud's aversion to dealing with these issues than of an initial lack of awareness (see Haynal and Falzeder, 1993, for a cogent discussion of these issues).

Chused's comments on acting out and repetitions (1991), while not directed specifically to Freud's paper, are relevant here: "acting out and repetition refer only to the patient's behavior; they imply that the analyst is an observer of the experience, not a participant in it" (p. 628). Chused takes the position that when patients undergo a regression they will attempt to actualize (i.e., gratify) their transference wishes through enactments, which can elicit in the analyst feelings, wishes, and impulses to act. Chused accepts the inevitability of the analyst's contribution to these enactments and sees his efforts to distinguish "the determinants based on his own psychology from those arising from the patient" (p. 618) as crucial to a more complete understanding of the transference.

Chused's comments are applicable to all patients but have particular relevance for work with patients like Ms. A, whose emotions are organized as preconcepts. For these patients, meaning is organized through action, and there is a marked propensity to draw the analyst into (re)enactments of archaic relationships. From the two-person perspective, the analyst can be drawn into the patient's "present moment of the past" (Eliot, 1919, p. 11, cited by Ogden, 1993, p. 3) through the process of empathy or through enactment with its defensive and gratifying aspect–for the analyst as well as the patient. These forms of participation are not mutually exclusive, and both occur in all analytic work. The analyst's goal, although it is one that can never be achieved completely, is to proceed through empathic understanding, containment, and eventual interpretation, not through actualization via enactment. In working with Ms. A, I came to understand that her preconceptual organization of experience, with its heightened potential for mutual enactment, was a compelling representation of the past characterized by an immediacy of the moment that was crucial to the analytic work. The more I was able to understand how Ms. A's emotions were constructed and the communicative function they served, in contrast to the words she used, the more I was able to deemphasize the resistant function of these emotional constructions. This was helpful in maintaining the patience required for the opening up of an analytic space in which interpretations could take on real meaning, rather than remaining mere words incapable of encompassing the intensity of Ms. A's preconceptually organized world. The only hope of resolving these ties to the past is through the transference. Emotions organized on a preconceptual level provide an opportunity for patient and analyst to address a past made manifest in the contemporary distortions of the transference.

# References

Arlow, J. (1991). *Psychoanalysis: Clinical theory and practice.* Madison, CT: International Universities Press.

Bach, S. (1985). *Narcissistic states and the therapeutic process.* New York: Jason Aronson.

———(1991). On sadomasochistic object relations. In G. Fogel & W. Myers (Eds.), *Perversions and near perversions in clinical practice* (pp. 75-92). New Haven, CT: Yale University Press.

Beilin, H. (1992). Piaget's new theory. In H. Beilin & P. Pufall (Eds.), *Piaget's theory: Prospects and possibilities* (pp 1-20). Hillsdale, NJ: Erlbaum.

Brenner, C. (1974). On the nature and development of affects: A unified theory. *Psychoanalytic Quarterly, 43:*532–556.

———(1982). *The mind in conflict.* New York: International Universities Press.

———(1991). A psychoanalytic theory of affects. *Journal of the American Psychoanalytic Association,* 39 (Suppl.):305–316.

Bruner, J. S., Goodnow, J. L. & Austin, G. A. (1956). *A study of thinking.* New York: Wiley.

Chused, J. (1991). The evocative power of enactments. *Journal of the American Psychoanalytic Association,* 39:615–639.

Eissler, K. R. (1953). Notes upon the emotionality of a schizophrenic patient and its relation to problems of technique. *Psychoanalytic Study of the Child,* 8:199–251.

Eliot, T. S. (1919) Tradition and the individual talent. In *Selected Essays* (pp. 3-11). New York: Harcourt, Brace and World, 1960.

Flavell, J. H. (1963). *The Developmental psychology of Jean Piaget.* Princeton, NJ: Van Nostrand.

Flavell, J. H. (1992). Perspectives on perspective taking. In H. Beilin & P. Pufall (Eds.), *Piaget's theory: Prospects and possibilities* (pp. 107-140). Hillsdale, NJ: Erlbaum.

Freud, S. (1900). The interpretation of dreams. *Standard Edition,* 4/5.

———(1912). The dynamics of transference. *Standard Edition,* 12:99–108.

————(1914). Remembering, repeating and working-through. *Standard Edition,* 12:147–156.

————(1915a). Observations on transference-love. *Standard Edition,* 12:159–171.

————(1915b). The unconscious. *Standard Edition,* 14:166–215.

————(1919). A child is being beaten. *Standard Edition,* 17:179–204.

————(1924). The loss of reality in neurosis and psychosis. *Standard Edition,* 19:183–187.

————(1926). Inhibitions, symptoms and anxiety. *Standard Edition,* 20:87–174.

Furth, H. (1992). The developmental origin of human societies. In H. Beilin & P. Pufall (Eds.), *Piaget's theory: Prospects and possibilities* (pp. 251-266). Hillsdale, NJ: Erlbaum.

Goldberg, A. (1994). Farewell to the object analyst. *International Journal of Psychoanalysis,* 75:21–30.

Greenspan, S. (1979). *Intelligence and adaptation: An integration of psychoanalytic and Piagetian developmental psychology.* New York: International Universities Press.

Grossman, L. (1993). The perverse attitude toward reality. *Psychoanalytic Quarterly,* 42:422–436.

Haynal, H. & Falzeder, E. (1993). Slaying the dragons of the past or cooking the hare in the present: An historical view on affects in the psychoanalytic encounter. *Psychoanalytic Inquiry,* 13:357–371.

Horowitz, M., Fridhandler, B. & Stinson, C. (1991). Person schemas and emotion. *Journal of the American Psychoanalytic Association,* 39 (Suppl.):173–208.

Hurvich, M. (1970). On the concept of reality testing. *International Journal of Psychoanalysis,* 51:299–311.

Kernberg, O. (1967). Borderline personality organization. *Journal of the American Psychoanalytic Association,* 15:641–685.

Lasky, R. (1993). *Dynamics of development and the therapeutic process.* Northvale, NJ: Jason Aronson.

Loewald, H. (1978). Primary process, secondary process, and language. In *Papers on psychoanalysis* (pp. 178-206). New Haven, CT: Yale University Press, 1980.

Mahon, E. J. (1991). The "dissolution" of the Oedipus complex: A neglected cognitive factor. *Psychoanalytic Quarterly,* 50:628–636.

McLaughlin, J. T. (1991). Clinical and theoretical aspects of enactment. *Journal of the American Psychoanalytic Association,* 39:595–614.

Meltzoff, A. (1985). The roots of social and cognitive development: Models of man's original nature. In T. Field & N. Fox (Eds.), *Social Perception in Infants* (pp. 1-30). Norwood, NJ: Ablex.

Moran, M. (1991). Chaos theory and psychoanalysis. *International Review of Psychoanalysis,* 18:211–221.

Ogden, T. H. (1994). The analytic third: Working with intersubjective clinical facts. *International Journal of Psychoanalysis,* 75:3–19.

Panel (1992). Enactments in psychoanalysis. Reported by M. Johan. *Journal of the American Psychoanalytic Association,* 40:827–841.

Piaget, J. (1951). *Play, dreams, and imitation in childhood.* New York: Norton.

———(1973). *The child and reality: Problems of genetic psychology.* New York: Grossman.

———& Garcia, R. (1989). *Psychogenesis and the history of science.* New York: Columbia University Press.

Pine, F. (1985). *Developmental theory and clinical process.* New Haven, CT: Yale University Press.

Rapaport, D. (1951). Principal factors determining intellectual evolution from childhood to adult life. In *Organization and pathology of thought* (pp. 154-175). Austen Riggs Monograph 1. New York: Columbia University Press.

Roughton, R. E. (1993). Useful aspects of acting out: Repetition, enactment, and actualization. *Journal of the American Psychoanalytic Association,* 41:443–472.

Sarnoff, C. (1976). *Latency.* New York: Jason Aronson.

Schafer, R. (1968). *Aspects of internalization.* New York: International Universities Press.

Sinclair, H. (1992). Changing perspectives in child language acquisition. In H. Beilin & P. Pufall (Eds.), *Piaget's theory: Prospects and possibilities* (pp. 211-228). Hillsdale, NJ: Erlbaum.

Skolnikoff, A. Z. (1993). The analyst's experience in the psychoanalytic situation: A continuum between objective and subjective reality. *Psychoanalytic Inquiry,* 13: 296–309.

Steingart, I. (1983). *Pathological play in borderline and narcissistic personalities.* Jamaica, NY: Spectrum.

Tolpin, M. (1978). Self-objects and oedipal objects: A crucial developmental distinction. *Psychoanalytic Study of the Child,* 33:167–184.

Winnicott, D. W. (1958). The capacity to be alone. In *The maturational processes and the facilitating environment* (pp. 29-36). New York: International Universities Press, 1965.

———( 1971). *Playing and reality.* New York: Basic Books.

Wolff, P. (1960). The developmental psychologies of Jean Piaget and psychoanalysis. Psychological Issues Monograph 5. New York: International Universities Press.

CHAPTER 2

# Narcissistic Injury and Sadomasochistic
# Compensation in a Latency-Age Boy

*Reflections on "Narcissistic Injury and Sadomasochistic Compensation in a Latency-Age Boy"*

**Phyllis Beren**

I did not know Allan well when I was putting together an edited book about children who suffered from a narcissistic disturbance. The aim of the book was to look closely at the inner life of children, including both their internal conflicts and their reactions to the environment and also the integral role of the family system. The more specific focus was on the many disorders of narcissism that occur in the children, adolescents and parents whom we see today for treatment. The collection would include previously published papers and also include cases of colleagues, where I believed that a broader narcissistic issue was in play. The therapist often found these children very challenging, and the treatment was characterized by intense enactments and countertransference.

I asked Allan to contribute an unpublished paper, and, in his gracious way, he did not disappoint. He began his chapter with an association between his young patient and Richard III: "Deformed, unfinished...lamely and unfashionable...so that dogs bark at me as I halt by them,..." [and] "Since I cannot prove a lover...I am determined to be a villain" (Act I, Scene I). Richard goes on to give a developmental history. "[I was] sent before my time into this breathing world, scarce half made up, cheated of feature by dissembling nature." Allan draws attention to the influence of the parent, noting: "It was mother (nature) that did him wrong—sent him out of the womb before his time. Richard's physical deformities are a metaphor for feeling unloved by his mother." And quoting her: "A grievous burthen was thy birth to me. Tetchy and wayward was thy infancy" (Act IV, Scene IV).

From here, Allan moves on to describe a treatment filled with intense and dramatic moments consisting of enactments where he and the child become engaged in a perverse relationship characterized by intimate and highly charged anal-sadistic expressions. In his own therapeutic journey, Allan finds himself grappling with the intense countertransference feelings evoked by his patient, whose need to humiliate and control him was the boy's only defensive means of staying alive. Allan handles all of this in an extraordinary manner, all the while not flinching from the raw feelings aroused in him.

Allan and I had several editorial discussions about his early drafts where I raised a number of questions, including ones about his countertransference responses to the boy. As he listened to my comments, I was impressed with his open, non-defensive manner and his willingness to re-examine his thinking. It was in these talks that I got a taste of Allan as an analyst, and my respect and admiration grew for his talents as a child psychotherapist.

This was the beginning of a close collegial friendship that spanned about twenty years. We served together on the IPTAR Institute Board, took turns as Dean of Training, sat on the Society Board together; and when I was president, Allan was the president-elect. As a colleague, I could with confidence refer adults and children to him, knowing they would be in fine hands. Early on I had gleaned his talent with challenging patients from his chapter in my book. With his calm, accepting, non-judgmental attitude and absolute dedication to his patients he provided an atmosphere of understanding, caring and containment. As time went on, my admiration only grew as I heard him present and publish very fine papers reflecting his theoretical openness and his belief in psychoanalytic treatment for most patients. Allan was an extraordinary psychoanalyst, an admired teacher, a supervisor, author, mentor and a very special human being. I miss him greatly.

*       *       *

# Narcissistic Injury and Sadomasochistic Compensation in a Latency-Age Boy

*Allan Frosch*

## Introduction

In the opening soliloquy of *The Tragedy of King Richard III* (1593), Shakespeare tells us of Richard's narcissistic injuries: "Deformed, unfinished . . .. lamely and unfashionable . . . so that dogs bark at me as I halt by them–and his attempts at compensation: "Since I cannot prove a lover . . . I am determined to be a villain" (Act I, Scene I, p. 113). If I cannot find gratification through libido, I will find it through the exercise of my aggression. Of course, Richard is talking not only about his physical deformities (which Shakespeare may well have exaggerated; see Smith [1957]) but about his emotional reaction to them. Richard tells us that something went wrong between him and his mother: " [I was] sent before my time into this breathing world, scarce half made up, cheated of feature by dissembling nature" (p. 113). It was mother (nature) that did him wrong sent him out of the womb before his time. Richard's physical deformities are a metaphor for feeling unloved by his mother:

A grievous burthen was thy birth to me ,
Tetchy and wayward was thy infancy (Act IV, Scene IV, p. 146).

If the Duchess of York had loved her son more, then Richard's school days might not have been so "frightful, desperate, wild, and furious" (p. 146).

Wildness and fury are Richard's attempts to compensate for the fearfulness and desperation of feeling unloved.

In this paper I will discuss my work with David, a latency-age boy whose "wild and furious" verbal and physically aggressive behavior is clearly atypical for someone his age. One way to understand David's actions is to view them in the context of a series of narcissistic failures and the compensatory strategies (defenses and restitutional measures) for coping with these failures.

At the oral, anal, and phallic stages of his development, David's parents displayed a repetitive pattern of less than adequate response to his needs. This was most pronounced with his mother who did not seem able to devote herself to David, so that he never became the center of her interests. David's aggression would seem a reaction to this. "If I cannot be loved, valued, and cared for, then you will hate and fear me, but I will certainly be a compelling presence in your life."

The inability of David's parents (particularly his mother) to contain his aggression in the first four to five years of life led David to develop a defensive strategy characterized by the rapid mobilization of rage directed at the other. The rage functions to ward off feelings of helplessness and a sense of annihilation, but also to maintain desire and involvement vis-à-vis the other. Unlike Richard, who eliminates his objects in order to feel alive, David devalues his objects but does not relinquish his longing to obtain narcissistic supplies from them "you must love me" screams the sadist as he beats his objects (Bach 1985).

The evolution of David's behavior into a sadomasochistic organization developed out of his attempt to get his mother (and later his father) to accept (i.e., understand the meaning of) his aggression. In the presence of his parents' failure to understand his anger, David felt more and more out of control. His sadomasochistic behavior was a way to create a sense of greater control by turning the passive experience of being engulfed by rage into the more active experience of directing the rage at others and getting a relatively predictable reaction.

In short, by making the other feel helpless and out of control, David can disavow such feelings in himself and feel more in control. For David, the movement from passively experiencing anger to actively directing it at someone—initially (and primarily) his mother—was an important step in turning unpleasure into pleasure. The anger became erotized. "How would you like it if I knocked over your bookcase?" David announced as he leaned against my bookcase on a day when he felt that "you and that bitch" (mother) were forcing him to come—"Tomorrow is the first day of my vacation. Why the fuck should I be here today?"

## History of Failed Narcissistic Aspirations and David's Reactions to Them

David is the second child born to a middle-class couple, both of whom work. His sister is four years older than David and is described by her parents as the all-American girl: an A student and excellent athlete, she is popular, personable, and "never a problem at home." When David was born, his mother had just completed her PhD and "landed the job of a lifetime." She went to work full-time when David was 2 months old. At that point she began drinking several mugs of coffee a day, as well as Coca-Cola. She continued to breastfeed David in the morning and in the evening when she returned home. She discontinued breast-feeding at 6 months when it became apparent that David was gaining only about a pound a month. In her words, "caffeine is a small molecule that goes right through to breast milk," so David's failure to thrive was a result of his mother's "bad milk."

I understand this story both as a factual piece of David's early history and as a metaphor for the mother's lack of libidinal connection to her son. The mother's involvement with her career, her excitement over her new job, and her own narcissistic issues interfered with the essential task of motherhood—what Stern (1995) calls the life-growth theme: "Can the mother keep the baby alive? Can she make him grow and thrive physically? It is this theme . . . that makes success at feeding so vital" (p. 175).

As I understand David's development, this is a crucial organizing event in his life. He is deprived of mother's good milk. What he had has been taken away. Some beginning sense of existence is threatened with annihilation and David fights for his survival. He is a "difficult" baby. He cries, has tantrums, is a "fussy" eater and is not easily soothed. He forces the environment to attend to him. He tries to elicit from the environment that which he has been deprived of by mother.

This breach in the early libidinal relationship between David and his mother represented a pattern that was to be repeated in various forms throughout David's life—first with mother and then with both parents. For example, from the age of 2 months David spent significant amounts of time with baby-sitters. His parents report that one of the sitters was a teenage girl so preoccupied with herself that she would watch TV for hours on end and pay no attention to David, who was left to cry most of the time. The parents fired the girl after a few months, but the story raises a number of questions.

Why was this girl hired or, at the very least, why was she kept on for several months? What does it mean for a child to express frustration and anger for hours on end and not be heard? David's anger was carried over into the relationship with his mother. She describes David as an extremely difficult child who sorely tried her patience. David's mother felt that there was something wrong with him. In the comparison with his sister, he did not fare well. The mother's inadequacies are externalized and David is the one who is impaired (Novick and Novick 1987). Without the libidinal investment in her son, David's mother's judgment is seriously impaired and it is David's fault. This was certainly the case around toilet training.

David's mother described his toilet training as relatively uneventful; nonetheless it was frustrating to her because he had had more difficulty than his sister. From his mother's point of view, David had taken too long, achieving bowel control about the age of 3. Following this there was a regression and he began soiling. His parents decided not to use diapers during this period, and for three to four months David soiled his clothes. The regression seemed coincident with his mother's increased involvement with her job (which meant longer hours away from home and frequent business trips). David's father had always traveled two or three months a year, one or two weeks at a time. Now mother began to take two- or three-week trips, over the course of a year totaling some three to four months. David's reaction to his mother's traveling was intense. He would not speak to her on the phone when she called and would often be enraged at her when she returned. This was in marked contrast to his father's leave-taking, which David seemed to take more in stride. David's mother was, in her own words, "totally oblivious" to separations, and her leave-takings occasioned temper tantrums as well as soiling.

David is not the good, loving, "clean" child who has a burgeoning sense of mastery over bodily functions, drives, and objects. What we see with David is a failure of these aspirations. The failure, however, was not complete. David's longing for his mother seems to have taken the form of an intensification of his aggressive relationship with her; his anger was met by an intensification of her anger toward him. Her attempts to compensate for this anger took the form of a technical relationship toward David where the emphasis was on doing the "right thing." Doing the "right thing" without a libidinal interest in the other is a prescription for failure, and David was treated as if he did not exist. David's sense of helplessness, associated with a failure of narcissistic aspirations, is here defensively altered through a process of reversal. David is the powerful one in the relationship with his mother. She can abandon him, but he can do the same to her and, in the process, deny that her leave-takings have any meaning for him at all. Narcissistic wishes to be loving were replaced by the erotization of wishes to be "bad." David's intense longing for his mother was replaced by an angry sadomasochistic relationship with her.

During the phallic/oedipal period, David's provocative sadomasochistic behavior increased dramatically. He would go often into his parents' bedroom and jump in bed with his mother in a sexual and aggressive manner. If he were asked to leave by either parent, an argument would ensue and David would become verbally abusive. By age 6 or 7 the mixture of sex and aggression was striking: "Take off your clothes, Mom, so 1 can play with your tits before Daddy gets home." Following such incidents, David's father would speak to him, chastise him, or physically carry him to his room. More often than not, David's response to his father's interventions was to say "go fuck yourself."

David's father became a vivid character only when the phallic/oedipal period was reached. Up to that point he remained a passive, shadowy figure who was not a source of support for David. During the latter part of the phallic/oedipal period, and extending into the years typically associated with latency, David's father is described by both parents (and David) as a forceful, highly competitive, and sometimes angry presence in relation to his son.

For David, the competitive situation of the phallic/oedipal period is associated with an earlier time of life when he was small, weak, and helpless in relation to powerful figures who were unavailable to him in a narcissistically enhancing and life-affirming way. The situation is potentiated during this crucial developmental period, at least in part, by his father's competition and anger toward David, which is clearly fueled by David's sadomasochism.

When he was very young David's temper tantrums drew attention, thereby allowing him to be involved with the other through the exercise of his aggression. The more elaborated versions of these temper tantrums when he was 6 or 7, however, represented a restriction of ego functioning that interfered with the gratification of narcissistic aspirations in a realistic way. David could not relinquish his infantile grandiosity so that he could compete with peers and take winning or losing in stride. Losing was tantamount to feeling annihilated and an occasion for attacks of rage; winning, for a grandiose display of elation invariably accompanied by a complete devaluation (i.e., annihilation) of the other.

It is easy to see how such behavior could provoke retaliation. It is a retaliation, however, that on an unconscious level David controls. He provokes the behavior. At home he could not play a board game and lose. He might throw the game all over the room, or accuse the other of cheating and start an argument. Given David's behavior, it is easier to see how he could feel himself feared and disliked rather than admired and the center of attention in a positive, narcissistically enhancing manner.

Bibring (1953) gives the example of a narcissistically vulnerable patient who warded off feelings of helplessness by having a fantasy of walking down the street with a large sword in her hand and cutting off the heads of the people passing by . . ." (p. 44). He makes the point that such aggressive fantasies can be narcissistically gratifying. To a significant extent this was the case with David. His sadistic behavior toward his parents defends against wishes to be loved and cared for, and provides him with a sense of pleasure and excitement associated with the discharge of aggression, and a sense of power associated with verbal and physical abuse of the other. The fantasies underlying these reversals of affects and role relations can reach grandiose proportions and compensate for a profound sense of vulnerability and helplessness. David does to others what he feels has been done to him. When he tells his mother that he would like to fuck her, or calls his father a bitch and throws cat litter all over the house, David is treating others as if they did not exist as people with needs and feelings. This was the situation that existed when David entered treatment a month or two short of his ninth birthday.

## Treatment

David presented as a somewhat short and overweight boy. His parents told me that David felt very uncomfortable about his weight and would not swim without a T-shirt. In the initial sessions there was a forced maturity as he sat in a chair, crossed his legs, and chatted about this and that. One of his favorite conversations was about food. David told me that he carried· prodigious amounts of jelly beans, candy bars, and other assorted treats in his backpack, and he would often open his pack during a session and devour bags of potato chips and candy. When I would make a comment about this, with the intention of exploring it a bit, David would tell me to "shut the fuck up," or he would put his hands over his ears and scream in a high-pitched voice that was deafening. When I commented on the piercing quality of the sound he seemed genuinely pleased and told me that he thought it must be deafening and that he was convinced he could eventually shatter my windows with it. All of this occurred during the first month of treatment.

## The Wannabe King: An Anal-Sadistic Fantasy

In the second month of treatment David decided he wanted to make a castle out of Legos. Construction of the castle was spread over a number of sessions, and David's creativity and skill were apparent in the final product. It was a large castle, with ramps for the guards and a dungeon for prisoners. The dungeon had one prisoner in it, and the reason for this man's imprisonment never became clear. What was clear, however was that the prisoner would escape. This was accomplished through bribing a guard and eventually killing the king who had placed him there. When this was done, the prisoner became king. He made friends with all the neighboring kings, as well as the guards of the former king, now deceased. Everyone seemed to be getting along very well. Then one day the former prisoner, now king, killed all the guards and all the kings and became king of everyone. He became all-powerful.

In David's fantasy he turns the tables on the king who imprisoned him. He does to the king what was done to him—he puts him in a hole. He kills him. In David's fantasy he is also a duplicitous person who kills his friends and colleagues. He is an anal-sadistic king, not an oedipal victor. The pleasure is in tricking and killing the other, not in being strong and victorious, or in getting the admiration of others through courageous deeds. David's victory is an empty one, and he is alone—he kills everyone and he must go on killing. David convinces others that they have a libidinal relationship with him when in fact they don't. He charms them with his libido and destroys them with his aggression. This is a situation that is familiar to David from his early relationship with his mother where he must have felt a sense of attachment, betrayal, and ultimately helplessness. Once again he does to others what he feels has been done to him. In real life, of course, David does not kill people. But he does turn his aggression on them so that he can set up a situation in which the other ceases to be a reliable object and David therefore feels alone—the way he must have felt as a very young child in the absence of a reliable maternal object. The past is re-created in the present like similar Russian dolls nested within each other.

As the work continued, the aggressive nature of David's behavior seemed to climb at an exponential rate. With great elation he would throw his empty food wrappers all over the office and threaten to rub his bubblegum into the couch. David, like Richard, was determined to be a villain. He communicated through action, as well as words, that I had to assume the passive role in our relationship. He was preoccupied with revenge, strength, and power. He might talk, for example, about how he felt that a friend had not treated him properly and how he would get that person back. At times a toy might be thrown at me as the session came to a close, or he might threaten to push all the books off the bookcase on his way out. It was as if he were taking revenge on me for ending the session. The behavior, clearly designed to provoke, did not cross the line where David became unmanageable.

To some extent, however, his provocations were successful. In David's story of the "Wannabe King," David ultimately is left alone because of his aggression. My countertransference was such that I found myself struggling at times to stay connected to him in a positive way, and even after two years of twice-weekly psychotherapy, I often felt apprehensive about seeing David. His abusive behavior made me angry. The work, however, was made most difficult for me because I felt so helpless. I doubted whether I could help David. I often felt as if I were a prop for his foils, and felt that his self-esteem seemed to ride on how he could devalue or provoke me. When not caught up in my countertransferentially induced despair, I could reflect that my feelings of vulnerability, helplessness, anger, and guilt were similar to feelings David has had all his life, feelings he in a sense "gave to me" to hold on to during our sessions. I thought that I was able to help David by containing these feelings for him–something his parents were not able to do.

David's sadomasochistic relationship with his mother was an attempt to adapt to a relationship that, for David, was filled with fears of being hurt or annihilated. This disturbance in the libidinal relationship between David and his mother was re-created in the transference. David felt I was beating him, that is, forcing him to talk about things and treating him as a "retard" or a "psycho." His response to these attacks was to beat me: David actively engaged me through the exercise of his aggression. The Novicks (1987) point out that the therapists of children with fantasies similar to David's often found the work "arduous, joyless, and ungratifying for a long time" (p. 356). I would add to this that I also found working with David an intensely intimate experience. He was never distant or withdrawn. Although David felt I was forcing him to come, he hardly ever missed a session and only rarely did he want to end early. On the contrary, David often wanted to beat me one more time at cards before he left, even if our time was up. He wanted to leave me, as he put it, "penniless, on the street without a dime so your own wife wouldn't bother to even look at you. You're nothing, a real piece of shit." The wish is to obliterate me or, at the very least, humiliate me. David wants me to feel as he has felt so much of his life. His way of relating to me is to engage in a perverse relationship. It is an anal-sadistic relationship that is highly charged and intimate.

At card games David would cheat openly. If I commented on this obvious behavior, he would deny it, become enraged at me, and accuse me of calling him a liar. What was particularly interesting was the fact that David's superior intelligence and need to win made him an excellent cardplayer. His strategy, concentration, and investment in the game would assuredly have led to victory without any recourse to cheating. It was the cheating, abusiveness, and overall provocative behavior that was the essence of David's perverse relationship with me and everyone else, particularly his parents. I believe that this way of relating provided David a certain distance from intense longings for intimacy that were terrifying to him. Patterns of sadism and masochism were repeated at different levels and took an endless variety of forms.

The following vignette exemplifies the sadomasochistic fantasies, the underlying sense of vulnerability, and the communicative value of an enactment when the therapist is able to extricate himself from the pull of countertransference and get back to the work of understanding rather than enacting.

### The Baseball Cap Enactment

During the second year of treatment, David spent a session showing me his voluminous collection of superhero cards. For the most part I listened and asked a question from time to time so that I could better understand the nature and function of each superhero. When I felt there was an opportunity to do so, I might offer a comment about the defensive and gratifying aspects of these fantasy figures, and muse aloud how anyone might feel strong and totally protected if he were like one of these superheroes or had some connection with them. My line of thought was not lost on David, and at some point he told me to "cut the cheap psychology crap, you fucking retard."

David experienced my comments as a narcissistic injury. His fragile sense of self seemed so dependent on the maintenance of grandiose fantasies of omnipotence that any suggestion of vulnerability was met by rage and devaluation. Overall, however, the session was colored in a distinctly positive, I would say libidinal, tone. David wanted to show me his card collection and clearly valued my interest in it. He was in no hurry to leave the session, and I did not feel a great need to *do* something with the material.

As the session drew to a close and David collected his things and started to leave, I noticed that he had left his baseball cap on the couch. I mentioned this to him as I picked it up and flipped it to him. He dropped it, picked it up, and left.

The next session began on the same positive note. David began to draw superheroes and asked if I had any Wite-Out he could use to correct a drawing. After he had used it, I noticed that he had left the cap off. I asked if he would put it on, and he did. The next thing I saw was the bottle of Wite-Out moving through the air at a considerable speed toward my head. I had the uncanny sensation that time had slowed down. As I watched the bottle moving toward me, I wondered how I would feel seeing patients for the rest of the day covered by Wite-Out. I put up my hand, caught the bottle, and had the sense that I might cry. I blurted out, "Why did you do that?" David calmly responded, "Because you threw my baseball cap at me."

David could not express in words the meaning of the previous day's experience. To say "because you threw my baseball cap at me" does not do justice to the intensity of the feelings he may have had. For David, throwing the Wite-Out and inducing certain feelings in me that were similar to his own was an essential step in the communicative process. Only after the action was performed could David try to approach the experience through the use of language. Freedman (1994) has written about the sequence of action followed by recollection and insight; he notes that increased levels of mental reorganization are often preceded by an action, acting out, or enactment. The terms are often used interchangeably. As I understand

Freedman, enactments are often related to a failure of language. Thoughts and impulses that cannot be represented through spoken language can achieve representation through action.

In a related vein, Mahon (1991) has outlined the advance from the more concrete and action-oriented thinking of the prelatency child to the more abstract thought and language of the child who has had a relatively successful resolution of the Oedipus complex and entered the psychological state of latency (Sarnoff 1976, pp. 115-121). Bach (1994) has argued that on a preoeidpal level the "child's words must 'pass through' a receptive or attuned parent and be endowed with affect and significance in the course of this passage before they return to the child as 'meaningful words'" (p. 145). The child must be heard by the parent in an emotionally meaningful way so that words can be used as symbols to communicate to others the child's experience of the world. David's language is skewed toward primary as opposed to secondary process; in Piagetian terms, it is preoperational rather than being at the level of concrete operations (Steingart 1983). In short, because words are inadequate to convey the intensity of his feelings, David switches to a different level of representation-action.

David's reliance on action makes the therapist's task of containment more difficult. It is one thing to have an intellectual appreciation for David's narcissistic difficulties and quite another when they present as actions that lead to powerful emotional responses in the therapist.

The therapeutic process takes the form of a mini drama played out between patient and therapist, one fueled by transference and countertransference distortions. McLaughlin (1991) has described such dramas as a mix of verbal and motoric behavior of such force and intensity that they influence the other to respond in a particular way. It is only when the therapist can extricate him or herself from the countertransference and metaphorically step back and return to the job of analyzing, rather than enacting, that he or she is in a position to understand the meaning the patient has given to the transference situation (Chused 1991, Lasky 1993). At some point, aspects of this understanding can be given to the patient in the form of a verbal intervention that can help explain, clarify, or organize the enactment. The verbalization of this action-oriented, effectively laden "thing" (i.e., enactment) is an attempt to make the unconscious conscious. For this to be successful, it must take place in an atmosphere of trust where David feels that his words and actions are important and have meaning. Only then can the words that I attach to the situation represent a new way to look at things, rather than a challenge to David's sense of reality and an invitation to continue the sadomasochistic enactment.

A necessary condition for the establishment of therapeutic trust is the therapist's ability to be attuned to the patient's inner emotional states, to think about these states, and to understand how the other views the experience before attempting to intervene. In short, the therapist must take the patient's feelings, thoughts, and actions very seriously. The therapist must avoid the establishment of a technical relationship (without minimizing the importance of good technique) and strive to libidinize the patient through the exercise of therapeutic love–a process where the therapist is "devoted" to deepening his understanding of the patient's psychic reality, his unconscious construction of the world (Steingart 1995). This is how I understand the process of containment.

David has organized the transference relationship in a way that is consistent with his unconscious representation of the world. In this situation the intricacies of personal meaning include for David his feeling that I am trying to hurt or humiliate him by throwing the baseball cap. For the work to proceed in a productive way, it is crucial that the therapist be able to use his feelings as signals that act as an affective dimension to the pattern of meaning created by the patient.

In this situation, my feeling that I might cry is crucial in understanding how I organized what went on between us. I felt hurt by someone I thought was my friend. I used these words because they help explain why I felt like crying. David had become part of my dynamic past. I did not feel like a therapist attempting to help a troubled child. I felt like a vulnerable child who had been betrayed. I became the container for David's feelings.

My initial evaluation of this situation was as follows: David dropped the baseball cap, and for him this represented a terrible humiliation. It is the emotional counterpart to beating me at cards and leaving me turned into a piece of shit on the street. Loss—the dropping of the cap, losing a board game or a game of cards—feels like an annihilation to David. Of course he felt hurt by me. Who wouldn't in such a circumstance? The word "hurt" does not even begin to capture the extent of David's unpleasure. It feels like the narcissistic humiliation experienced by a baby crying for attention only to be ignored; by a 2-year-old who feels terrible shame and humiliation when an unempathic parent scolds him over a loss of bowel control; or by a child who feels humiliated when he must walk around in soiled clothing, or ignored and filled with impotent rage when his mother leaves on a business trip. All of these childhood calamities may be condensed into the baseball cap incident.

The act of throwing the Wite-Out at me, though very dramatic, in fact follows a set pattern in David's overall behavior. The incident exemplifies David's use of aggression to defend against feelings of vulnerability and helplessness. In this case the immediacy and intensity of my own emotional response allowed me to understand that the enactment was also David's struggle for survival, a desperate attempt to be heard, to be understood. It is David's way of trying to maintain a meaningful relationship with me. He needs to let me know that I hurt his feelings in order for this relationship to have any value to him. And David must feel that I can welcome, understand, and eventually help him with these feelings–in short, that I can contain his feelings of being hurt and angry.

## The Dialectic between Psychic and Material Reality

Before the therapist can help the patient understand the enactment, a crucial question concerning the nature of reality must be addressed. For example, is David's father in actuality a monster who wants to kill his son ("break his neck") and therefore someone who David must ward off through the use of aggression? Or is it more accurate to say that David takes his fantasies about his father and turns them, through the use of projective identification, into a virtual reality that induces the other to act in a way consistent with the fantasy? (Here I refer to projective identification as an interpersonal maneuver, as opposed to limiting it to fantasy. The extension of this concept from fantasy [Klein 1946] to behavior has been elucidated by Ogden [1979]).

But I began this discussion by saying David dropped the cap. I could just as easily have asked why I threw the cap. Does the flip of the cap really represent my unconscious wish to hurt David? Or is it a friendly gesture, that is multiply determined, that may therefore contain sadistic elements that David selectively responds to because of his unconscious mental set?

It is in the heat of the transference, where the therapist can look at himself as well as at the patient, that questions concerning the nature of reality can best be answered. In this case I have no doubt that it is David's psychic reality, his unconscious organization of the world, that defines the present along the lines of the past. For David this past includes significant narcissistic insult early in life. His response to the baseball cap incident is understandable from this perspective. David's dynamic organization of the present fits into the pattern of meaning established earlier in life and is reinforced through his compensatory and defensive strategies.

It is the exercise of aggression that is David's primary and automatic defense against these narcissistic injuries. While oedipal issues are clearly present, it is David's excitement in humiliating the other, in wiping the other out, that is the primary driving force behind his fantasies and behavior.

David's anal-sadistic organization is a compromise position that defends against longing to be a passive little boy who will be loved and cared for, on the one hand, and fears of being ignored and humiliated— "Wited-Out," if you will—on the other.

For a child to begin to master the Oedipus complex and move out into the larger world and say, in effect, "this is who I am and this is what I want, and I am not all-powerful–I know that my father is bigger and stronger than me and that his relationship with my mother is different from mine," there must be some basic sense of self-worth and trust about himself and others. The development of trust and self-worth is initiated very early in life and speaks to a certain kind of relationship in which the child can receive narcissistic supplies, which leads to libidinal investment in self and object representations. This process was interfered with in David's development. To become the center of attention, he provokes the other. Thus he receives attention with a negative sign: hate not love. This is the masochistic counterpart of his sadistic behavior. This situation is very familiar to David and has, as the Novicks put it, "the smell of home" (1987, p.363).

With David's need for love in mind, I would like to entertain another interpretation of the enactment. In this scenario David did not become upset when I flipped the baseball cap to him. His positive affect at the beginning of the next session can support such a consideration. Instead he became upset when I asked him to put the Wite-Out cap back on the bottle. Why didn't I assume that he might use the bottle again, or that he would put the cap on when he finished drawing? Was I afraid of David's aggression and treating him like a time bomb about to explode? If this is so, it is a clear example of how the past actively organizes the present through the inducement of certain feelings, attitudes, and behavior in the other that are similar to feelings, attitudes, and behaviors of significant objects from the past.

Another way of looking at this situation is to consider that my motivation for asking David about the Wite-Out cap was a maneuver on my part to push him away. Was I uncomfortable with the intensity of his positive feelings? With someone like David the narcissistic defenses (e.g., rage and devaluation) can so dominate the clinical picture that the underlying longing for love (narcissistic supplies) can fade into the background. David's need to get attention and involvement from the other is reflected by the intensity of his defenses, particularly his aggression. In my work with David I have learned that it is his libidinal feelings, his need for me to *want* to be with him (he has accused me of seeing him only because I am paid to by his parents), that is often a factor in the transference/countertransference constellation. It is David's need to be loved (i.e., his wish to be comforted, to be held in high esteem) as well as his hatred that must be contained by the therapist.

## Summary

David, like Richard, was ripped out of his state of narcissistic omnipotence before his time. Mother's bad milk (factually and metaphorically) was an impingement that shattered David's fragile sense of narcissistic omnipotence and did not allow for "optimal disillusionments" and a gradual abstraction of infantile omnipotence in the form of a positively cathected ego ideal (Blos 1979, Freud 1914). 1t is the narcissistically enhancing sense of omnipotence of infancy and early childhood that is the "foundation on which trust in oneself and the world is built. Indeed, it is when these *experiences of omnipotence* are lacking and the object's failures impinge on the child that a reactive *defensive omnipotence* arises to deny and overcompensate for feelings of annihilation and death of the self" (Bach 1994, p. 172).

I have suggested that a failure of narcissistic aspirations in infancy and early childhood was met with by a mobilization of aggression on David's part. Initially the aggression was a way of expressing frustration and attracting his mother's attention. Over time the aggression became pleasurable in its own right and was used in the pursuit of grandiose fantasies of omnipotence. The narcissistic rage and devaluation of the other also turned passivity into activity and served to defend against longings for intimacy that threatened to reactivate feelings of helplessness and despair. The fantasy of the Wannabe King was seen as a compromise formation with primarily preoedipal determinants. In this fantasy the wish to sadistically attack the other represents an anal sadistic organization that fuels oedipal conflicts. In this fantasy David's murderous rage puts him in a position where he is alone. It was suggested that in real life David potentially "kills off" the other by inducing aggression or fear in them; this, while exciting to David in his anal struggles, carries with it the threat of abandonment. This was particularly clear in the clinical process referred to as an enactment.

An analysis of my reaction to David can suggest that wishes to hurt David or to move away from his intense feelings, libidinal as well as aggressive, may have played a role in the baseball cap incident. I also speculated that these feelings may have been implicated in my initial reaction to the Wite-Out cap.

All patients attempt to actualize the transference by converting their wishes to actions that can induce the therapist to behave in ways that confirm the patient's psychic reality. These actions, or mini dramas, are compromise formations that are related to the gratification of, or defense against, transference wishes (Boesky 1982). These issues are crucial in our work with all patients, but are accentuated with a child like David who can feel easily hurt and humiliated.

David's narcissistic vulnerability, the propensity to experience the present along the lines·of failed narcissistic aspirations of the past, leads to the rapid mobilization of aggression, with a heightened potential for action. This action potential is directly related to the consistent failure of narcissistic aspirations, which has led to a less than adequate mastery of the Oedipus ·complex. This has a direct bearing on David's thought and language, which is skewed toward an archaic organization and cannot be used to convey the intensity of his affective state.

For David to remain in a meaningful relationship he must be able to express his feelings about the other. When this expression is organized primarily around action, the demand on the other (therapist, parent, friend) not to respond in kind becomes very great. In the therapeutic situation, the therapist's capacity to contain David's emotional expressions and tactfully convey the meaning of the transference situation is crucial to therapeutic success. With patients less narcissistically vulnerable, the process of containment can often remain in the background; it is both necessary and, for the most part, readily available. With patients like David, however. It is more likely to be the focus of the therapist's attention throughout the treatment.

## Sadomasochism–Another Perspective

The theme of loss and restitution runs through David's sadomasochistic enactments. One form it takes is David's provoking the other to attack him. This would be tantamount to a loss of the reliable object, the contemporary representation of bad milk. In these enactments David does not quite go over the edge—he doesn't push the bookcase over. When he does push the other too far he is able to re-establish the libidinal aspects of the relationship. He oscillates between order and disorder, between maintaining libidinal connections, severing them, and bringing them back to life. Of course, I am describing the external manifestations of David's internal world.

David's sadomasochistic world is something he knows very well. It is a world where one is beaten or does the beating, and it represents "a perversion of reality" (Frosch 1995, Grossman 1993, Steingart 1983) where fantasy and aggression take precedence over reality and libido. The fantasies are organized around sadomasochistic constructions that hold out the promise of redemption—the mother of pain is associated with the mother of pleasure. As the protagonist in Pauline Reage's (1965) *Story of O* says—"It is only when you make me suffer that I feel safe and secure." It is only when O's sadistic "master" is about to leave her that she chooses to die. The painful blows of the sadist's whip defend against the greater pain of loss and annihilation.

In David's fantasies the suffering is typically associated with the de-valued other. Narcissistic trauma and self-annihilation have been transformed into a grandiose affirmation of the self. David can do anything he wants, with anyone he wants, in any way that he wants, and particularly in ways that are forbidden. Negativism has become the object of idealization (Bach 1984, pp. 145-146). Loss and restitution take place in the destruction and restitution of the all-powerful object. In David's fantasy world of anal omnipotence, self and object are always interchangeable. Sadism and masochism are different sides of the same coin. Self and object exist as complements, or they do not exist at all. This sadomasochistic world of suffering and redemption, loss and restitution, is a reflection of the disturbance in the pleasure economy between David and his mother and is re-created in the transference.

## Concluding Comments

For David thought and language are still skewed toward archaic levels of organization. Therefore his use of action instead of words allows the therapist an opportunity to see his narcissistic vulnerabilities in an emotionally charged way. This provides an occasion for containment and the potential for insight-oriented interventions. At the same time, however, the therapist's capacity for containment can be compromised during affectively charged and action-oriented dramatizations of David's internal world directed at the person of the therapist. At these times the potential for action, as opposed to analysis, on the therapist's part can be destructive to the therapeutic process. It is a dangerous thing if reality fulfills repressed wishes. The phantasy becomes reality and all defensive measures are thereupon reinforced" (Freud 1928, p.186). David exerts pressure on reality to bend to his fantasy expectations. That is to say, he tries to induce *material reality* (current experience with others) to fit into the pattern of expectations based on *psychic reality*—his collection of narcissistically informed archaic unconscious fantasies organized as compromise formations.

## References

Bach, S. (1985). *Narcissistic states and the therapeutic process.* New York: Jason Aronson.

———(1994). *The language of perversion and the language of love.* Northvale, NJ: Jason Aronson.

Bibring, E. (1953). The mechanism of depression. In H. Greenacre (Ed.), *Affective disorders* (pp. 13-48). New York: International Universities Press.

Blos, P. (1979). The genealogy of the ego ideal. In *The adolescent passage* (pp. 43-88). New York: International Universities Press.

Boesky, D. (1982). Acting out—A reconsideration of the concept. *International Journal of Psycho-Analysis,* 63:39-57.

Chused, J. (1991). The evocative power of enactments. *Journal of the American Psychoanalytic Association,* 39:615–639.

Freedman, N. (1994). More on transformation: Enactments in psychoanalytic space. In A. K. Richards & A. D. Richards (Eds.), *Spectrum of psychoanalysis: Essays in honor of Martin S. Bergmann* (pp. 93-110). Madison, CT: International Universities Press.

Freud, S. (1914). On narcissism: An introduction. *Standard Edition,* 14:67–104.

———(1928). Dostoevsky and parricide. *Standard Edition,* 21:175–196.

Frosch, A. (1995). The preconceptual organization of emotion. *Journal of the American Psychoanalytic Association,* 43(4):423–447.

Grossman, L. (1993). The perverse attitude toward reality. *Psychoanalytic Quarterly*, 42(3):422–436.

Klein, M. (1946). Notes on some schizoid mechanisms. *International Journal of Psycho-Analysis*, 27:99-110.

Lasky, R. (1993) *Dynamics of Development and the Therapeutic Process.* Northvale, NJ: Jason Aronson.

Mahon, E. J. (l991). The "dissolution" of the Oedipus complex: A neglected cognitive factor. *Psychoanalytic Quarterly*, 50:628–636.

McLaughlin, J. T. (1991). Clinical and theoretical aspects of enactment. *Journal of the American Psychoanalytic Association*, 39:595–614.

Novick, K., & Novick, J. (1987). The essence of masochism. *Psychoanalytic Study of the Child*, 42:353-384.

Ogden, T. (1979). On projective identification. *International Journal of Psycho-Analysis*, 60:357–373.

Reage, P. (1965). *Story of O.* New York: Ballantine Books.

Sarnoff, C. (1976). *Latency.* New York: Jason Aronson.

Shakespeare, W. (1593). *The Tragedy of King Richard III.* In W. Wright, (Ed.), *The complete works of Shakespeare* (pp. 111-156). Garden City, NY: Garden City Books, 1936.

Smith, G. (1957). *A history of England.* New York: Charles Scribner's Sons.

Steingart, I. (1983). *Pathological play in borderline and narcissistic personalities.* Jamaica, NY: Spectrum.

———(1995). *A thing apart.* Northvale, NJ: Jason Aronson.

Stern, D. (1995). *The motherhood constellation: A unified view of parent-infant psychotherapy.* New York: Basic Books.

# Psychoanalytic Realities

The ideas outlined in Allan Frosch's earlier developmental papers took a jump forward with the invitation to participate in a *Festschrift* for Norbert Freedman, organized to honor his contributions to the widening scope of psychoanalysis. Via Bert's research, theory and technique around the central role of symbolization in the analytic process, Allan began to articulate his view of the dialectical tension between psychic and material reality. This nascent articulation evolved to become a unique frame of reference and central current in his thinking and experience that would continue over the course of his career.

In this series of papers written and published over just two years, Allan's capacity to both honor and make creative "use" of Bert's work, of Freud's constructs of primary and secondary process, and of Winnicott's focus on the parallels between the earliest relationship and its echo in the clinical setting are all at play. The word "play" is key as he described in his first paper in the case of sadomasochistic compensation in a child therapy. Things can and indeed must get rough at times. The analyst must become an essential character and a co-constructor in the dramatic action, participate in an emotionally meaningful way and, most importantly, survive the concrete reality of what he would later crystallize as a patient's "unbearable psychic pain."

Richard Lasky articulates this aspect of Allan's thinking and clinical approach as a core receptivity to, and containment of, all the hating and loving aspects that a patient may bring to the transference. He underscores Allan's conviction that when the analyst is immersed in the primary process experience of the patient, and even when interpretations cannot be heard and emotionally experienced in the secondary process, analysis is still possible. This notion was taken up by Neal Vorus in describing this next iteration in Allan's ideas as the construction of a "conceptual bridge"—between classical and relational views of symbolization of transference and countertransference—a non-linear systems approach to the dyad as an intimate, intersubjective relationship.

Tessa Addison captures Allan Frosch's unique capacity to immerse himself in the clinical encounter and conceptualize this experience in his writing, but also to transmit on a broader scale his hope and trust in the transformative power of analysis. She notes that in her analytic supervision with him, he was a collaborative, collegial witness and mentor who conveyed an emotional honesty about the analytic process that fostered her own development as an analyst.

# CHAPTER 3

# Psychic Reality and the Analytic Relationship

## Reflections on "Psychic Reality and the Analytic Relationship"

### Tessa Addison

In "Psychic Reality and the Analytic Relationship," Allan Frosch takes us through the history of "psychic reality" as an analytic concept. It is a cogent and pithy theoretical walk-through and would stand alone as such. But Allan does not leave it there. His focus in the paper's second half, illuminated with the thoughtful elaboration of clinical material, is what I take to be core to Allan's concerns: the transformational power of the analytic relationship.

Allan was my supervisor and mentor, not my analyst. We can all agree that the analytic and supervisory processes are significantly different. Nonetheless, rather than recapitulate Allan's arguments or do his nuanced explication the injustice of summarization, I would like to use this introduction to suggest that some of the same conditions Allan lays out as necessary to analytic impact on psychic reality are also critical for growth within the supervisory setting.

In moments, for example, when my countertransference made maintaining my "loving desire to understand the patient's mind" difficult, I believe Allan's interest and "belief in the efficacy of the analytic enterprise" held space for me to regain my own. And when it came time to write my final case report and I despaired of ever being able to do so, I felt Allan holding hope for me. Constrained by the rigidities of my own psychic reality, I struggled to see a way forward. Like the woman in this paper's opening vignette, I had the wish, the inhibition, and the substitution of alternative action. I wanted to write, but would do almost anything else, including, occasionally, going back to bed instead of going to supervision.

What allowed me, ultimately, to finish that paper, graduate and become the analyst capable of writing this essay? Or to put the question in the terms of this paper, what allowed my fantasies and patterned behaviors around writing to shift enough to make the closed system of this aspect of my psychic reality a more open one? My analyst's sustained and sustaining interest, surely. But also, I believe it was my experience of Allan, of his remarkable intelligence, tremendous patience, and easygoing humor, and of "the action, the back-and-forth ways of going at things, both verbal and nonverbal" of the supervision and the "build-up of a particular kind of safety and trust" that allowed me not only to take in and metabolize his contributions to my understanding of the case, but also to "modify the affective core of [my] basic orientation to the world." It is my loss not to have understood the impact Allan had on my psychic reality soon enough to convey my appreciation to him more fully; it is our community's loss that he is no longer with us and available to form similarly transformative relationships with future generations of analysands and supervisees.

\*　　\*　　\*

# Psychic Reality and the Analytic Relationship

*Allan Frosch*

> Psychic reality is the world as we perceive it; and fantasy is the way we
> give meaning to experience (Friedman, 1995).

A thirty-one-year-old woman is in an analysis with a female analyst. The
woman is unemployed and in a session talks about how she got out of
bed that day with every intention of looking for a job. After a moment
or two she decided to go back to bed. Here we have a wonderful paradigm for viewing psychic reality. There is a wish (I want to get a job
today), an inhibition of a goal-directed action, and a substitution of
another action—going back to bed. Between the wish and the ac-
tion/inaction lies psychic reality—the meanings the patient
unconsciously ascribes to the world. For this woman looking for a job
means that she will either get a job that is "mundane and boring …
empty" or one where she will "bite off more than I can chew." We are not
surprised that her experience of the analysis is that it is also useless and
empty, but yet she cannot wait to come every day. Sometimes the desire
to come feels like it is too much to bear. Over time the analyst understands that this alternation between a sense of deprivation and
emptiness on the one hand and feelings of being overwhelmed and out
of control on the other may be related to her relationship with a depressed, alcoholic mother and a very exciting but relatively unavailable
father. It is a pattern of organizing experience, or giving meaning to the
world, where her earliest relationships with significant others have been
altered and maintained over the course of a lifetime. The analyst's take of
how the past presents in the here and now of this woman's life is a construction put together by patient and analyst.

So what we are talking about with this woman's organization of the
present represents an intermingling of past and present, internal and
external, imagination and actual event. As we grow up we try to make
sense of the world, primarily our experiences with others. We develop
beliefs about how things work, and in psychoanalysis many of these

beliefs are called fantasies. These fantasies are compromise formations where wishes and defenses are organized around intense emotions. Our ideas about ourselves and others, our self and object representations, are constructions that carry certain expectations as well as strategies for minimizing unpleasure and maximizing pleasure—for providing what Joseph Sandler (1960) called "a background of safety." This sense of safety was not available for this woman as she grew up, and her expectation of self and other, or self in relation to other, is that she will be traumatized, and feel empty or overwhelmed.

The format of this article also moves between past and present. Freud's ideas from different time periods are presented alongside the ideas of contemporary theorists so that we can see how earlier formulations of psychic reality are altered and maintained—how they are embedded, so to speak, in our contemporary ideas, and how later concepts alter the meaning we give to earlier formulations of psychic reality. In the first half of the article I will highlight what I believe to be a uniquely psychoanalytic perspective: Namely, that in its essence, psychic reality always reflects a person's earliest experience with significant objects, what the French analyst H. Faimberg (1995) refers to as a psyche "constituted in relation to primordial others" (p. 10). The meaning of these experiences are transformed, that is, altered and maintained, over the course of one's life. To the extent that they are maintained, contemporary experience is assimilated into this schema for giving meaning to the world, and psychic reality is understood as a closed system. To the degree that contemporary events (or objects) can be experienced as different, the organization of meaning from the past can accommodate new experience and we can think of psychic reality in terms of a relatively open system. In the second half of the article I will talk about the analyst's role in this process of assimilation/accommodation.

I will also address some of the implications of the idea that our unconscious construction of the world is always, to a greater or lesser extent, a new edition or "merely a new impression or reprint" (Freud, 1905a, p. 116) of our earliest relationships with significant others. This is particularly important in the analytic situation where the idea of a continuum with new editions on one end and mere reprints on the other roughly translates into symbolized or desymbolized versions of earlier experience. In my opinion the concept of such a continuum is often "forgotten" by the analyst, particularly when we move toward the more linear reprints or desymbolized forms of the transference.

## *Psychic Reality*

In a letter to Fliess in December of 1896 Freud talked about what he thought was essentially new about his theory of mind: "the stratification of memories through translations across developmental epochs. ... [I am working on the assumption] [that] our psychic mechanism has come into being by a process of stratification: the material present in the form of memory traces being subjected from time to time to a rearrangement in accordance with fresh circumstances ... to a retranscription .... [M]emory is present not once but several times over ... [and] the successive registrations represent the psychic achievement of successive epochs of life" (Masson, 1985, p. 207). Here, at least in outline form, is what Grossman (1992) called Freud's recursive representational model: Memories are rearranged in accordance with fresh circumstances and contemporary events represent earlier ones. This recursive representational model of mind is a maker of meaning. The stratification of translations refers to a relation of meaning with successive translations becoming more complex and abstract (cf. Schimek, 1975; Vorus, 1998). One's experience of a current object (or event) represents an earlier one organized on a different level of complexity. The meaning of the past is nested in the present, but it is a past that is both altered and maintained. If these translations went well, the current object could stand for the archaic one but still be seen as an object in itself (Rycroft, 1956). In short, the contemporary object represents or symbolizes the archaic one. Psychopathology is seen as a failure of translation due to the traumatic nature of the early event so that contemporary events are experienced as the earlier traumatic one. We could say that the current event is not a representation of the past, but is a re-presentation of it. At this point in 1896 Freud believed in his "neurotica" or seduction theory, so sexual traumas and the pathological defensive efforts directed toward their memory were understood to lead to a situation where the past was alive in the present.

By the following year, however, Freud confided to Fleiss that he no longer believed in the seduction theory: "There are no indications of reality in the unconscious; so that we cannot distinguish between truth and fiction that has been cathected with affect" (Masson, 1985, p. 264). By 1899 he questioned "whether we have any memories at all from our childhood: memories relating to our childhood may be all that we possess" (Freud, 1899, p. 322). I would paraphrase this and say that we do not have memories of reality but about reality, and that all of our perceptions, like all of our memories, are best understood as amalgams of fact and fiction (Fogel, 1993). This reflects an active view of perception where reality is always a complex intermingling of inner and outer, the external event and the subjective context. This complex intermingling is what "really" happened as far as the person is concerned (Michaels & Roughton, 1985), so that psychic reality is, for each of us, our only reality. In the 1880s and well into the 1900s Freud favored a more passive (or copy) model of perception. Within the limitations of our sensory system our perceptions were seen as an accurate reflection of reality. The memories of these perceptions, however, acquired a personal and subjective meaning because they were imbued with wishes and fantasies. Wishes distorted the contents of memories, not the perception of reality. Thus reality (perceptions) and fantasy (drive-cathected memories) were in opposition to each other (Schimek, 1975, p. 174). For Freud, there was the world of external, factual, or material reality and the separate inner subjective world of psychic reality.

The opposition between inner and outer was evident in all of Freud's discussions of psychic reality. In 1900 he introduced the concept of "psychical reality" in *The Interpretation of Dreams*: "When we look at unconscious wishes reduced to their truest shape, we shall have to conclude, no doubt, that psychical reality is a particular form of existence not to be confused with material reality" (p. 620). Unconscious wishes were conceived of as impulses that seek to reestablish the situation of the original, or actual satisfaction (p. 566), and it is only these primitive (or primary process) presentations that were considered psychic reality (cf. Vorus, 1998, p. 206). If, as Freud said to Fleiss in 1889, fantasy was the key to it all (Masson, 1985, p. 340), it was not quite the key in 1900. Fantasies were more apt to be seen as transitional or intermediate thoughts, the secondary process elaborations used to infer the primary process wishes that were the true psychical reality.

Over the next decade Freud sketched out a model of mental development based on a child's earliest relationship with its mother. "The child sucking at its mother's breast has become the prototype of every relation of love. The finding of an object is in fact a refinding of it" (1905b, p. 222). What is also a part of this love relationship is the child's experience of being treated as a sexual object: "A child's mother strokes him, kisses him, rocks him, and quite clearly treats him as a substitute for a complete sexual object" (p. 223). By 1910, in his paper on Leonardo da Vinci, Freud talked about the "organic impression" (p. 87) of the infant sucking at the mother's breast as one that remains with us in disguised forms throughout our lives.

With the idea of a highly charged reciprocal relationship between mother and infant—adult and child—Freud was developing a model that is very much in accord with contemporary models of mind. His idea of action patterns (mother strokes, baby sucks) associated with the earliest events of infancy is consistent with aspects of attachment theory (cf. Fonagy, 2001, pp. 48–50), and some of the mother-infant research that emphasizes the reciprocal regulatory system between mother and infant that lays the foundation for self-regulation later in life (Beebe, Lachmann and Jaffe, 1997; Silverman, 1998). In a series of papers Fonagy and Target (Fonagy, 1995; Fonagy & Target, 1996; Target & Fonagy, 1996) have argued that the development of self-regulation and a subjective world (psychic reality) is related to the parents' capacity to think about thoughts, feelings, and desires in the infant's mind and in their own mind in relation to the infant (Fonagy & Target, 2002, p. 321). What they call mentalization or representations of psychological states in the mind of the infant is related to the caregivers' mindfulness of the child's mental states (Fonagy & Target, 2002, p. 321).

Freud's thinking did not go in this direction, and by 1913, in *Totem and Taboo*, he moved from the mother of infancy to the father of our prehistoric past, and the killing of the father by the primal horde became the prototype for the oedipal drama, with the important difference, of course, that neurotics "are above all inhibited in their actions: with them the thought is a complete substitute for the deed" (p. 161). In this work Freud returned to the concept of psychic reality for the first time in over a decade: Our phylogenetic ancestors did as they intended to do, whereas neurotics respond to psychical reality "and are punishing themselves for impulses which were merely felt" (p. 161).

If, as Freud said in 1897, the past is a preparation for the present (Masson, 1985, p. 274), it is now the very distant past in the form of inherited schemata of these prototypical events carried by "primal phantasies" (a concept he introduced in 1915 [See Freud, 1915a] and more fully elaborated in 1917) that is becoming the basis of mind. The primal fantasies are given shape by this prehistoric past and simultaneously act as organizers for contemporary experience. By 1917 psychic reality had evolved from referring to an unconscious wish to fantasies that "possess a reality of a sort. ... The phantasies possess psychical as contrasted with material reality, and we gradually learn to understand that in the world of neuroses it is psychical reality which is of the decisive kind" (1917, p. 368).

It was Freud's movement toward phylogenetic memories (in the form of rough outlines or schemas of prototypical events such as castration and the killing of the father), as misguided as most people felt (and feel) it to be, that allowed him the conceptual freedom, so to speak, to develop a purely subjective construction of mind which, at least from my perspective, argues against a clear distinction between psychic reality and material reality. In his article on "Negation" Freud (1925) moved away from a passive or copy theory of perception: "perception is not a purely passive process" (p. 238). The unconscious sends out feelers into the external world that select and organize, that is, construct a world of "reality." He relates this process to the child's earliest experiences in the world: "Expressed in the language of the oldest instinctual impulses, the judgement is: 'I should like to eat this'/or 'I should like to spit it out,' and put more generally: 'I should like to take this into myself and to keep that out'" (p. 237). Here Freud returns to the infant sucking at its mother's breast to discuss the process of our active construction of the world. Instinctual impulses are now equated with fantasies (cf. Vorus, 1998). These ideas about our earliest construction of the world were first presented in "Instincts and Their Vicissitudes" (1915b), two years after the publication of *Totem and Taboo* and the very same year Freud sent what he called his phylogenetic fantasy to Ferenczi. In that document the father persecuted his sons and castrated them (at least the older ones), and the sons eventually killed the primal father (Grubrich-Simitis, 1988).

Most contemporary analysts would agree that fantasies, oedipal or otherwise, can be shaped or given form via the parent or caretaker's attitude, thoughts, and ways of handling the child, without any need to rely on phylogenetically acquired schemata. This was certainly the point of view of Schimek (1975) who, like Freud, rooted the world of fantasy to actual experience—although for Schimek the deed was much closer to home. It is the infant's relation to its mother, conceptualized as an affectively charged sensorimotor schema, that organizes our unconscious construction of the world. These early constructions ascribe meaning to the world in the form of what Schimek called regulatory principles, or organized ways of going at things, what we might call today procedural memories or presymbolic representations which become part of dynamically organized unconscious precursors of self and object representations that early in life are pointed toward survival (cf. Silverman, 1998).

Wilma Bucci's (2002) idea of a system of subsymbolic nonverbal organized thought based on somatic, sensorimotor processes is a creative transformation of some of Schimek's thinking into the language of information processing, cognitive psychology, and neuropsychology. Bucci believes that patient and analyst communicate profoundly in this early mode of thought, which she likens to intuition. It is this very early form of thought that makes up the affective core of what Bucci calls "emotion schemas."

Emotion schemas are built and rebuilt through repeated interactions with mother-other from the beginning of life, and constitute one's knowledge of one's self in relation to others (Bucci, 2002, p. 771). For Bucci (see also Schimek, 1975; Fonagy & Target, 2002; Schore, 2002), these early emotional configurations can also be represented on a neurological level in the form of firing patterns in the brain. This is consistent with a recursive representational system where events are represented at different levels of organization (or abstraction). Thus the infant's organic impressions at its mother's breast may be thought of in somatic or neurophysiological terms as well as being conceptualized as elaborations of such impressions in the form of fantasies. A person's psychic reality must include all of these at different levels of representation. Fantasy is the product of a mind whose function is to represent experience, that is, to give meaning to the world. Let me give you an example of what I mean through a vignette presented in a paper by Anne Marie Sandler (1975) that I will use as a segue into the second half of this paper.

A young man who had been in analysis for many years presented with a pattern of behavior that Sandler saw as a defense against sexual feelings for his mother and death wishes toward his father. He would study and do well but would not complete the final part of his examinations. He would become engaged and break the engagement when the emotional involvement became too close. This pattern was repeated in the analysis where he would first absorb the analyst's interpretations with a great deal of pleasurable understanding and then, towards the end of the session, recapitulate the interpretations "and would, so to speak, fling them in the analyst's face" (p. 368). One day the patient reported that his roommate had bought a bicycle and now there were two bicycles in the hallway, but this was too much and the landlord would surely insist on both bicycles being removed, whereas he previously tolerated one. He then went on to speak of his difficulties in fitting all his cooking equipment into his kitchen, and mentioned that he felt that he had always had the problem of fitting too much into too little space. Sandler felt, "without quite knowing why," that there must have been some very early experience behind the patient's pattern of functioning and asked the patient whether he had suffered from episodes of vomiting in his childhood or infancy. The patient replied that he did not know. The next day he reported that he had asked his mother about his first year of life, and she had said that as an infant he had suffered from pyloric stenosis (a blockage in the passing of food to the stomach):

68

He would take his feed but after a certain point would suddenly vomit it all out. It suddenly became clear to both patient and analyst that the patient's whole life had been coloured by a pattern of functioning in which he could tolerate only a certain quantity of feeling or excitement and that when the limit had been reached he had to "get rid of everything," as he put it. Following this piece of insight there were marked changes in his life and he could permit himself to complete things which he could not previously finish (p. 368).

For Sandler each stage of development has laws and logic of its own, or different procedures for organizing the world; like Schimek, she believes that these early sensorimotor experiences are part of fantasies elaborated at a later time.

Let me organize some of the ideas I have presented as they might relate to Sandler's patient: In response to repeated trauma related to feeding—a function directly connected to survival—there is an organization of affectively charged memories centered around bodily experiences and action. These presymbolic thought processes (or procedural memories) defined the infant's world and persisted throughout this man's life as an essential aspect of his psychic reality. He could not put this very basic sense of himself in relation to others into words and, at best, only indirectly through fantasies. His life became organized to protect himself from the expectation of trauma that is reflected in every situation including, and perhaps especially so, in the analytic situation. He would, so to speak, have his subsymbolic sensors activated to pick up the analyst's thoughts, feelings, and attitudes toward him that might be experienced as toxic and a prelude to the violent vomiting up of experience. Sandler, of course, described how she could be pulled into his psychic reality and feel like the analytic mother whose interpretive milk was rejected and flung back in her face. These contributions (countertransference) from the analyst's side of the dyad may not be reflected by what is said, but can be sensed through the analyst's tone of voice, body orientation, gestures, choice of words, and a variety of other less than direct forms of communication. Here I find it helpful to think of Schimek's idea that early schemas forged through action can lead to the notion that sometimes action may precede insight(1975, p. 185n; see also Freedman, 1994; Frosch 1998). I would say that it is the action, the back-and-forth ways of going at things, both verbal and nonverbal, of the analytic relationship, that can allow for a build-up of a particular kind of safety and trust so that patients can take in the analyst's contributions in a way that has the potential to modify the affective core of our basic orientation to the world.

Along these lines I think it must have been Sandler's interest in her patient, by which I mean her emotional involvement, that was the key to the therapeutic success. This does not contradict Sandler's take on the situation that the knowledge of the vomiting up of mother's milk shifted the patient's orientation to the world. I would argue that without her ongoing investment in the patient, Sandler might not have been receptive to something in his story about the bicycles and cooking equipment that led her to believe in earlier feeding difficulties. Sandler's interest was an entree into her patient's psychic reality.

To my way of thinking, one of the very best descriptions of how crucial the analyst's interest is has been provided in a recent paper by Ted Jacobs (2002). Jacobs talked about his analysis with Edith Jacobson as

> a lifesaver. ... [She] displayed a kind of investment in the treatment that produced a feeling, not formulated in our theories, that one was truly cared about. This intangible factor, conveyed by dedicated analysts largely through the quality of their listening and the affect that they communicate, ... is a therapeutic agent of the greatest importance ... one of the key factors that cuts across schools of thought ... and very possibly may be the one essential quality that is shared by the most effective and valued practitioners in our field (p. 13).

I believe what Jacobs is talking about is the reciprocal of the patient's love for the analyst. The positive transference, which Freud maintained was a necessary condition for analytic work, represents the patient's love for the analyst. This allows for the analyst to be experienced as someone who can be both loved and hated (cf. Schafer, 1977). I believe that a necessary condition for the continuation of the patient's healthy love is the analyst's capacity to love his or her patient. This would include the analyst's thoughts and feelings about the patient as well as the analyst's reactions to his or her own thoughts and feelings. This love, or interest, or, as Irving Steingart (1995) has put it, the analyst's loving desire to understand the patient's mind—his or her psychic reality (pp. 126–127), certainly includes the analyst's ongoing self-analysis of his or her countertransference (cf. Rothstein, 1999). I also think it must include the analyst's belief in the efficacy of the analytic enterprise, a belief that must go back to the analyst's own experience as a patient. This is crucial to all analytic work, but particularly so when early preverbal and unconscious regulatory procedures play an increasingly important role in the treatment process. It is the waxing and waning of the analytic relationship, the cycles of transference and countertransference, or those periods when analyst and patient may experience hopelessness and despair that the analyst must confront the countertransference, to be sure, but also must be able to draw on his or her own analytic experience as a source of hope.

Let me give you an example from my own practice. I met "Jeffrey" when he was thirty-six years old and had just completed a PhD in economics. He had been in psychotherapy in his twenties and specifically requested an analysis. We agreed to meet five times a week, and within a few months worked out very early morning hours to accommodate his work schedule. Jeffrey said that he felt depressed, and had trouble completing things on time. This was a pattern that led people to feel nervous and angry with him at school as well as in his personal relationships. Jeffrey had, he said, a "string of women," and this was also a pattern in his life. He quipped that he liked the feeling that there was at least someone "out there" thinking about him when she woke up every day.

Jeffrey came from a relatively affluent background and his family traveled a lot because of his father's work. He lived in three or four different cities in the first six to seven years of his life. He described his parents as distant and critical, and his fondest memories were of various caretakers whom he was very attached to. Separation was always difficult.

Jeffrey established a pattern early on in treatment of missing sessions. He would come regularly and then miss a number of sessions. Sometimes he would miss an entire week. If psychoanalysis is the talking cure, I had some troubles with Jeffrey. We did not talk that much about his missed sessions. It was not for want of trying on my part. Jeffrey would listen and consider what I had to say, usually with complete disdain. It was (at least most of the time), "psychobabble" to him. Over time I felt dismissed, angry, and impotent, and questioned whether I was doing an analysis and whether this guy was capable of this sort of work. In my thoughts I punished him for his actions that made me feel uncomfortable. He was not coming to his sessions. Jeffrey was resistant and we could not talk about it. Over time I changed my mind about this, and I was better able to appreciate the wishful as well as defensive aspects of this compromise formation. I came to believe that in his ways of going at things with me, this man was bringing into the analysis what was most meaningful in his life. On the deepest level of his psyche the other-than-symbolic visceral experience of being left is replicated in different form via his girlfriends (whom he leaves) and his analyst who longingly waits for him. And we remember him; we think about him. I certainly did in the mornings when he did not call or come. I was one of Jeffrey's women who woke up and thought about him. My awareness of the role I played in Jeffrey's world—his psychic reality—shifted my perspective and allowed me to see my doubts and concerns as countertransference rather than as a reality response to a patient I had experienced as thwarting my analytic efforts. More and more I was able to understand Jeffrey's action as an essential part of the treatment process. It was a reflection of his earliest experiences of separation and loss being played out in a transitional (or transformational) space. Sometimes we could talk about Jeffrey's belief that the only way to get ahead in life—professionally, personally, and in his analysis—was to submit—to lose his balls—to come to his sessions; or we talked about the importance of me keeping him in mind when he did not come. And sometimes we could not use language to talk about the meanings of Jeffrey's comings and goings— and my waiting.[1] When words lacked meaning for Jeffrey I thought my

---

[1] The movement between wishes and fears organized at different levels of psychosexual development highlights the dynamic stratification of memories that is an essential

understanding of his action patterns must have provided what Kohut (1968) called "the needed narcissistic echo" (p. 110), so that Jeffrey sensed that I knew who he was and what he was going through, and that I had some understanding of his psychic reality.

A condition for loving for Sandler's patient, or Jeffrey (or for any of us at some time), may be directly related to unconscious regulatory processes that, if they could be verbalized, might be put as follows: "If I reject your interventions, or if I accept them and treat them as if they were meaningless, will you still have an interest in me? Will I be able to experience this relationship as one that is safe? Will you be able to help me to regulate my feelings, my overall state of being in the world?" I believe that all patients at one time or another will push us to think out of the box, to look at things differently. Each patient will have his or her own way of going at things, and analysts, like everyone else, can have trouble getting out of their comfortable routines. I have described some of Jeffrey's ways of going at things, his unconscious spirit that has been called up from the depths. It behooves us not to try and send it back.

It should not be so difficult for any of us to understand what this man was struggling with. We are all more similar than different. Although I did not miss my sessions, I certainly wondered how my analyst could keep her interest in me, how she could care for me. I thought her interpretations were (usually) correct, but I continued to repeat things in my life and in the analysis. Like Jacobs, however, I always felt that she was interested in me, and liked me. I felt safe in my sessions. I was not the center of her life and she could not undo the traumas of my childhood.

---

aspect of the Freudian model of the mind. Jeffrey's memories are always (as they are for all of us) a part of a dynamic system where the arrangement of wishes and defenses is fluid, not static. At times not coming to sessions was certainly Jeffrey's way of coping with castration anxiety; at other times castration anxiety defends against oral longings. A more accurate reading of the situation is that Jeffrey's action is not a way of coping with this or that, castration or merger, but it is what we, analysts, think it is. It is our construction—our way of organizing the data of the analysis. It becomes something more when the patient modifies our construction and comes up with his or her own rendering that seems right to both participants in the analytic dyad. When analyst and patient resonate in this way the potential for transformation--growth-- is actualized.

But, like Jeffrey, I could bring these early experiences into the session in the form of repetitive patterns of behavior, and my analyst put into practice the clinical implications of Freud's revolutionary concept of the dynamic stratification of memories. She interpreted wishes and defenses associated with oedipal and preoedipal fantasies. There was no magic to this. It was solid analytic technique that focused on helping me to understand the world I had constructed—my psychic reality.

## Summary

In this article 1 have argued that the more linear transformations or desymbolized expressions of one's earliest relationships are always a part of psychic reality and represent a unique opportunity in the analytic situation to transform a person's emotional orientation to the world. A necessary condition for this to come about is the analyst's capacity for sustained interest in the patient. This interest, which goes well beyond an intellectual one, can be threatened by counter-transference as well as certain assumptions the analyst has about the nature of the analytic process. The analyst's belief in the analytic process, a belief that can only come from his or her own analysis, is seen as crucial in helping the transformational process that occurs in a successful analysis.

## Acknowledgements

The author wishes to thank Lillian Gordon, Ruth Oscharoff, and Dr. Neal Vorus for their help in the preparation of this article.

## References

Beebe, B., Lachmann, F. & Jaffe, J. (1997). A transformational model of pre-symbolic representations: Reply to commentaries. *Psychoanalytic Dialogues*, 7:215-224.

Bucci, W. (2002). The referential process, consciousness, and the sense of self. *Psychoanalytic Inquiry*, 22:766–793.

Faimberg, H. (1995). Misunderstanding and psychic truths. *International Journal of Psycho-Analysis*, 76:9–13.

Fogel, G. (1993). A transitional phase in our understanding of the psychoanalytic process: A new look at Ferenczi and Rank. *Journal of the American Psychoanalytic Association*, 47:85–602.

Fonagy, P. (1995). Playing with reality: The development of psychic reality and its malfunction in borderline personalities. *International Journal of Psycho-Analysis*, 76:39–44.

——(2001). *Attachment theory and psychoanalysis*. New York: Other Press.

——& Target, M. (1996). Playing with reality: I. Theory of mind and the normal development of psychic reality. *International Journal of Psycho-Analysis*, 77:217–233.

——& ———(2002). Early intervention and the development of self-regulation. *Psychoanalytic Inquiry*, 22:307–335.

Freedman, N. (1994). More on transformation: Enactments in psychoanalytic space. In A. K. Richards & A. D. Richards (Eds.), *Spectrum of psychoanalysis: Essays in honor of Martin S. Bergman* (pp. 93–110). Madison, CT: International Universities Press.

Freud, S. (1899). Screen memories. *Standard Edition*, 3:303–322.

——(1900). The interpretation of dreams (second part). *Standard Edition*, 5:339–625.

——(1905a). Fragments of a case of hysteria. *Standard Edition*, 7:3–122.

——(1905b). Three essays on sexuality. *Standard Edition*, 7: 25–243.

——(1910). Leonardo da Vinci and a memory of his childhood. *Standard Edition*, 77:63–137.

——(1913). Totem and taboo. *Standard Edition*, 73:1–161.

—— (1915a). A case of paranoia running counter to the psycho-analytic theory of the disease. *Standard Edition*, 14:263–272.

——(1915b). Instincts and their vicissitudes. *Standard Edition*, 74:109–140.

——(1917). Introductory lectures on psycho-analysis (Part 3). *Standard Edition*, 76:243–496.

——(1925). Negation. *Standard Edition*, 79:235–239.

Friedman, L. (1995). Psychic reality in psychoanalytic theory. *International Journal of Psycho-Analysis,* 76:25–28.

Frosch, A. (1998). Narcissistic injury and sadomasochistic compensation in a latency-age boy. In P. Beren (Ed.), *Narcissistic disorders in children and adolescents: Diagnosis and treatment* (pp. 263–280). Northvale, NJ: Jason Aronson.

Grossman, W. (1992). Hierarchies, boundaries, and representation in a Freudian model of mental organization. *Journal of the American Psychoanalytic Association,* 40:27–62.

Grubrich-Simitis, I. (1988). Trauma or drive—drive and trauma—a reading of Sigmund Freud's phylogenetic fantasy of 1915. *Psychoanalytic Study of the Child,* 43:3–32.

Jacobs, T. (2002). Secondary revision: On rethinking the analytic process and analytic technique. *Psychoanalytic Inquiry,* 23:3–28.

Kohut, H. (1968). The psychoanalytic treatment of narcissistic personality disorders: Outline of a systematic approach. *Psychoanalytic Study of the Child,* 23:86–113.

Masson, J. (1985). *The complete letters of Sigmund Freud to Wilhelm Fliess 1887–1904.* Cambridge, MA: Belknap Press of Harvard University Press.

Michels, R. & Roughton, R. (1985). Perspectives on the nature of psychic reality. *Journal of the American Psychoanalytic Association,* 33:645–659.

Rothstein, A. (1999). Some implications of the analyst feeling disturbed while working with disturbed patients. *Psychoanalytic Quarterly,* 65:541–558.

Rycroft, C. (1956) Symbolism and its relationship to the primary and secondary processes. *International Journal of Psycho-Analysis,* 37:137–146.

Sandler, A. (1975). Comments on the significance of Piaget's work for psychoanalysis. *International Review of Psycho-Analysis,* 2:365–377.

Sandler, J. (1960). The background of safety. *International Journal of Psycho-Analysis,* 47:52–356.

Schafer, R. (1977). The interpretation of transference and the conditions for loving. *Journal of the American Psychoanalytic Association,* 25:335–362.

Schimek, J. (1975). A critical re-examination of Freud's concept of unconscious mental representation. *International Review of Psycho-Analysis*, 2:171–187.

Schore, A. (2002). Advances in neuropsychoanalysis, attachment theory, and trauma research: Implications for self-psychology. *Psychoanalytic Inquiry*, 22:433–485.

Silverman, D. (1998). The tie that binds affect regulation, attachment, and psychoanalysis. *Psychoanalytic Psychology*, 15:187–212.

Steingart, I. (1995). *A thing apart*. Northvale, NJ: Jason Aronson.

Target, M. & Fonagy, P. (1996). Playing with reality: II. The development of psychic reality from a theoretical perspective. *International Journal of Psycho-Analysis*, 77:459–479.

Vorus, N. (1998). *The concept of fantasy in psychoanalysis: An examination of the place of reality in the Freud-Klein controversies*. Unpublished dissertation, City University of New York.

# CHAPTER 4

# Transference, Psychic Reality and Material Reality

## Reflections on "Transference, Psychic Reality and Material Reality"

*Neal Vorus*

In this chapter, Allan Frosch's primary subject is *psychic reality*, an elastic concept with various meanings in the analytic literature. Allan defines it broadly while giving it his own particular spin, and in doing so sketches a crucial point of convergence between Freudian and Relational approaches. He first defines psychic reality as "an organization of unconscious fantasies, encoded as compromise formations, that actively structures the present" based on the past (p. 604). Psychic reality is an "unconscious structure for producing meaning" comprised of a pattern of unconscious fantasies, a structure that encodes new experiences in the form of repeated variations of the same childhood themes. This definition roots the concept in the American classical tradition of Arlow and Brenner (1964, 1990).

Where Allan breaks new ground is in his incorporation of the Relational and Interpersonal perspectives of thinkers such as Aron (1990) and Levenson (1981) who insist that the transference is always a "joint creation" of patient and analyst reflecting the "real matrix of events and personalities." The analyst's countertransference is just as much an active ingredient in the ongoing interaction as the patient's transference, and thus *who the analyst is* has as much impact on the treatment process as anything coming from the patient. In this view, the classical primacy of psychic reality over material reality is upended, with mutually constructed enactments in the *present* taking the place previously held by the patient's unconscious fantasies rooted in the *past*. Material reality, in the form of current interaction, replaces psychic reality as the bedrock of psychoanalytic investigation.

Rather than resting with this simple dichotomy between classical and relational perspectives, Allan Frosch erects a conceptual bridge through the inclusion of nonlinear dynamic systems theory (cf. Gleick, 1987). This is a model that emerged in the 1970s in the work of mathematicians and physicists studying "near repetitive activity" observable within the chaotic output of complex dynamic systems. From this perspective, two apparently paradoxical processes characterize any complex dynamic system: 1) small changes cascade through the system to produce large effects, and 2) dynamic systems move toward self-replicating patterns observable over both small and large scales. In applying this approach to psychoanalytic data, Allan retains both the relational view of analytic interaction as co-constructed and the classical emphasis on the deterministic power of unconscious fantasy. As a dynamic system, analytic interaction includes both the substantial effects of changes in material reality, including the reality of the analyst's countertransference, and the self-replicating role of the patient's psychic reality.

It is with this notion of countertransference as "material reality" producing large effects in the complexity of analytic interaction that this paper makes perhaps its greatest contribution. With rare candor, Allan offers a clinical example in which a patient's transference-driven provocations (e.g., the patient running a credit check on her analyst) led to a loss of reflective function in the analyst. "My interest was in controlling what happened rather than deepening my understanding of the transference, that is, psychic reality.... . I became the complement of Ms. B's transference scenario, and she became part of my infantile past" (p. 622).

Allan acknowledges the relational view that this enactment was clearly a "joint construction" of patient and analyst. He describes responding to the patient's provocations by shifting to a stance that (in retrospect) had a blaming, defensive quality, generated by his growing sense of panic and anger and consequent diminishment of symbolic understanding. The patient responded to these changes in her analyst's tone by 'upping the ante' in her anger and provocativeness, and a "sadomasochistic power struggle" ensued that was co-constructed by patient and analyst in their contemporaneous interaction, not simply determined by the patient's unconscious past.

Again referring to the study of complex non-linear systems, Allan describes a recurring pattern detectable within the chaos of immediate interaction. He notes that the patient's response to his changes demonstrated a self-similar pattern, "a different aspect, shape, or form of psychic reality that is similar to all other manifestations" (p. 625). While the material reality of his countertransference clearly produced large effects, these eventually assumed the shape of a familiar pattern that had recurred throughout the patient's life.

One point that Allan does not make in his paper, but is apparent upon re-reading, involves another type of large change produced by the analyst's participation, his "material reality." In addition to participating in the difficult enactment described so evocatively, Allan also played a crucial role in finding a way out of the impasse through the restoration of reflective, symbolic understanding. One assumes this, too, became a repeated pattern, not only in the immediacy of patient-analyst interaction, but also within the psychic reality of the patient. Perhaps this is another factor to be considered from the standpoint of non-linear dynamic systems theory: in addition to the staging of recurrence amongst chaos, one also sees, in a well-functioning analytic dyad, the possibility of an alteration of recurrence, a movement toward a new, healthier equilibrium.

# References

Arlow, J. & Brenner, C. (1964). *Psychoanalytic concepts and the structural theory.* New York: International Universities Press.

_____&_____(1990). The psychoanalytic process. *Psychoanalytic Quarterly*, 59: 678–692.

Aron, L. (1990). One person and two person psychologies and the method of psychoanalysis. *Psychoanalytic Psychology*, 7: 475–485.

Gleick, J. (1987). *Chaos: Making a new science.* New York: Penguin Books.

Levenson, E. (1981). Facts or fantasies: On the nature of psychoanalytic data. *Contemporary Psychoanalysis*, 17: 486–500.

\*     \*     \*

# Transference: Psychic Reality and Material Reality

## Allan Frosch

*This article explores the impact of material reality in the form of the analyst's unrecognized and enacted countertransference on a patient's psychic reality (PR) as it presents in the transference. PR refers to a patient's experience in the transference and to an organization of unconscious fantasies, encoded as compromise formations, that actively structures the present and can be inferred from the data of psychoanalysis. Clinical material is presented in support of the author's belief that PR plays the central role in the construction of the transference and that material reality can influence both the nature and form of the transference through the activation or inhibition of different sets of fantasies in the analyst and the patient.*

> When I was at home in my parent's house, I used to make a list of all the things I was quite sure would not follow me if only I could cross the vast ocean that lay before me; I used to think that just a change in venue would banish forever from my life the things I most despised. But that was not to be so. As each day unfolded before me, I could see the sameness in everything; I could see the present take a shape—the shape of the past.
>
> —Jamaica Kincaid (1991, p. 90)

My aim in this article is to explore the impact of material reality, in the form of the analyst's unrecognized and enacted countertransference, on a patient's psychic reality as it presents in the transference. The term *psychic reality* refers to a patient's experience in the transference (i.e., a subjective experience), as well as to an organization of unconscious fantasies, encoded as compromise formations, that actively structures the present and can be inferred from the data of psychoanalysis. Psychic reality, in the words of the poet, is the shape of the past. The major window of observation for this exploration is four summarized sessions of clinical process that I will refer to as an *enactment*.

83

The article is organized into four sections. In the first section the terms psychic reality, countertransference, and enactment will be briefly discussed. There will also be a limited discussion of the emphasis on psychic reality and material reality as seen from different theoretical perspectives. The second section contains the clinical material, and the third section is devoted to a discussion of this material as it relates to the theoretical ideas presented in the body of the article. The final section is the summary and concluding comments.

## Psychic Reality

Freud (1917/1963) thought of psychic reality as a collection of unconscious fantasies, which he distinguished from material reality. "The phantasies possess psychical as contrasted with material reality, and we gradually learn to understand that in the world of the neuroses it is psychical reality which is the decisive kind" (Freud, 1917/1963, p.368).[1]

These unconscious fantasies are organized around childhood wishes, defenses, and experiences with material (i.e., external or "actual") reality. Interactions with material reality, particularly those interactions with significant others, become organized within this subjective construction of the world. These "amalgams of fact and fiction" (Fogel,1993, p. 594) represent the "personal meanings the analysand ascribes, especially unconsciously, to events and actions in the past and present" (Schafer, 1985, p. 537) and are organized according to the laws of the primary process.

They are understood to be affect-laden sensory motor images that are primarily, but not exclusively, visual in nature. Freud often referred to these nonlinguistically encoded images in spatial terms (e.g., shapes and forms, Freud, 1900/1953b; plates, 1912/1958a; things, 1915/1957b;

---

[1] Vorus (1998) has discussed the evolution of psychic reality from an unconscious wish "to a redefinition of psychic reality no longer exclusively pertaining to unconscious wishes, but now extended to all manifestations of phantasy" (p. 206). It is this latter formulation, captured in this citation from Freud (1917/1963), that is used throughout this article.

and objects, Freud 1937/1964b), and argued that they do not become linked to words until they move toward consciousness (Freud, 1915/1957b). He believed that these unconscious fantasies were reprinted throughout a person's life (Freud, 1912/1958a). That is to say, the organizing influence of these unconscious fantasies leads to patterns of meaning from the past that actively structures the present.

Psychic reality is a structure for producing meaning. New experience is attracted to this archaic meaning structure and organized accordingly. If we think of this meaning structure in spatial terms, then meaning can be conceptualized as a pattern of organizing experience. Present experience can never be organized exactly like past experience. The mind is not a structure that repeats itself exactly (Moran, 1991). Present experience is organized so that it fits into this pattern. The pattern, therefore, is stable but not static. It can change but it will always maintain the essence of what it is. This is consistent with Freud's notion that *"psychical reality too has more than one form of existence* [italics added]" (Freud, 1900/1953b, p. 620n). Although Freud did not use this phrase in relation to psychical reality after 1909 (see Editor's note, Freud, 1900/1953b, p. 620n), the idea that psychic reality can take different forms is central to a psychoanalytic perspective and has been discussed in some detail in a recent article by Grossman (1992), who argues that, from Freud's "recursive representational" model of mind, "early experiences are retained in later organizations, but shaped to later content" (p. 51).

In a recursive process, each event or representation is based on and similar to the previous one. It is a self-similar pattern within a pattern so that the past is embedded in the dynamics of the present (Arlow, 1991b), like similar Russian dolls nested within each other (Grossman, 1992; see Gleick, 1987, for a similar description from the perspective of chaos theory). Wishes, fears, and defenses from early childhood "are part of unconscious fantasies that seek resolution in the present through compromise formation" (Bachant, Lynch & Richards, 1995, p. 75).

In this recursive model of the mind, psychic reality is given prominence over material reality, and the exploration of these unconscious fantasies is central to a psychoanalytic understanding. Freud knew that our inferences from the data of psychoanalysis could never lead to a complete understanding of these unconscious fantasies. A limiting factor was the person of the analyst. The interfering effects of the less-than-ideal analyst were always an issue for him (e.g., 1910/1957a, 1937/1964a).

## *Countertransference*

Freud (1910/1957a) used the term "counter-transference" to refer to those unresolved issues in the analyst, which were responsive to the patient's transference and interfered with the progress of an analysis. This view of countertransference as a pathological interference with the analytic process is sometimes referred to as the "classical" (Kernberg, 1965) or more "limited" (Lasky, 1993) view of countertransference. Analysts subscribing to this perspective differentiate those feelings of the analyst that are bound up in reactivated conflict from those feelings that are not. Although both sets of feelings can provide information about the patient (e.g., wishes or active strivings directed toward the analyst), the feelings that remain embedded in the analyst's own reactivated infantile conflicts are seen to represent an impediment toward increased understanding. From a limited point of view, countertransference is a resistance to the analyst's use of his or her own unconscious as an instrument to receive communication from the patient's unconscious (Freud, 1912/1958b; 1951/1973c; 1960/1973b; 1966/1973a; see Lasky, 1993, for a discussion of how reactivated conflict can be constructively used as part of the analytic instrument as differentiated from its disruptive interference as expressed in countertransference).

From this perspective the key to understanding countertransference is the analyst's personal analysis (Brenner, 1985, 1996) and a willingness to look at one's own conflicts as they present in the analytic situation (Reich, 1960/1973b).[2] The analytic goal is to minimize the impact of

---

[2] For Brenner (1985), countertransference, like transference, is ubiquitous and inescapable. His focus, however, is consistent with a limited perspective: "When we are asked to give examples of countertransference, we know what we are being asked for is examples of the kind of countertransference Reich was referring to, the kind that interferes with the conduct of analysis or makes it impossible altogether" (p.156).

countertransference or, as Reich (1951/1973c) put it, to "tame" the countertransference so that it remains "shadowy and in the background" (p. 154).

In what has come to be known as a broadened (Lasky, 1993) or totalist (Tansy & Burke, 1989) point of view, countertransference moved into the foreground of the analytic situation and all of the analyst's feelings were covered by this term (Fosshage, 1995; Heimann, 1950; Tansy & Burke, 1989).

> A totalistic concept of counter-transference does justice to the conception of the analytic situation as an interaction process in which past and present of both participants, as well as their mutual reactions to their past and present, fuse into a unique emotional position involving both of them (Kernberg, 1965, p. 41).

The influence of the Kleinians in England led to an emphasis on countertransference as a creation of the patient (Heimann, 1950). The emphasis shifted from countertransference as an interference with the analytic process to countertransference as "a highly significant tool" (Heimann, 1977, p. 318) in the analytic work. The danger is not that the analyst will fail to look at what he or she brings to the situation as much as the belief that an emphasis on the analyst's self-analysis of his or her reactions might "not consider sufficiently the specific way in which the patient provokes the reaction in the analyst" (Kernberg, 1965, p. 42).

Transference and countertransference were seen as inseparable aspects of an ongoing process. The analyst responded to the patient's transference, and the patient responded to the analyst's countertransference (Little, 1951). "Transference and countertransference are products of the combined unconscious work of patient and analyst" (Little, 1951, p. 40).

In this country, Sullivan's (1954) idea that the data of psychoanalysis does not reside in the patient or the analyst "but in the situation which is created between the observer and his subject" (p. 3) was the foundation for the emerging concept of countertransference as part of an ongoing transaction in which "the attitudes and responses of each participant are complex entities arising from the transaction" (Gill, 1983, p. 218).

Many of these ideas came together in an article by Hoffman (1983) titled "The Patient as Interpreter of the Analyst's Experience." In this article, Hoffman argued that the patient not only elicits countertransference but also attends to and interprets overt and covert responses by the analyst that are consistent with the patient's unconscious viewpoint and expectations. Thus, the patient's reaction to the analyst's countertransference becomes incorporated into the transference. "The transference represents a way not only of construing but also of constructing or shaping interpersonal relations in general and the relationship with the analyst in particular" (Hoffman, 1983, p. 394).

The shift in emphasis, from countertransference as a resistance to countertransference as part of an ongoing communication between patient and analyst, provides the context for Hoffman's proposed shift in technique so that "the free emergence of multiple transference-countertransference scenarios" replaces free associations as the central focus of analytic attention (Hoffman,1996, p. 113).

## Psychic Reality and Material Reality— Different Points of View

It is clear that with the broadening of the concept of countertransference, there has been an intensified interest in the analyst's subjective involvement in the analytic process and what this means for the data of psychoanalysis. This interest has focused on, but is not limited to, the transference. For many analysts, for example Boesky (in Hurst, 1995), "reality considerations" such as the real behavior of the analyst are not seen as contributing to the formation of transference or otherwise fueling the analytic process (p. 534). In a similar vein, Steingart (1995) sees a patient's psychic reality as "existing independent of the analyst and the real person he or she is, and the investigatory procedure that is the psychoanalytic relationship" (p. 75). Arlow (1985) puts it as follows: "Transference may be understood as representing how the individual misperceives, misinterprets, and misresponds to the data of perception in terms of the mental set created by consistent unconscious fantasy derivatives" (p. 526).

For all of these analysts the emphasis is on the patient's intrapsychic contribution to his or her experience in the transference, and they would argue against the notion that transference is the result of analyst influence. Transference represents the patient's infantile construction of the world that has been transformed via the materials of the present, for example, the person of the analyst. Analysts who take this position are associated with a more limited view of countertransference.

Other analysts see the psychological impact of the analyst as a crucial determinant of the patient's conflicts and fantasies in the analytic situation.

> If we begin with the assumption that the analyst is as much an emotional participant in the analytic process as is the patient, then the concept of psychic reality applies to the analyst's thoughts and behavior as well as to those of the patient. (Skolnikoff, 1993, p. 296)

Aron (1990) argues that from the perspective of a "two-person psychology," infantile wishes and conflicts revealed in the patient's associations are not only or mainly remnants from the past, artificially imposed onto the therapeutic field, but are rather reflections of the actual interaction and encounters with the unique, individual analyst with all of his or her idiosyncratic features (p. 479).

In a similar vein, Levine (1994), while clearly acknowledging the importance of the patient's contribution to the analytic material, sees "the fundamental data of analysis as a continual stream of jointly created events" (p. 669). For Levenson (1981), it is "who the therapist is and what he brings to the therapy encounter"—the "real matrix of events and personalities" (p. 492) that is crucial to an understanding of transference. For Levenson (1981) the idea that transference is a product of our infantile construction of the world "is dead wrong" (p. 492).

Analysts who believe that transference is a joint creation of patient and analyst are more likely to fall under the rubric of a more broadened concept of countertransference. For these analysts the present can be illuminated by the past but is, to a greater or lesser extent, independent of the past (Gill, 1995). In this formulation "material reality is given new prominence in relation to inner experience" (Grey, 1995–1996, p. 14; see also Gill, 1995, p. 105). The opposite is the case for those analysts who view the past as determining the present. In this formulation psychic reality is emphasized over material reality. Mitchell (1988) has expressed these differences as a ratio between intrapsychic and interpersonal:

> all psychoanalytic theories regard experience as a mixture of something brought to the experience by the subject and actual phenomena in the real world. No one believes in a totally naive observer simply recording actuality; no one believes in a totally programmed observer only projecting his internal reality. But there are many differences in how one sees the ratio between these two factors in the construction of subjective experience (p. 489).

This difference in emphasis represents opposite end points on a conceptual continuum related to the impact of the analyst's subjectivity on the analytic process. In all of these formulations, the emphasis is on the degree of participation of the analyst. The question is always how much. The argument against a codeterminist hypothesis is that for the well-analyzed analyst, the ongoing monitoring of countertransference will minimize analyst impact, and these small influences will be insignificant in the context of what the patient brings to the situation (Brenner, 1996, esp. pp. 28–29).

The idea of trying to quantify the analyst's participation is fraught with difficulties, and Gill (1983) has argued that the patient's "mental set" organizes the analytic situation and the analyst's behavior takes place within this context. What the analyst thinks, or what an external observer might think, or even what the patient might think of the analyst's behavior are all beside the point. The patient's emotional response is the only valid unit of measurement.

Gill's position highlights the complexity of an interactive system. The idea that very small influences can be ignored rests on the assumption that variables are added together. In other words, the small influence of the analyst is added on to what the patient brings to the situation so that a "small" degree of participation will have a small impact. However, in a complex dynamic system, such as the psychoanalytic model of the mind or the psychoanalytic situation, the variables are interactive, not additive, and a "small" change in conditions (e.g., countertransference) can "cascade" (Moran, 1991) through the system so that the small change can have a large impact. Therefore, the moment-to-moment behavior of the system, for example, the analysand's experience of the transference, cannot be predicted.

If we return to some of the ideas presented earlier about the organizing influence of psychic reality, how infantile wishes embedded in fantasies actively imbue the present with meanings from the past, we can argue that the meaning one gives to the present should reflect one's unconscious construction of the world. In other words, a characteristic pattern should be discernible across all situations. Psychic reality is not dependent on the situation, but the form it takes is.

These two ideas—sensitivity to change and movement toward a discernible pattern of functioning that emerges from the multiplicity of behavior—are characteristic of complex or nonlinear systems (i.e., systems in which multiple variables interact) and have been applied to psychoanalysis by a number of authors (e.g., Fogel, 1990; Galatzer-Levy, 1995; Moran, 1991; Spruiell, 1993).[3] Together they give rise to a very particular kind of prediction: We cannot predict the status of a system on a moment-to-moment basis, but we can predict an emergent pattern characteristic of that particular system. Stated differently, we cannot predict how a person will think, act, or feel in a particular situation (or a particular session), but we would expect a particular view of the world to be articulated throughout a person's life. The "paradox" of moment-to-moment unpredictability in the context of a deterministic system is characteristic of enactments.

---

[3] Brenner's (1976,1985) discussion of the unpredictability of countertransference is consistent with the one outlined above even though he comes to different conclusions about the analyst's "small" countertransference contribution (cf. Brenner, 1996).

## Enactment

The term enactment is relatively new to the analytic literature (McLaughlin, 1991). It is related to the concept of acting out in that some conflict that has been activated or intensified by the analytic process is expressed in behavior rather than in words (Roughton, 1993). It differs from acting out, however, by avoiding the negative connotations usually associated with the latter concept. Another important difference refers to the point of initiation. Whereas acting out was seen as something the patient did, enactments are seen as interactive phenomena that can be initiated by either member of the analytic dyad (Chused, 1991; Jacobs, 1986; Roughton, 1993). Enactments represent the dramatization of a wish or "an interpersonal happening" (McLaughlin, 1991) in which each of the participants attributes what is happening to the behavior of the other and each of the participants tries to force the other into a reciprocal action or a particular role that is related to unconscious wishes, conflicts, and fantasies in the transference–countertransference matrix.

Analytic enactments are compromise formations that always contain the essential elements of the unconscious pattern of organizing the world that is referred to throughout this article as psychic reality. Enactments can be subtle and remain out of the analyst's awareness (Katz, 1999) or they may take a more dramatic shape that is difficult to miss. Roughton (1993) gives a number of examples that suggest that in some cases the more dramatic forms of enactment represent the end point in a series of covert enactments that may have gone on for quite some time.

The particular form an enactment takes is not directly related to how it is used in an analysis. Enactments are symbolic interactions that have unconscious meaning for the patient and the analyst (McLaughlin, 1991), and their usefulness is related to the analyst's being able to view them as such. I put it this way because I believe it is crucial for the analyst to experience in the transference–countertransference matrix aspects of the patient's feeling states and feelings in himself or herself related to the patient without losing the capacity to remain in a relative state of secondary process symbolization. It is this capacity, which is constantly lost and regained throughout the analytic endeavor, that can act as an agent that transforms the patient's potential for symbolization into an actuality (cf. Frosch, in press).

In this article the term enactment refers to forms of analytic discourse in which meaning is organized around action. Action in its broadest sense refers to words as well as motor behavior. The key element in the behavior or behaviors is to force the other into a particular role or stance. The form a particular enactment takes is unpredictable but its occurrence is not unexpected given the fact that there is inherent unpredictability in all complex systems.

The psychoanalytic situation is not stable. We can think of this instability as part of the interpretive process whereby the equilibrium of a patient's psychic organization is disrupted (Arlow, 1979/1991a) or, as I do here, as a consequence of the repetitive feedback of transference and countertransference that is the hallmark of an enactment.

A characteristic of complex systems, such as the psychoanalytic model of mind or the psychoanalytic situation, is that output and input variables can be interchangeable (Moran, 1991). Here transference and countertransference are viewed as output and input variables constituting the "flow" of the psychoanalytic situation during an enactment.

Psychic reality is seen as a pattern of organizing influence in the non-linear dynamic system referred to as the mind; and enactments are seen as irregular shapes the pattern of psychic reality can assume. If we examine these enactments we would expect to be able to detect the similarity between these particular moments and the overall pattern of psychic reality: "The mind contains patterned regularity embedded in the unpredictability of momentary particulars" (Fogel, 1990, p. 90). Enactments are one type of these particulars.

## Clinical Material

### History

Ms. B started her analysis when she was 29 years old. She presented as an attractive, petite woman who felt her personal and professional life "sucked." Ms. B had no difficulty meeting men but because of her constant devaluation of them she did not find any to be interesting. The exception to this was any man who was not interested in her. A graduate of a prestigious law school at 25 years of age, Ms. B immediately took a position on the staff of a major financial corporation. She was at this position for nearly 4 years and felt she was "stagnating in my own anger." Ms. B was passed over for advancement and thought that she might have to leave the firm.

The eldest of five sisters and two brothers, Ms. B came from a middle-class neighborhood in New York City where her parents owned a "mom and pop candy store that everyone called 'Pop's' because my mother was always pregnant." She describes her mother as depressed, living in fantasies, and preoccupied with having children. Ms. B's first sister (C) was born when Ms. B was 2 years old. She recalls the years following C's birth as being filled with a constant need to be with her mother and a sense of panic and rage at her mother's "unavailability." She longed for her mother's exclusive attention and would have temper tantrums when her mother could not be with her. Separation, even for a short time, was experienced as traumatic.

When she was 7 years old, Ms. B went into the hospital for some tests and had to stay overnight. She desperately wanted her mother to sleep in the room with her. When her mother said that she could not do this, Ms. B became enraged and, as she recalls, from that time on dismissed her mother as a helpless, anxiety-ridden woman. More and more she experienced her mother as "repulsive" when the latter would touch or kiss her. Ms. B decided that she did not need her mother. This defensive alteration of Ms. B's dependent relationship with her mother remained in effect until the latter's death nearly 20 years later.

Ms. B always felt that her mother loved her—just not enough and, therefore, she viewed her mother as useless. This was not the case with her father. Ms. B felt rejected by and enraged at him. She felt that her father always ignored her and preferred her younger sisters: "He ignored the boys and loved the girls—except me." She recalls wanting her father's attention, being furious at him for not getting it, and provoking him through name-calling, contempt, and criticism in an attempt to get some attention. Her father responded by withdrawing and shifting his attention to the other children: "He was indifferent to me." Occasionally he became overtly angry.

Ms. B described her father as a very outgoing man who could not pass up a drink. "He was the life of the party. Everyone loved him—but he loved the bottle." Her father's excessive drinking was an ongoing subject of concern in the family, and when Ms. B was 14 years old, her father drove his car off a bridge and died: "He died drunk. I think he probably did it on purpose, but who knows? Everyone was upset except me. It was the only fantasy I had that came true." Toward the end of her 7-year analysis. Ms. B was able to talk about the pain of this loss and her feeling that if her father had loved her he would never have done such a thing.

### Treatment

During the first year and a half of treatment, the major part of the analytic work was focused on Ms. B's professional relationships with two male superiors. With her immediate superior, Mr. A, Ms. B acted out her wishes to be cared for and comforted. She would constantly ask for reassurance, go to Mr. A's office, and spend the major part of a business meeting declaring her need for "you to help me to make things better." Ms. B always felt that Mr. A, like her mother, cared for her but, in effect, not enough. She felt that he favored other staff more and that his ultimate allegiance was to Mr. J, his superior. She felt that Mr. J ignored her and preferred the other members of his staff, particularly the women. Ms. B used the same methods to get Mr. J's attention that she used to get her father's attention, that is, she argued, baited, and provoked him. Ms. B was furious and, at times, openly contemptuous of Mr. J. She was convinced that he disliked her and would hold her back from advancing her career. She felt that Mr. J was a grandiose, arrogant, and stupid man: "If he drank I'd swear he was my father."

### Transference

Ms. B felt that I was an empathic and reliable person who was available to her in a special way. She also felt that I did not like her and was bored by her. When I was quiet during a session she felt I was punishing her.

"Sometimes you're like my mother and sometimes my father."

### The Enactment

In the 4th year of her analysis, Ms. B expressed her concerns about regression and the reactivation of issues with her mother:

> It scares me ... I don't want to get back into it... so many bad feelings.... I went to see my sister and her two-month-old daughter. I felt so depressed ... she reminds me of my own mother. I had dinner myself at this restaurant. I saw this mother and her kid sitting at a booth. She looked so worn out ... ignoring the kid. I lost all my energy ... just like me and my mother. I always tried to get attention, reassurance, validation.... My mother was always turned inward.

As our work continued, the transference oscillated between Ms. B's view of me as being "indifferent" toward her and more interested in other female patients (particularly her "arch rival"—a patient she would see in the waiting room) and her view of me as not comforting her, not telling her that everything will be all right:

> I want you to get rid of that woman ... you're indifferent to me. Make me feel better.... it feels just like mother. You don't tell me everything will be all right. I want a man—but it would be more useful to have peace of mind.

The desire to have peace of mind began to dominate the work. Ms. B wanted me to make her feel better. She spoke of seeing her niece,

> a wimp—crying and screaming and whimpering. I'm so self-centered. When you ask me a question I feel you don't understand what I'm saying. I think "what the hell's the matter with you?" I'm furious at you right now. I want you to make me feel better. I know this is what Ann [a very "needy, dependent, and demanding" colleague who enrages Ms. B] wants me to do for her. When you don't help me I feel all by myself. No one cares or knows I'm alive. Nothing feels real.

At this point Ms. B talked about how frightened she was of "warm feelings." She might become like her mother—a weak, phony hypocrite. This would be like "falling between the cracks," a phrase that came to be understood as a derivative of a wish to have a close, empathic, nurturing relationship with her mother that was associated with fears of feeling more helpless and dependent. "If I'm too dependent on you, you would not be available to me ... like my mother and her next pregnancy." She thought friends and family all wanted her to be a warm, caring person: "I have to spite them or I'll become like my mother ... weak." She angrily said that she did not feel she was getting enough from me:

> You know on my insurance claim forms you put down your social se-
> curity number and I can do a credit check on you. And I will when I get
> angry at you. It will serve you right. Try and stop me if you can.... I pay
> you plenty of money each month and I feel you don't give me my dues
> [*sic*]. I feel panicky on the weekends.

As the work continued, Ms. B's need to be in contact with me was more and more associated with a sense of panic and anger. I said that I thought the anger made her feel out of control:

> Ms. B: You misconstrue cause and effect. I feel needy. I can't envision
> not seeing you for three days. You say I feel panic because of my feel-
> ings of dependency and then I have a wish to get you. That's not it. I
> feel dependent and fear that there's nothing there. I do want to hurt
> you and I am afraid of driving you crazy ... like Ann does to me at
> work with her demands that I understand everything she wants.

> AF: You've told me that you don't like Ann when she makes these de-
> mands and perhaps you feel that I don't like you and you're going to
> get me.

> Ms. B: Yes, I feel helpless ... you're not fulfilling my needs ... you don't
> like me. I'm at your mercy; you hold all the cards. All I can do is be a
> pain in the neck.

AF: As you did with your father?

Ms. B said yes and went on to tell me that she didn't like me because I rubbed her nose in my "indifference."

During this session and the sessions leading up to it I felt a growing sense of panic and anger. I became increasingly unable to keep the symbolic nature of the interactions in mind. The intensity of my own feelings overwhelmed whatever objective understanding I had or could have. I "blamed" Ms. B and saw the situation as one that could be corrected if she would listen to my interpretations. What I wanted to say to her was: "Look here you've lost your capacity to see me as a representative of the past. I have become the archaic object." Of course, this is exactly what happened to me. Why was I so frightened of the intensity of this woman's feelings and threats? What, in reality, could happen? It is clear, at least in retrospect, that Ms. B had become one of my archaic objects. As such she had the power to humiliate me. I felt that I had to stop her. I believe that she felt very much the same way toward me. We each blamed the other. The communicative value of our words was organized around a desire to force the other to do something. My comments during this period did not reflect an analyst who was emotionally present, involved, and interested in seeing the situation from Ms. B's perspective. Ms. B was bringing in her past in a way that had meaning for her and I said, in effect, "Not that way, do it my way."

In the next session, Ms. B announced that she had run a credit check on me.[4] She felt justified because of her

---

[4] There are a number of reasons why Ms. B may have chosen a credit check as the vehicle of enactment. Her work situation, for one thing, lent itself to this. It was part and parcel of her professional life to run and review credit reports. For Ms. B, money was a mark of one's worth, and she often questioned my worth by how much money she thought I had. My office was in a very fashionable building, but it was a rather modestly furnished office. Was I well off financially or not? I suspect that the credit check was a way of inducing a sense of impotency and humiliation in me. There was nothing I could do about it just as there was nothing she could do about seeing me on the weekends. I think she may have harbored fantasies that she would find out the worst things about me, both personally and financially, and I would be humiliated by this. If she felt humiliated by the intensity of her feelings to get more from me, the credit check could

voracious hunger for attention.... Your credit is far from perfect. If you came to my company for a loan I'd make you pay through the nose ... that's not the point. I need to have an illusion of a connection. I know it's a break of trust. I found out where you live, your apartment number, all kinds of financial information ... it's taking unfair advantage of you. Sorry, but this is what I have to do.... [silence] I read this article about group homes for children. They're like orphanages. These children have this tremendous need for love. They have to hold on to a fault... [they] want to hold on.

Here Ms. B was beginning to put into words something very important. All I was capable of doing, however, was to ask what thoughts she had about this story and the credit check. "I shouldn't expect you to see it... [it's] making contact. I think you're pissed. [Question from AF] Because it's a rotten thing to do and because of the dry way you ask the question."

Ms. B talked about her sense of deprivation as a child, her feeling that she was not getting her due from a male customer that she had a crush on—and how she had sent him a nasty letter. And she talked about how she felt she was spying on my personal life and was worried that I would throw her out of treatment. I commented on her anger toward her father, the customer at work, and myself.

What I am is hungry for attention ... contact. There's a vacuum in my stomach. You don't see this the way I do. For me it's an expression of my hunger for attention not anger. This gave me a sense of connection.

She went on to talk about how cut off she felt, as if she did not exist, and how she wanted to feel special and connected. She said that her secretary had not been giving her her undivided attention and she yelled at this woman and made her cry. Ms. B was sure that no one in her office liked her. I said that I knew how cut off she felt and when this happened

---

be an attempt to reverse the situation. This was, as she put it, taking unfair advantage of me. This is exactly what she felt I was doing to her. My susceptibility to this particular threat was an essential part of the enactment.

she became very angry. I talked about her anger at her secretary and me and how she was so afraid of retaliation.

By the end of the session she was telling me how frightened she was of the upcoming weekend:

Ms. B: It scares me, the weekend. I feel so needy. You're freezing me out.

AF: I know the weekends are hard for you because you don't feel connected to me. Now you are concerned that I will retaliate and freeze you out, that I will not be able to understand and be empathic to your needs.

This reenactment of the traumatic past felt like a life-and-death struggle for Ms. B as well as myself. In the situation I have described both of the participants experienced the present as an actual replication (not representation) of the past. The psychoanalytic situation had lost its symbolic meaning and we were both motivated by anxiety and anger. A compromise was reached which was characterized by an oscillating sadomasochistic power struggle which we "survived." That is to say, over time I was better able to look at my reaction to the analytic situation and Ms. B was able to look at the feelings she brought to the situation. Before ending this section of the article, I would like to present some clinical material that, as I see it, highlights the notion of sameness amidst change.

When we resumed our work after the summer break (6 months after the credit check), Ms. B began talking about her "resistance ... to these needy, dependent feelings." I asked her about this and she reported a dream of being in a bakery and not feeling wanted or needed. She interpreted the dream as having something to do with how she felt being back in treatment. She wanted to get something from me and was frightened that I would reject her. The dream was an entrée to a discussion of Ms. B's desire to integrate the "regressed, demanding and infantile" side of her and the "more intellectual and mature" side. This had now become a focus of treatment. It was not without danger: "To give up my claims on you risks falling into the abyss." This notion of falling into the abyss is Ms. B's metaphor for feeling totally alone and unsupported.

Ms. B went on to tell me how she often wrote me love letters, which she never mailed. In her letters she felt very warmly toward me and saw me as a potential source of support and understanding. I had become an "ally" in her quest to know herself better. She was struggling to see the world differently:

> My life is changing. I feel excitement and terror. I wrote you a letter on Monday ... about chipping away at my delusions to you. It means giving up these fantasies of having an intimate and exciting personal relationship to you. I'm supposed to gain real interactions—possibly with an actual man. This probably will never happen ... not possible. Tuesday and Wednesday I couldn't stand the tension of feeling good. I scared myself.

Ms. B said that she felt uncomfortable when she felt good, and feeling depressed was a way of regaining her equilibrium. In December she brought in a dream.

> I am lying on the couch in your office. The couch is a bed. I'm dressed in a slip, bra and underwear. I'm skinnier by twenty pounds and younger by ten years. You're bringing a kid to your office ... every day ... your one-year-old son. You were breast-feeding. You had well-developed breasts. I wanted to leave to get cake and tea. You said— "No, lie down and tell me your sexual escapades." You stopped breast-feeding and returned to your usual appearance. The kid was tearing around ... showing off ... uninhibited ... fun loving ... wonderful kid ... or you were showing off ... wonderful parent ... happy, vigorous, fun loving kid.

Ms. B talked about this dream as part of her ongoing conflict with me. On the one hand she did want to use me as an ally. On the other hand, however, the dream reminded her how she "can't give up my delusions of intimacy with you. I don't want to go to work. I want to stay in bed and be allowed to have an intimate relationship with you." The wish to have a more intimate relationship with me brought up intense fears: "The breast-feeding was yucky. It made me feel like a clown. Nothing makes sense." I believe that these dreams and the discussion of the love letters were related to internal changes that allowed Ms. B to experience things differently. Her struggle to define the analytic relationship had more clearly become a process of looking at herself. Who I was continued to be an issue for Ms. B, but it was an issue that she now saw through the prism of her inner world.

In January Ms. B said that she felt a real shift in how she experienced her treatment:

> I feel there's been a turning point in therapy. I'm hoping it's for the better. It doesn't feel like it right now. Now it feels panicky.... I'm not enraged at you anymore ... not in a long time. That came from a feeling you were abandoning me—my insistence on a merged relationship.... These new feelings ... I have constant doubts ... a different level of self-doubt. I used to leave and eat—an emotional hunger—physical—not now. Now it feels like I'm going crazy—crazy at the same time I'm getting saner. It feels hopeless ... get better so I can go crazy.

One of the things that scared Ms. B was her feeling that if she allowed herself to feel positively toward another person she would be "dropped like the nothing I really am." Her relationship with a man that she had been dating was fraught with difficulties: "Physical intimacy is disgusting ... sex ... aging... bodies ... bathroom matters." Her relationship to me was terrifying as well:

> You think I'm disgusting. I'm such a pain in the ass. I'm difficult and miserable, a real monster. That's the problem. I feel needy and dependent on you. I feel you're repulsed by me ... an inhuman monster. I want you to look at me with tenderness, affection and forbearance. I want you to have patience with my anger and immaturity.

At this point in our work together Ms. B felt very good about the analysis. She saw me more and more as an ally who was on her "wavelength." She felt she could use the analysis to begin to get the things she wanted out of life. Ms. B had begun to solidify an important relationship with a man and to have unprecedented success professionally. Less than a year after these feelings emerged, Ms. B talked about ending her treatment.

Ms. B had often commented on other female patients. She had wondered whether I might be sexually attracted to them and not her, whether I cared more for them, and the like. At times during the analysis this had led to intense anger toward me, which alternated with regressive longings for me to be a powerful and comforting mother. At this point in the treatment Ms. B had an early morning session. It was my second session of the day and Ms. B had sometimes seen a man leaving the office. In this session Ms. B was 5 min early and saw that my previous patient was now a young and attractive woman. She did not look at this woman in the waiting room and did not comment on the fact that there was a new patient, and that the new patient was a woman. There was a 2–3-minute silence before Ms. B spoke of how tired she was of "being analytical." She felt shy and inhibited and thought these feelings held her back in the analysis. When I asked about this she cut me off and angrily said that it was a "structural blockage … a personality structure." She remembered what her mother often said: "Don't try— don't make a fool of yourself." I asked if she were concerned that some of her feelings here might make her feel like a fool—and if her feeling angry with me was a reaction to my intervention, which might have led to a discussion of these feelings. She said that she felt frightened being around a friend who was so needy and depressed. "I don't want to talk to her. I don't understand emotional connectedness out of a sexual context." She denied being anxious about rejection and then caught herself: "I'm so afraid of intimacy and, logically, rejection is the flip side. I can't deal with needy people." She reported a dream where her boyfriend slept with another woman.

I guess I am afraid of rejection. I don't have emotional relationships. I eat pastries.

103

With Donald I can feel torn like when my mother died. I want to cling to him and I'm terrified he'll walk out. At the same time I feel he's not good enough. Let's get rid of him. I feel this conflict in my own body.... Not the case with you. I always blame you ... I'm tired of therapy. I'll put it on hold. I have so many problems. There's nothing therapy can do.... What am I doing here? I want to go home to bed. Therapy feels irrelevant... it's such an annoying feeling, such a pain in the ass to get rid of you. You'll fight me all the way. It makes me angry.

I certainly felt the impulse to argue with Ms. B, to say that a continuation of the analysis represented an opportunity for her to resolve issues in the transference that would continue to play a crucial role in her life. I thought that Ms. B's anger was a reaction to the new "arch rival" and to the intensification of regressive longings in the transference. She ostensibly gets rid of the man and looks for a woman. One can think of this as a regression from an oedipal to a more preoedipal position. From my point of view a separation of these issues is artificial. For Ms. B the representation of a man is infused with longings to be mothered.

This [i.e., the analytic relationship] is ultimately unsatisfying like my relationship with my mother. I always felt dissatisfied. It embodies my mother—nothing is enough.... I can't relate to friends on an emotional basis. Only Donald. Before that it was you. I need to have a fantasy relationship with whomever. I have these infantile ambitions for a merged relationship. That's all I want.

The man is mother. In the dream I have breasts. Ms. B's intense fear of rejection is filled with fears of falling into the abyss or falling between the cracks. She will be totally alone with no lifeline. I understood this to be a dynamic pattern that is repeated in different forms throughout this woman's life.

From my point of view the termination was premature. I thought important work remained to be done and that it was in Ms. B's best interests to continue the analysis. When I talked with her about this, two major transferential themes became apparent. Ms. B said that she did not want to feel consumed by fantasies of me and added, most importantly I thought, that she would probably seek out treatment at some point with a female therapist on a once-a-week basis to "get some concrete advice." Although the nature of the advice remained unclear, I understood this wish to be an attempt at finding some compromise to the unresolved issues with her mother that were being reactivated in the transference at this time. She was frightened that the intensification of these transference wishes would, in her words, so "consume" her that she would have nothing left for her relationship with Donald. Although I did not believe this to be the case, I certainly understood her concerns. Ms. B's analysis had been filled with intense longings for a "merged" (her word) relationship with me and equally intense periods of hating me and wanting to hurt me. Her image of chewing me up and spitting me out when she was finished captures the oral aggressive theme that played such an important role in the work.

The second transferential theme was Ms. B's conviction that my motivation for wanting her to continue the analysis was based on my own narcissistic needs for perfection. In her thinking she became my trophy, and the emblem of my greatness was reflected in her psychological well-being. In Ms. B's version of the analysis I wanted to explore her thoughts and feelings about ending the analysis for my personal gain. It is not that I do not want to help her, it simply is not my primary goal. She feels that I am forcing her into a situation in which she would lose all control, become overwhelmed and, ultimately, be totally alone and dependent on me. I am the sadist and she is the masochist. It is a situation that Ms. B is very familiar with; and it is not surprising that she wants to reverse it. Ms. B takes control and actively imposes her will on me. She is the "sadist" who is depriving me of my hard-earned fame and glory, albeit at her expense. I am the passive "masochist" who can do nothing. It is a different version of the credit check and, like the credit check, has the potential for another reversal of the sadomasochistic situation. In the credit check situation Ms. B felt frightened that I would retaliate and freeze her out. If unresolved issues seriously interfere with her life in the future (as we both thought they might), it is easy to imagine that Ms. B might feel that I let her down (froze her out) by not somehow preventing her from leaving. Was I indifferent to her like her father? Perhaps I, like her mother, really cared for her, but just not enough. I saw her wish to terminate as an enactment in which Ms. B could find her past in the present moment of the future.

## Discussion

During the credit check, my anxiety about the patient's intense feelings— her anger and threats, as well as her voracious needs—led me to focus on Ms. B's anger, as opposed to her sense of panic, and to move away from the immediacy of the situation and to make genetic interventions. If the "love" of the analyst is expressed through his or her love for the patient's psychic reality (Steingart, 1995), then it is clear I did not love this patient during this time. My interest was in controlling what happened rather than deepening my understanding of the transference, that is, psychic reality. When Ms. B said that I was angry with her she was right; I was. I experienced her as a real "pain in the neck." I became the complement of Ms. B's transference scenario, and she became part of my infantile past. I was stuck. In this situation is it correct to say that Ms. B's experience in the transference was a joint construction of patient and analyst? I would say that this is a correct statement, but a limited one. Here I am drawing on the work of Berger (1995), who makes an important distinction between *correct*, "which refers to limited understandings and perceptions that are attainable from within a narrow, constrained perspective," and *true*, "which refers to wider understandings that are available from the standpoint of a broader and deeper framework…. The latter sees and takes into account critical features that are unavailable, omitted, or concealed in the former" (p. 442). What is "concealed" in this situation, to put it in these terms, is that the enactment is a relatively out-of-the-ordinary manifestation of a pattern of organizing the world (i.e., of imbuing self and object representations with particular meanings) that extends well beyond the immediate situation. It is a compromise formation that, in a variety of forms, appears throughout this woman's life. In the psychoanalytic situation it allows the patient to present her longing for a warm, loving, and nurturing relationship in the context of anger. My contribution to this process is part of the compromise.

When Ms. B said that she would run a credit check when she got angry with me, it would certainly suggest that when she made this threat she was not feeling angry with me or, perhaps more accurately, not as angry as I thought she was. It is reasonable therefore to wonder what went on in the transition between relative stability—the verbal statement that she would run a credit check—and the increased turbulence—that is, actually running the credit check.

In the session before the credit check, Ms. B said that she felt dependent on me and was afraid that there was nothing there. She said that she felt helpless and at my mercy, and that there was nothing she could do but be a pain in the neck. I responded that this was similar to what she did with her father. Ms. B agreed and said that I was rubbing her nose in my indifference. I think she is making an important point here. Her earlier statement can now be understood as follows:

> I am trying to get through to you the way I tried to get through to my mother and later my father. My threats are not to be understood as only an expression of my frustration and anger. If you are an empathic person you should be able to hear me trying to establish a certain kind of meaningful relationship with you—a relationship where you can acknowledge my psychic reality and deepen my understanding of it. When you go on to tell me that I am angry at you the way I was with my father, I know you are right. But that doesn't address the issue I have with you. That feels like you are saying all of these feelings I am having are not real, they are merely a reflection of the past. That feels like you are intentionally trying to hurt me by acting totally indifferent to me, and then I have to increase the pressure I am putting on you. You can say it's my anger; I feel it's my voracious need to make contact.

In other words, my defensive response to Ms. B's feeling that she cannot survive without getting more from me was a crucial factor in determining the form of the transference at this moment in time. Ms. B's construction of the analytic relationship, her amalgam of fact and fiction, was potentiated by my own construction, which was driven by fantasies of being hurt and humiliated. The psychoanalytic situation had lost its symbolic meaning for both participants. The question, therefore, is not only whether my countertransference influenced Ms. B's construction of the transference. It did. A "broader/deeper" question is whether we can observe a pattern in the meaning Ms. B gave to self and object representations that extended beyond the immediate situation and, simultaneously, encompassed the present.

Ms. B has used an aspect of material reality to express her unconscious fantasy construction of the world. My countertransferentially driven intervention or interventions acted as a piece of material reality that has been transformed into an action-oriented, affectively laden, externalized representation of Ms. B's psychic reality. The transformation was crucial. The image of me rubbing her nose in my indifference is very different from that of an analyst who (a) is making a mistake, (b) is unempathic or angry, or (c) harbors sadistic wishes. From her point of view, her psychic reality, I was intentionally hurting her. Such behavior on my part deserved nothing less than Ms. B trying to hurt or humiliate me.

There was a reversal here between material and psychic reality; and the determining factor was the dynamically driven past that actively structured the present. To the extent that Ms. B could induce feelings and attitudes in me that were similar to those of significant objects from the past, there was a consistency and stability between present and past. Her anger was crucial to this link. In this situation, meaning was organized around affect, and Ms. B's sense of justifiable rage was a determining factor in the "reality" of the experience for her (cf. Frosch, 1995). Ms. B's belief that I wanted to hurt her could also be very exciting to her. She turned passive into active and did to me what she felt I was doing to her. It allowed for a discharge of her aggression: "It's like a shot in the arm" is a phrase Ms. B often used to signify the sense of excitement and aliveness she felt when angry. A good feeling, it represents what Freud (1937/1964b) called the "finer structure" of psychical objects (p. 261). Here masochistic fantasies and sadistic fantasies are interchangeable (cf. Steingart, 1995, esp. pp. 24–25). Love and hate are similar parts of a pattern. She beat me because she loved me and wanted me to love her. Her anger was an attempt to get through to me, to make sure I was not indifferent to her. If I could respond with love, that is, get beyond the anger (mine as well as hers) and understand her, then I could love her as she beat me. This is the kind of love dreams are made of (cf. Bach, 1985, esp. pp. 129–150 —the Dream of the Marquis DeSade). Thus, Ms. B's sadomasochistic fantasies expressed and defended against her wish for a more intimate (i.e., "merged") relationship. They were compromise formations that were automatically invoked in situations in which Ms. B felt threatened. In this context I understand threat to refer to moments when Ms. B felt she was being treated with indifference or when she felt she was loved.

This is one view of Ms. B's psychic reality. It is my construction on the scale of the transference of an aspect of an underlying dynamic pattern that determines the shape of this woman's life. At times it also represented, to a greater or lesser extent, Ms. B's understanding of her psychic reality. Ms. B came to analysis because of this dynamically determined pattern of behavior. The compelling nature of the credit check enactment should not obscure our view of Ms. B's unconsciously determined primary process organization of the present based on the past. Her behavior during the transference enactment was consistent with Ms. B's pattern of behavior throughout the transference, as well as with her parents and her superiors at work, discussed in an earlier section of this article. The enactment can be seen as a relatively out-of-the-ordinary example of Ms. B's psychic reality. It is, at a particular moment in time, a different aspect, shape, or form of psychic reality that is similar to all other manifestations. The enactment exemplifies that psychic reality has many forms of existence.

In this situation, to say that material reality, my countertransference, was merely a hook for Ms. B's psychic reality may be correct, but not true. How the analyst responds to his or her intense emotional states during an enactment; how, in effect, the analyst unsticks himself or herself can either facilitate the work or inhibit it. Here I would agree with Levenson's (1981) comment that it is who the analyst is and what he or she brings to the analytic situation that is crucial. If the patient must give up his or her desire to gratify transference wishes for the sake of love for the analyst (Friedman, 1991), then the analyst must do the same with his or her resistance (i.e., countertransference—from a more limited perspective) for the sake of love for the patient's psychic reality. Resistance interferes with self-awareness and the acquisition of knowledge (Renik, 1995).

In the psychoanalytic situation, the analyst's resistance interferes with an increased understanding of the patient's unconscious fantasies. The analyst's resistance is also part of an ongoing process that influences subsequent manifestations of the transference. In other words, there is an ongoing process of reciprocal influence through the activation or inhibition of fantasy sets—that is, transference and countertransference—in the patient and the analyst. The form the transference (or countertransference) takes at a particular moment in time influences and shapes the activation or inhibition of different aspects of the patient's psychic reality that can emerge in the transference-countertransference matrix. By placing Ms. B's unconscious fantasies in the context of the transference-countertransference matrix, I am including a qualitative dimension that can accrue to form. That is to say, if we think of form as an arrangement of separate elements in a particular way (Webster's, 1964), then the separate elements in Ms. B's psychic reality are the different sets of fantasies that can be activated or inhibited in the transference-countertransference matrix. Thus the quality and shape (i.e., nature and form) Ms. B's transference takes at a given point in time cannot be independent of my countertransference. The analyst's task is to discern a dynamic pattern in the patient that cuts across situations. It is a given that what the analyst comes up with will always be influenced by his or her unconscious fantasies and their corresponding emotions. The analyst's construction of the patient is an amalgam of fact and fantasy just as we would say psychic reality is so constructed. There is no one way of defining who the patient is, and we hope that our way will have a good enough fit so that it can be helpful.

The issues that came up around termination are a case in point. I saw the termination as premature, and I followed Ms. B's resistance to exploring the wish to terminate for as long as I thought I could without risking an irreparable rupture in the therapeutic relationship. Ms. B made it clear, however, that this was the way it had to be. I came to believe that she was right; and I wondered whether my newfound belief was a collusion with a defensively oriented enactment. After all, my initial impulse to argue with Ms. B occurred in the context of previously unmastered countertransference at the time of the credit check. Was I inhibited or restricted as an analyst because of my concerns about my countertransference? I thought that Ms. B's expectation that I would fight her all the way about termination was also a wish that I prevent her from a premature termination of a therapeutic process that might enable her to prevent future disappointments and unhappiness. She did not, however, present her thoughts about termination in a way that we could discuss. It was a done deal delivered in an argumentative and devaluing manner. If I had been less uncomfortable with the induced counter-transference, could I have helped this woman explore her wish to terminate in a way that might not have been experienced by her as an attempt to force her into submission? Or, more accurately, could we have worked through this sadomasochistic fantasy and viewed termination from a variety of perspectives?

Let me add a corrective to this pessimistically colored picture. The fact that I could view Ms. B's termination as a sadomasochistic enactment does not take away from her perspective that it was the right thing to do at the time. She may have gone as far as she could in her analysis with me. I understood very well the predicament that Ms. B felt she was in. She really did believe that there were analytic issues to be resolved that had the potential to impact on every aspect of her life. She also felt that if she continued the analysis it would be an act of submission and, therefore, an absolute humiliation. It was an untenable situation. She had to leave, and she needed to feel that I really saw this from her point of view. Her need to control the final phase of the analysis can be seen as indicating a lack of trust of the analyst. At the same time, however, her control at the end of the analysis can lead to an increased capacity on her part for self-regulation and the further development of analytic trust. For Ms. B, analytic trust was variable and its solidification may be seen as an outcome rather than a precondition of treatment (cf. Bach, 1998; Ellman, 1991; Settlage, 1977). From this perspective Ms. B's identifications with my capacity to see things from her point of view can go a long way toward contributing to psychic regulation through internalization (see Freedman, Hoffenberg, Vorus & Frosch, 1999, esp. pp. 767–769). In this scenario, internalization is highlighted and stakes its claim on the analytic stage alongside conflict resolution. The distinction between these two ways of looking at the analytic situation is perhaps better stated as interrelated aspects of the same coin. From a conflict model I thought that the reworking of the past in the heightened atmosphere of the transference led to shifts in the arrangement of wishes and defenses in central compromise formations. The modification of these compromise formations increased Ms. B's capacity to experience positive feelings in the analysis and in her more extra analytic world. By the end of our work together she was better able to come to terms with the good enough quality of the analytic relationship. She was, from a different perspective, better able to internalize me as a benign object. She felt our work had been productive and experienced me as someone who had her best interests in mind. Ms. B said that she felt she "got her money's worth." Coming from someone whose world revolved around money, I thought that this was a statement reflective of deep positive feelings. In the past, money, in the displaced form of the credit check, had been used as a weapon. Here it may be used, at least in part, as reparation. Ms. B repairs the damage that she believes she is inflicting on me by depriving me of my narcissistic triumph.

## Summary and Conclusion

In discussing how transference came about, Freud (1912/1958a) said that an individual produces what might be described as a stereotype plate (*"or several such* [italics added]"), which is "constantly reprinted afresh—in the course of the person's life" (pp. 99–100). These stereotype plates are fantasies organized around prototypical self and object representations from the patient's past, which attach themselves to the person of the analyst. The unconscious pattern that we refer to as psychic reality will take on a different form or shape depending on what fantasies are active, that is, invested with instinctual energy, at that moment in time. In other words, the organization of fantasies that we call psychic reality is a cathectic distribution. From moment to moment, session to session, the shape of psychic reality can vary like variations on a theme. In this context "form" or "shape" contains a qualitative dimension. In the clinical situation this is seen in the different manifestations of the transference. In the long run, however, these different shapes will be self-similar, and a pattern of meaning characteristic for each person will be discernible.

Throughout this article, I have tried to show that the mind, like any complex system, has patterned regularity in the context of unpredictability. The analyst's task is one of pattern recognition (Spruiell, 1993), that is to say, to recognize the underlying pattern of psychic reality as it presents on different levels of observation and takes on many different forms. The forms are determined by the activation or inhibition (cathexis or decathexis) of particular sets of fantasies in the patient that are related to the analyst's interpretive work, as well as his or her unrecognized and enacted fantasy set, that is, countertransference. In this context I have highlighted the reciprocal relationship between transference and counter-transference while giving central importance to the patient's psychic reality as it transforms the present into a version of the past.

An example of this transformation is the sadomasochistic compromise formations that are related to Ms. B's wishes for emotionally intimate relation-ships. These compromise formations appeared in Ms. B's screen memories, discussed earlier, as well as in her actual contemporary relationships—including the relationship with the analyst. To the extent that she could draw the other into these fantasies, Ms. B reconstructed the past using the materials of the present. The analyst's recognition of his or her role in these "new editions" (Freud, 1905/1953a, p. 116) of the past is a necessary part of a process in which the reliving and reworking of psychic reality leads to shifts in the organization of compromise formations that affect the quality of a person's life. The organization of compromise formations is conceptualized as the relation between wishes and defenses that colors the adaptive and mala-daptive aspects of the compromise formations (Brenner, 1985), as well as the hierarchical arrangement of compromise formations (i.e., the psychic value given to oral, anal, and phallic oedipal constructions). In this context the same kind of thinking used earlier in regard to countertransference can be used in a discussion of "analytic cure." Small changes can have profound consequences. Subtle shifts in the arrangement within and between com-promise formations can lead to significantly different "enactments with reality." That is to say, the other can become a different "model ... object...

helper (or) opponent" (Freud, 1921/1955, p. 69), in the patient's psychic reality and this can lead to further interactions that are colored by this new experience. A continuation of this process can shift the quality of a person's life. (This idea is explored in some depth by Grossman, 1998, in his discussion of the complemental series as a general principle of psychoanalytic theory.) This is what happened to Ms. B. By the end of the analysis she had not only come to terms with the good enough quality of the analytic relationship but also saw her boyfriend in a new light. Donald was not perfect but Ms. B saw him as someone that she could possibly build a life with. The less-than-perfect other could now be experienced as rewarding rather than traumatic. This shift in the experience of self and object representations can also be seen from the perspective of analytic trust and the capacity to internalize more benign object representations.

## Acknowledgements

I thank the following people for their valuable input into this article: Donna Bassin, Joseph Cancelmo, Gil Katz, Richard Lasky, Ruth Oscharoff, and Neal Vorus. I would also like to thank Daisy Franco, who supervised the case of Ms. B.

## References

Arlow, J. (1985). The concept of psychic reality and related problems. *Journal of the American Psychoanalytic Association*, 33:521–535.

———(1991a). The genesis of interpretation. In *Psychoanalysis: Clinical theory and practice* (pp. 279–288). New York: International Universities Press, 1979.

———(1991b). Methodology and reconstruction. *Psychoanalytic Quarterly*, 40:539–563.

Aron, L. (1990). One person and two person psychologies and the method of psychoanalysis. *Psychoanalytic Psychology*, 7:475–489.

Bach, S. (1985). *Narcissistic states and the therapeutic process*. Northvale. NJ: Jason Aronson.

———(1998). On treating the difficult patient. In C. Ellman, S. Grand, M. Silvan & S. Ellman (Eds.), *The Modern Freudians—Contemporary psychoanalytic technique* (pp. 185–195). Northvale, NJ: Jason Aronson.

Bachant, J. L., Lynch, A. & Richards, A. (1995). Relational models in psychoanalytic theory. *Psychoanalytic Psychology*, 12:71–88.

Berger, L. (1995). Grunbaum's questionable interpretation of inanimate systems: "History" and "context" in physics. *Psychoanalytic Psychology*, 12:439–449.

Brenner, C. (1976). *Psychoanalytic technique and psychic conflict*. New York: International Universities Press.

———(1985). Countertransference as compromise formation. *Psychoanalytic Quarterly*, 34:155–163.

———(1996). The nature of knowledge and the limits of authority in psychoanalysis. *Psychoanalytic Quarterly*, 65:21–31.

Chused, J. (1991). The evocative power of enactments. *Journal of the American Psychoanalytic Association*, 39:615–639.

Ellman, S. (1991). *Freud's technique papers—A contemporary perspective*. Northvale, NJ: Jason Aronson.

Fogel, G. (1990). [Review of the book Chaos: Making a new science]. *Bulletin of the Association of Psychoanalytic Medicine*, 29:89–94.

———(1993). A transitional phase in our understanding of the psychoanalytic process: A new look at Ferenczi and Rank. *Journal of the American Psychoanalytic Association*, 41:585–602.

Fosshage, J. (1995). Countertransference as the analyst's experience of the analysand: Influence of listening perspectives. *Psychoanalytic Psychology*, 12:375–391.

Freedman, N., Hoffenberg, J., Vorus, N. & Frosch, A. (1999). The effectiveness of psychoanalytic psychotherapy: The role of treatment duration, frequency of sessions, and the therapeutic relationship. *Journal of the American Psychoanalytic Association*, 47:741–772.

Freud, S. (1900). The interpretation of dreams. *Standard Edition*, 4/5:1–751.

——— (1905). Fragment of an analysis of a case of hysteria. *Standard Edition*, 7:1–122.

———(1910). The future prospects of psycho-analytic therapy. *Standard Edition*, 11:139–151.

———(1912). The dynamics of transference. *Standard Edition*, 12:97–108.

———(1912). Recommendations to physicians practicing psychoanalysis. *Standard Edition*, 12:109–120.

———(1915). The unconscious. *Standard Edition*, 14:159–215.

———(1917). Introductory lectures on psycho-analysis. *Standard Edition*, 16:243–483.

———(1921). Group psychology and the analysis of the ego. *Standard Edition*, 18:69–143.

———(1937). Analysis terminable and interminable. *Standard Edition*, 23:209–253.

———(1937). Constructions in analysis. *Standard Edition*, 23:255–269.

Friedman, L. (1991). A reading of Freud's papers on technique. *Psychoanalytic Quarterly*, 40:564–595.

Frosch, A. (1995). The preconceptual organization of emotion. *Journal of the American Psychoanalytic Association*, 43:423–447.

———(2002). Survival, symbolization, and psychic space. In R. Lasky (Ed.), *A Festschrift in honor of Norbert Freedman* (pp. 366-386). New York: Other Press.

Galatzer-Levy, R. (1995). Psychoanalysis and dynamical systems theory: Prediction and self similarity. *Journal of the American Psychoanalytic Association*, 43:1085–1113.

Gill, M. (1983). The interpersonal paradigm and the degree of the therapist's involvement. *Contemporary Psychoanalysis*, 19:200–237.

———(1995). Classical and relational psychoanalysis. *Psychoanalytic Psychology*, 12:89–107.

Gleick, J. (1987). *Chaos: Making a new science*. New York: Penguin Books.

Grey, A. (1995–1996). Sullivan's contribution to psychoanalysis: An overview. *The Review of Interpersonal Psychoanalysis*, 1:14–16.

Grossman, W. (1992). Hierarchies, boundaries, and representation in a Freudian model of mental organization. *Journal of the American Psychoanalytic Association*, 40:27–62.

———(1998). Freud's presentation of "the psychoanalytic mode of thought" in *Totem and taboo* and his technical papers. *International Journal Psycho-Analysis*, 79:469–486.

Heimann, P. (1950). On counter-transference. *International Journal Psycho-Analysis*, 31:81–84.

———(1977). Further observations on the analyst's cognitive processes. *Journal of the American Psychoanalytic Association,* 25:313–333.

Hoffman, I. (1983). The patient as interpreter of the analyst's experience. *Contemporary Psychoanalysis*, 19:389–422.

———(1996). The intimate and ironic authority of the psychoanalyst's presence. *Psychoanalytic Quarterly*, 65:102–136.

Hurst, D. (1995). Toward a definition of the term and concept of interaction [Panel report]. *Journal of the American Psychoanalytic Association,* 43:521–537.

Jacobs, T. (1986). On countertransference enactments. *Journal of the American Psychoanalytic Association,* 34:289–307.

Katz, G. (1999). Where the action is: The enacted dimension of the analytic process. *Journal of the American Psychoanalytic Association,* 46:1129–1167.

Kernberg, O. (1965). Notes on countertransference. *Journal of the American Psychoanalytic Association,* 13:38–56.

Kincaid, J. (1991). *Lucy*. New York: Penguin Books.

Lasky, R. (1993). *Dynamics of development and the therapeutic process.* Northvale, NJ: Jason Aronson.

Levenson, E. (1981). Facts or fantasies: On the nature of psychoanalytic data. *Contemporary Psychoanalysis*, 17:486–500.

Levine, H. (1994). The analyst's participation in the analytic process. *International Journal of Psycho-Analysis,* 75:665–676.

Little, M. (1951). Counter-transference and the patient's response to it. *International Journal of Psycho-Analysis,* 32:32–40.

McLaughlin, J. T. (1991). Clinical and theoretical aspects of enactment. *Journal of the American Psychoanalytic Association,* 39:595–614.

Mitchell, S. (1988). The intrapsychic and the interpersonal: Different theories, different domains, or historical artifacts. *Psychoanalytic Inquiry*, 8:472–496.

Moran, M. (1991). Chaos and psychoanalysis: The fluidic nature of mind. *International Review Psycho-Analysis,* 18:211–221.

Reich, A. (1973a). Empathy and countertransference. In *Annie Reich: Psychoanalytic contributions* (pp. 344–360). New York: International Universities Press, 1966.

———(1973b). Further remarks on countertransference. In *Annie Reich: Psychoanalytic contributions* (pp. 271–287). New York: International Universities Press, 1960.

———(1973c). On countertransference. In *Annie Reich: Psychoanalytic contributions* (pp. 136–154). New York: International Universities Press, 1951.

Renik, O. (1995). The ideal of the anonymous analyst and the problem of self-disclosures. *Psychoanalytic Quarterly*, 34:466–495.

Roughton, R. (1993). Useful aspects of acting out: Repetition, enactment, and actualization. *Journal of the American Psychoanalytic Association*, 41:443–472.

Schafer, R. (1985). The interpretation of psychic reality, developmental influences, and unconscious communication. *Journal of the American Psychoanalytic Association*, 33:537–554.

Settlage, C. (1977). The psychoanalytic understanding of narcissistic and borderline personality disorders: Advances in developmental theory. *Journal of the American Psychoanalytic Association*, 25:805–833.

Skolnikoff, A. (1993). The analyst's experience in the psychoanalytic situation: A continuum between objective and subjective reality. *Psychoanalytic Inquiry*, 13:296–309.

Spruiell, V. (1993). Deterministic chaos and the sciences of complexity: Psychoanalysis in the midst of a general scientific revolution. *Journal of the American Psychoanalytic Association*, 41:3–44.

Steingart, I. (1995). *A thing apart*. Northvale, NJ: Jason Aronson.

Sullivan, H. (1954). *The psychiatric interview*. New York: Norton.

Tansy, M. & Burke, W. (1989). *Understanding counter-transference from projective identification to empathy*. Hillsdale, NJ: Analytic Press.

Vorus, N. (1998). *The concept of fantasy in psychoanalysis: An examination of the place of reality in the Freud—Klein controversies*. Unpublished doctoral dissertation, City University of New York.

*Webster's new twentieth century dictionary* (unabridged; 2nd ed.). (1964). Cleveland, OH: World.

# CHAPTER 5

# Survival, Symbolization and Psychic Space

## Reflections on "Survival, Symbolization and Psychic Space"

### Richard Lasky

In this paper Allan tackled the relationship of love and hate in David's treatment and how the management of aggression both set back and facilitated that work.

On "love's side" was Allan's containment and metabolization of David's aggression and sustaining support, continuing over years. Allan wrote "in the transference I became a more narcissistically gratifying mother" (p. 373), and he described an attempt to find ways to be "in sync" with David's basic frame of mind and psychic requirements. That was a long-term undertaking that ultimately led to an improved capacity for symbolized secondary-process thinking.

On "aggression's side" Allan thought David believed that Allan had the capacity to survive the hate directed at him. Indeed, it was the belief that Allan would survive any amount of aggression that allowed David to take greater emotional risks. Toleration without retaliation, unaccompanied by interpretation because David was not ready for it and would experience it as an attack, was Allan's model. Allan put it this way: "a receptivity to David's sadism will facilitate the potential for transformation. By receptivity

I do not refer to a masochistic submission. There must be an acceptance on the analyst's part, however, that David's immersion in this primary process mode of the symbolic process is the only way he can maintain and tolerate the therapeutic relationship at this point. The analyst's receptivity must also include a willingness to carry on the analytic process internally rather than communicate understanding before the patient is ready to take in new meaning" (p. 379).

Allan didn't make these arguments to reduce the role of interpretation, but to show how analytic work is possible when interpretation is not. This is somewhat reminiscent of Bion's emendation of Klein's concept of projective identification, in that the mother not only contains but also metabolizes projected unacceptable content until it is palatable for the baby.

Throughout, Allan addresses the clinical integration of desymbolized experience and symbolizing capacity. He describes the need for the analyst to contain and experience but also to gain psychic distance from the patient's raw, purely affective, sensory-motor, pre-operational functioning, including over-reliance on primary process, non-representational thinking and feeling . He repeatedly emphasized that love and hate both represent necessary aspects of repeating cycles of transformation associated with incremental gains in symbolic functioning. Like Winnicott, Allan thought that hate was frequently a prerequisite to love (p. 381), and that the object's survival of the patient's destructive wishes/actions, was often necessary for the patient to be able to place the object outside the self. And for Allan, "the term psychic survival [in this context] refers to the analyst's ability to remain a reliable object in the face of the patient's desymbolized [that is, the primitive aggression-laden action-dominated] transference" (p. 368). By surviving the patient's hate and becoming an object separate from the patient's self, it would be possible for the patient to invest the analyst with love; and Allan believed that "it is only through the patient's love for the analyst that a certain kind of investment can be made in reality [that will ultimately] lead to a broadening of perspectives and a shift in the relationship of wishes and defenses" (p. 381).

Allan wanted to illustrate how symbolizing capacity in treatment is a direct consequence of how analytic possibility itself and the therapeutic relationship actively hinge upon each other. He was concerned with how that which goes on between analyst and patient permits and fosters the transformation of meaning structures that are primitive, and essentially primary-process based, into ones that are nuanced and reliant on secondary-process thinking. He defined this as "transformation…along the continuum of the symbolic process" (p. 368).

David stimulated many painful feelings in Allan. Allan described his feelings with honesty, and the intensity of treating David comes through even in the language of his metapsychological descriptions, "the *visceral* (my italics) lived-through present is a representation of the past and a template for the future" (p. 381). I have long been convinced that an analyst's capacity to allow a patient to express aggression, irrational and disproportionate aggression, is critical to the welfare of the patient and of the work; I believe that the ability to tolerate and contain this without responding defensively or inhibiting it or reacting to it in a retaliatory fashion is one of the truest measures of an analyst's fitness to do this work. Allan's ability to abide, contain, metabolize and transmute David's hate into love, into a constant never-diminishing concern for and interest in David's psychic reality, shines through in this paper from beginning to end. It illustrates not only that he was a brilliant theoretician but also how and why Allan was such a gifted and remarkable clinician.

\* \* \*

# Survival, Symbolization and Psychic Space

*Allan Frosh*

## Introduction

From a particular perspective psychoanalytic theory is elegant in its simplicity. The infant or child, and perhaps fetus, has certain needs and wishes that constitute desires. Depending on how the environment responds to these desires, we begin to form certain ideas and expectations of others and ourselves. We develop strategies to maximize pleasure and minimize unpleasure. These expectations, strategies, and desires are organized into an unconscious construction of the world that represents the personal meanings we give to events and actions in the past and present (Schafer 1985). These constructions are organized according to the laws of the primary process and are understood to be affect-laden sensory motor images that are primarily, but not exclusively, visual in nature. Freud referred to these unconscious constructions as "psychic reality" and believed that new editions of psychic reality were reprinted throughout one's life (1912), and in psychopathology the person had a greater investment in psychic reality than in material (i.e., external or "actual") reality (1917).

In the psychoanalytic situation the analyst begins to develop certain ideas about the patient's psychic reality. That is to say, the analyst may believe that a certain pattern of organizing experience imbues the patient's life with a meaning that transcends any particular situation. The analyst's ideas are informed by what the patient brings to the situation and by how the analyst reacts to the patient. In this paper the reciprocal relation between transference and countertransference is referred to as the transference/counter- transference matrix. The analyst's ideas about the patient's psychic reality are understood to be compromise formations that reflect conscious/unconscious and symbolized/desymbolized aspects of this matrix.

At particular times and with a reasonable amount of tact and empathy, the analyst offers up these ideas to the patient in the form of an interpretation, hypothesis, or conjecture, depending on one's style and belief system. At certain times these clinical conjectures are offered up as psychic reality unfolds in the heat of the transference. The idea is that with sufficient trust and safety the patient can look at the transference and see past, present, and future in an emotionally meaningful way. This can allow for the possibility of some alteration of psychic reality in terms of a modification of the relationship between wishes (desires) and defenses (strategies), and/or some modification of the emotional investment in psychic reality vs. material reality.

We know only too well, however, that our interventions are not always experienced by patients in a way that has therapeutic value. Sometimes patients can feel overwhelmed when asked to self-reflect, or, alternatively, feel that they understand exactly what the analyst says but this understanding is so devoid of affect that it is meaningless. The person feels the same. We also know from our experience on both sides of the couch, as well as from our research efforts (Freedman et al. 1999b), that over time patients do feel helped by the therapeutic experience, and this feeling of being helped is very much tied to the nature of the therapeutic relationship. How then do we understand the process that goes on between therapist and patient that facilitates the transformation of a meaning structure based on the primary process to one based on the secondary process? This is exactly the kind of transformation we talk about as we move along the continuum of the symbolic process.

The purpose of this paper is to discuss the symbolic process in relation to the therapeutic relationship. It is in the transference/countertransference matrix where issues of psychic survival can play a crucial role in the emergence of a more symbolized therapeutic relationship. The term *psychic survival* refers to the analyst's ability to remain a reliable object in the face of the patient's desymbolized transference. This will be discussed further and illuminated by case material where particular attention is given to the therapist's recognition and working through of countertransference issues as a necessary condition for the emergence of a symbolic process in the patient.

## Symbolic Process

The symbolic process is seen as an ego function or general capacity of the mind, which may be used by the primary or secondary process (Rycroft 1956). When the symbolic process is dominated by primary process activity the perceived object (e.g., the analyst) stands for an archaic object but is not well differentiated from it. The affects directed toward the contemporary object are the same as those associated with the archaic one (Segal 1957). In this situation self and object, past and present, and internal and external are not well differentiated. The object does not exist as an independent entity. There is no psychic space between self and other.

When the symbolic process is dominated by secondary process activity the affective charge toward the contemporary object is not the same as it was toward the archaic one. When a substitute in the external world is used as a symbol infused with secondary process activity, it can be distinguished from the original object. It stands for the archaic object but is also recognized as an object in itself (cf. Segal, p. 43). There is greater differentiation along all of the dimensions I have just touched upon. In this situation the person can go beyond the immediacy of the moment and begin to view contemporary experience from a number of perspectives. This is not the case when symbolic activity is organized according to the laws of the primary process. In this case the immediacy of the moment is "frozen" so that it cannot be decentered. It can *only* be seen from the person's subjective experience. Rycroft (1956) argues that when the symbolic process is infused with primary process activity the relationship to the object is "fundamentally autistic," whereas symbolic functioning organized around the secondary process leads to "communication, contact and interaction with the external object" (p. 139). This latter kind of symbolic functioning will be referred to as *symbolization*. Symbolic functioning that is organized along the lines of the primary process will be referred to as *desymbolization*. Desymbolization is characterized by a lack of secondary process activity that can be a result of developmental issues and/or a shift away from a more symbolized position. Desymbolization, like symbolization, is considered a compromise formation with multiple functions.

Movement along the continuum of the symbolic process toward a more optimum level of symbolization is marked by a number of trans-formations in the patient's relationship to the analyst as well as in the level of symbolic functioning. These are best understood as cycles of incremental gains and have been discussed in some detail by Freedman (1994, Freedman et al. 1999, Freedman and Karliner1999). In this paper I will show the cycles of transformations of fantasy/enactments as they occurred in the treatment of an adolescent boy. These enactments occurred in the fifth and sixth years of David's twice-weekly treatment when he was 12 to 14 years old, and were related to shifts toward a more optimum level of symbolization. The term *fantasy/enactment* refers to the content of the patient's fantasies that sometimes became dramatized between the two of us. That is to say, sometimes I actively participated in the drama. The phrase "a more optimum level of symbolization" refers to a particular use of the therapist by the patient.

## Clinical Material

### Brief History

David was referred for treatment when he was 8 years old (Frosch 1998) because he was verbally abusive at home and seemed on the edge of losing control physically. He threatened people, had trouble engaging in activities unless he was assured of being the best, and seemed completely distracted in school. David had difficulties with both of his parents, but these difficulties were particularly pronounced in relation to his mother. I saw David as a youngster with narcissistic vulnerabilities related to early, primarily maternal failures. He compensated for these early fail-ures with aggression. In the treatment situation David expressed his anger through a barrage of verbally abusive comments, devaluations, and provocations, as well as physical threats. I felt I had to prepare myself for these onslaughts, and I often did not look forward to our sessions. In short, David's behavior and my feeling state reflected what was going on in his family and, to a lesser extent, in school and with friends. Over the years there has been a gradual shift in how David experiences the psychotherapeutic situation, and my experience of it as well. I conceptualize these shifts as consisting of a number of transformations in the transference/countertransference matrix and in David's capacity to utilize secondary process thinking, which is a necessary condition for the emergence of symbolization. The shifts do not follow a clear linear progression. They are part of oscillating cycles that move between desymbolization and symbolization with corresponding affective states of hate and love.

### Treatment

When he was 12 years old David told me about a game he was playing on his computer called "The Age of Explorers." The point of the game was to capture a city. David decided to do this by taking control of the surrounding countryside and eliminating the city's food supply. When the people were nearly dead from starvation, David's forces, which were hidden in the city, slaughtered everyone. During this period of time David talked about his own relationship to food. Because his mother often worked late during the week, David sometimes cooked for himself at home. He excitedly described the wonderful meals he would make and took great delight in telling me how he had second or third helpings at his school cafeteria. Food has always played a crucial role in David's life and in a previous paper (Frosch 1998) I have discussed David's experiences at his mother's "less than optimal breast" as both fact and metaphor. During the first few years of our work together David viewed me as a decidedly less than optimal breast. I could give him nothing. What I did give him was devalued to the point of turning it into shit, which is how David described it. His whole manner of relating to me was along the lines of an intense power struggle in which David was always in the driver's seat. The content of the fantasy in the "Age of Explorers" game could be seen as a symbolic representation of David's early experiences with his mother. These early memories have been transformed so that now David is the sadist who deprives others of food and then slaughters them. In this sense the sadomasochistic dynamics organized around early feeding experiences with mother were very much active at this time. The feeling tone of the sessions, however, was of a more positive nature, and I had the distinct impression that David's pride in telling me his strategy and skill at playing this game was a reflection of a different use of me as a transference object. With David's entree into puberty and the need to disengage from the archaic mother, I became the symbolic father that David could use in his struggle against the regressive pull of the early maternal object. David's need to turn me into shit and his intense competition organized around issues of castration diminished in intensity, and a more positive transference developed.

Over the next few months David began to bring his laptop computer into the sessions and played car-racing games. He wanted me to actively participate and use the computer. He responded to my anxiety about my ability to play these games with a certain amount of contempt and scorn, but also with patience and support. The emotional tone was weighted toward David's being a benevolent teacher. A more wishful reversal in fantasy between parent and child was now enacted with me.

The use of the computer ushered in a new phase of the transference cycle. Shortly after my hands-on experience with the computer, David began bringing in his CD collection of "Gangsta Rap" music and playing it on the computer. A short time later he brought in a CD player and one set of earphones. David gave me one earphone and he used the other. There we sat with an earphone plugged into one of David's ears and the other plugged into mine. And a common wire joining each of the earphones with the CD player connected us. The CD player eventually gave way to a tape deck, but the common earphone set that joined David and me remained. The shift to the tape deck was significant. Now David could play tapes that he mixed. He told me he wanted to be a DJ and he enthusiastically explained the many technical skills he had learned and was continuing to learn. The earphone enactment represented a very important shift in the transference cycle. The structure of our sessions at this time could be seen as a regressive reenactment of the early mother-child relationship, which was so traumatic for David. A qualifying comment is needed here. If I had been unable to view David's presentation of his music in a less than positive way, it could well have led to a replication of the early trauma of the less than optimal breast, now enacted with a contemporary object. Fortunately this was not the case, and I was able to view David's presentation in a more symbolic way. My distaste of gangsta rap music very quickly gave way to an appreciation of David's interest in it and his burgeoning technical skills, including his ability to create his own lyrics and, most important, I understood how important it was for David to show me this. I believe a necessary component in David's increased capacity to use symbolization was my own capacity to anchor my reaction (i.e., my distaste) in a secondary process context so that a "working space" (Freedman and Lavender 1997) could be created within me that allowed for a particular kind of focus on the other.

As an infant David nearly fell into the category of a failure-to-thrive child because his mother's milk was not nourishing. As mentioned earlier, I view this as both fact and a metaphor for David's very difficult relationship with his mother, particularly during his early years. In the transference I became a more narcissistically gratifying mother. More accurately, of course, I became a symbol that David could use in the process of working through some of the early trauma. What I am describing is a secondary process context that could facilitate a particular form of thinking called symbolization. It is a repeated observation of analysts interested in the adolescent process that the regressive swings of this period can lead to greater structuralization (what Blos [1979] refers to as the second individuation process) only when these regressions occur in the context of a relatively healthy ego. David had been in therapy for four years at this point, and the therapeutic gains complemented the consolidation of ego functioning that characterized his latency period. His ego strength, conceptualized here as the use of secondary process thinking that could support symbolizaton served David well. I came to represent aspects of his parents that David could symbolically use to work through early trauma. I believe the preparatory work for this was accomplished during the previous four years of therapy where David often experienced me as a more direct representation of a negatively cathected parental imago. Where David's early years were characterized by a struggle for psychic survival, I felt our early years of working together were characterized by my own struggle for psychic survival in the context of David's rage, and the shifts in my countertransference between relative states of symbolization and desymbolization.

### The Wanna-Be-Rapper and the Lyrics of Psychotherapy

David's transformations from "The Age of Explorers" to the earphone enactment can be seen as a series of incremental risks. With each shift he puts more on the line. How will I respond to his desire that I think well of his talents, his interest in "gangsta rap" music, and his wish to be a DJ?

In the fantasy/enactment of the earphones the analytic relationship was characterized by an increased ratio of libido to aggression. Love more than hate. From my side of the dyad I looked forward to my sessions with David and could well remember a time when I did not. From David's side he often did not want to leave when the time ran out. And he talked more about pressing issues in his life. He spoke of girls—his libidinal interest in them as well as his sadism. David wanted to provoke and humiliate older women as well as girls his own age. Sometimes I could comment on this in terms of his relationship with his mother as well as his relationship with me. In the past David might simply curse me out if I did this, but at this point he usually would not curse or yell at me. At times he would smile and agree. These moments of "interpretive work" were actually few and far between, and the major topic of conversation was David's relationship with Jimmy.

Jimmy was the biggest kid in David's class and clearly the strongest. He was also the leader of a clique that David belonged to. As I understood the relationship between David and Jimmy, the most important thing for David was to be Jimmy's good friend. David was also frightened of passively submitting to Jimmy. On the one hand David wanted to feel protected, loved, and admired by Jimmy, but, on the other hand, he fought with him, sometimes physically, a good deal of the time. This was a not-so-thinly-veiled repetition of the dynamic between David and his father as well as with me. David might call his father at the office two or three times a day to ask some questions about music. At the same time he would denigrate his father's taste in music and aggressively provoke him. With me David would clearly want me to listen to his mixing of music and to recognize and admire the various techniques he had perfected. And just as he often left after the hour was up, he would sometimes announce that he had enough and leave before the hour was over. A barrage of provocations and angry insults often accompanied this. Thus with his father, with me, and with Jimmy, this pattern of moving toward the object and then moving away through aggressive and sometimes sadistic behavior was played out repeatedly.

It was with Jimmy, however, where we could most often talk about these conflicts. When I say talk about them I mean exactly that. We would talk about what went on between David and Jimmy. What I said was informed by my understanding of David's unconscious dynamics. Our conversations took place in the context of my thinking in an interpretive mode. What I would like to emphasize here is that these were my private thoughts that went beyond the immediacy of the moment and, for the most part, they remained private. I found that the closer I could stay to the concrete issues—what happened and who did what to whom—the more the dynamic issues could be represented.

Two factors were clearly associated with the series of fantasy/enactments culminating in the "earphone enactment": (1) there was a clear shift in David's ratio of libido to aggression and (2) there was an increased capacity for David to move beyond the concrete "realities" of the therapeutic situation. Psychotherapy was still something that David consciously did not want to come to. But this feeling did not determine his sense of reality as completely as it had in the past. (See Frosch 1995 for a discussion of the relationship between a person's sense of reality, affects, and archaic thinking.) David came and was eager to talk about things that were going on in his life that had meaning for him. And he wanted to communicate these things to me. Language began to share the stage with action. I thought that David was moving toward a new level of symbolization, a level that Freedman and Karliner (1999) call *discursive symbolization.* He was developing self-awareness in connection to others, a nascent self-reflectiveness in the context of relationships. Incremental gains in symbolization and the complexity of the therapeutic relationship go hand in hand.

## Symbolization and Complexity

In the elements of betrayal and sadism that characterized "The Age of Explorers" David may have been repeating what he felt had been done to him while simultaneously expressing the sadistic things he would like to do if the parent-child situation were reversed (cf. Klein 1932). In the earphone enactment David also remembers the early trauma through repetition but this time the compromise formation has been shifted. The wish for a more narcissistically gratifying relationship with mother is represented by the earphones, which join us together. I listened to David. I am tuned into him—after all, we share a common cord. The verbal associations to the fantasy represent David's longings toward his father who, in point of fact, is extremely knowledgeable about music. The movement between "The Age of Explorers" and the earphone enactment may be viewed as an attempt to integrate love and hate. In this sense the cycles of love and hate may be "regarded as an attempt at cure, an endeavor to reconcile the divided Ego—divided by the trauma—with the rest and to unite it into a strong whole that will be fit to cope with the outer world" (Freud 1937, p. 97).

The integration of love and hate has led to a shift in the complexity of David's objects. They are no longer either all good or all bad. David can see the relationship with Jimmy from multiple perspectives. He is better able to decenter himself from the immediacy of the moment and put himself in Jimmy's place. David's transference to Jimmy is tempered by David's secondary process thinking. Jimmy stands for the archaic object, but he is not that object. David can also see Jimmy as a person in his own right. This is also happening in David's transference to me. I am not only the person who forces David to come and, therefore, deprives him of instinctual gratification, that is, of an opportunity to go home, eat, and watch TV. I am beginning to become someone David wants to talk to about things that feel important to him. David has made an incremental gain along the continuum of the symbolic process.

## Transformations: The Modification of Temporal Parameters

In the first year of our work together David played out an elaborate fantasy with Legos where he killed all of his friends and became king of everyone. Two years later David was very interested in drawing super heroes in sessions. In my previous report (1998) I described a particular session with David.

> [T]he session was colored in a distinctly positive, I would say libidinal, tone. David wanted to show me his card collection and clearly valued my interest in it. He was in no hurry to leave the session, and I did not feel a great need to *do* something with the material. As the session drew to a close and David collected his things and started to leave, I noticed that he had left his baseball cap on the couch. I mentioned this to him as I picked it up and flipped it to him. He dropped it, picked it up, and left. ... In the next session he threw a bottle of Wite-Out at me: "Because you threw my baseball cap at me." [pp. 271–272]

This oscillating pattern of sadism and libido has been described in the present paper. A computer replaced Legos and Gangsta-Rap super heroes replaced comic book super heroes. What I would like to empha-size here is the notion that the temporal parameters of these new editions of earlier dynamic representations have been modified. This is most clearly presented in the earphone enactment where David's confi-dence in the analyst's capacity to survive his sadism allowed David to take greater emotional risks. David talked about his conflicts with Jimmy, his wishes and insecurities with girls, and a variety of other emotionally significant issues. He began to represent his inner world through language and began to stretch the temporal parameters of the cycles of love and hate. That is to say, he spent longer periods of time in a more libidinized transference and his *recovery* from his sadistic attacks toward me was more rapid. It is not that David's aggression disappeared. His aggression was always a part of the ongoing process and would present intermittently in a session or completely color the emotional tone of many sessions. I highlight the word "recovery" because it is often easier to see the therapeutic value of a patient's positive feelings, which do seem associated with a greater capacity for symbolization. My emphasis in this paper, however, is that love and hate both represent necessary aspects of repeating cycles of transformation associated with incremental gains in symbolic functioning.

## Symbolization and the Capacity to Use an Object

To "use me" in a therapeutic sense, David must recognize me as existing independently of him. In the process that leads to my existence as an independent object, David's sadism is crucial. If I can survive David's destructiveness, his fantasies as well as his overt behavior, something new is created. Winnicott (1971) puts it as follows: "A new feature thus arrives in the theory of object-relating. The subject says to the object: 'I destroyed you,' and the object is there to receive the communication. From now on the subject says: 'Hullo object!' 'I destroyed you.' 'I love you.' 'You have value for me because of your survival of my destruction of you'" (p. 90). For Winnicott the patient's destructiveness and the object's survival is crucial to placing the object outside of the self. Winnicott's discussion of the patient's destructiveness focuses on the object's "liability not to survive" (p. 93). Survival in its broadest sense means not to retaliate. However, it also refers to the therapist's overall feelings toward the patient that color the quality of the therapeutic relationship.

Here the question of David's sadism is not how to overcome it through interpretations, which David might (perhaps correctly) see as defensive. Hate and love coexist. Without the hate David cannot love and, ultimately, integrate the two. And I do not survive the hate in any absolute sense. I survive from moment to moment, from session to session. The ongoing quality of the relationship, that is, my attitude toward David and my overt behavior, are indices of survival/nonsurvival. Put into the language of this paper, they are indices of symbolization or desymbolization. Over time the individual moments blend into cycles of transference, which are characterized by a particular event that stands out. The particular eye-catching event should not obscure our view of the similar micropatterns embedded in the daily work. David plays his latest mix and in the middle of a piece he turns the volume up full blast. At this moment the earphone is not in his ear but it is in mine! David and I talk about his work, and he tells me that I don't even know what he is talking about. "You're pathetic." And then he goes back to the music and excitedly points out the technical skills that he has developed.

## Survival and Desymbolization

David's desymbolized experience is a communicative act. "I dislike you because you force me to come here, and you tell me I am crazy. If you say anything to me I will devalue it and you. I negate your therapeutic function. You don't exist. I have killed you off. Are you still alive?" The analytic task here is to remain alive, interested, and in the mode of symbolization. The task is to be able to go beyond the moment and believe that a receptivity to David's sadism will facilitate the potential for transformation. By receptivity I do not refer to a masochistic submission. There must be an acceptance on the analyst's part, however, that David's immersion in this primary process mode of the symbolic process is the only way he can maintain and tolerate the therapeutic relationship at this point. The analyst's receptivity must also include a willingness to carry on the analytic process internally rather than communicate his understanding before the patient is ready to take in new meaning.

One does not forget David or take him lightly. He makes his presence known through his desymbolized experience of the transference. As an infant David was "forgotten." In other words, he may have experienced his mother's less than adequate milk and a variety of other experiences in his early childhood as if he was forgotten, as if he did not exist. David's sadomasochism compensates for this by doing to others what was done to him and by making the kind of impression where he cannot really be forgotten. This is the adaptive aspect of a compromise formation that is easily seen as pathological.

### The Analyst's Inner Space

David's aggression in the form of his devaluing comments about me and the time we spent together was an important stimulus for my own self-reflections. Am I, as David so often told me, worthless to him? Is there any value to what we do together? David has spent nearly half his life in psychotherapy with me. How many of my interventions has he actually been able to make use of? Over time I have been able to formulate some idea of how our time has been useful to David. The word "formulate" may be misleading, because this has not been an entirely intellectual process for me. I often feel that I would like to jump up and scream when he turns the volume up and the music feels like it's going to crash through my eardrum. When David pours his potato chips all over the couch and floor, I have had fantasies of opening the door and telling him to leave. When he tells me to "shut the fuck up" after I have made what I think is a sensitive and thoughtful intervention, I have wanted to say something equally nasty to David. In retrospect I can recognize that these impulses to do something have been a prelude to my construction of an inner space—a more secondary process level of symbolization in relation to David. In short, David has a profound impact on how I think about myself and how I think about him. At some point this process allows me to sink into the moment with David without worrying what to say or how I can formulate something and offer it up to him. When this happens I believe there is a greater chance that my own unconscious can, so to speak, be inspired by the moment. I speak or I do not speak; I listen to the music and may say something about it, about Jimmy, or about David's latest attempt to provoke his mother into losing her temper.

### The Patient's Inner Space

David's need to feel omnipotent through devaluing or controlling me by ridding himself of unwanted parts and attributing them to me is a way of creating a space between us. It is as if David says, "Look here, I provoked you and you did not retaliate. I killed you and you are still alive. You contain me but are not me. I have filled you with these unwanted parts but you do not act like I think I would act if you did this to me.

When you act this way, it must mean that you love me. Now I can risk having different feelings toward you."

By creating a space between us David can begin to create an inner space. Now something can happen, in the sense that Herzog (1996) uses this phrase. That something has to do with the availability of David's inner world, which can now be presented to me in the form of a verbal narrative. For this something to happen there must be an overlap between David's availability and mine. Neither is static nor to be taken as a given. This is the meaning of Winnicott's notion of survival. It is a moment-to-moment proposition. Survival and overlap mean that the analyst must be emotionally present, involved, and willing. His or her feeling state is of critical importance here. It is only then that David can begin to take more emotional risks. This is certainly not a conscious process on David's part. What begins to happen in such a situation is that we have increased the potential for a range of optimal linking of past and present, self and object, symbol and what is symbolized. This optimal linking is called *symbolization* and is marked by a capacity to experience the past in the presence of the other in such a way that the experience itself becomes an object of one's thoughts. The visceral lived-through present is a representation of the past and a template for the future. The present moment can be seen from a variety of perspectives and its emotional coloration is not the same as it was in the past. The new experience is imbued with secondary process activity and is part of a psychic space between the analyst and patient and within the patient as well as the analyst. We have moved toward a dialogue between two symbolizers (Freedman 1988). The cycle of the analytic process has shifted and, at some point, it will shift again in the direction of the primary process level of desymbolization. This is the very nature of the work.

## Survival, Symbolization, and Psychic Space: A Recapitulation

Although hate and love both represent an investment in the therapist, they are not equivalent. Hate may be a prerequisite to love, but it is only through the patient's love for the analyst that a certain kind of investment can be made in reality, that is, in the person of the analyst, that can lead to a broadening of perspectives and a shift in the relationship of wishes and defenses. On the other side of the dyad it is the analyst's commitment to the patient or, as Steingart (1995) puts it, "the analyst's steadfast devotion *only* (italics added) to understanding the analysand's psychic reality" (p. 113) that is at the very center of the therapeutic relationship. This devotion, conceptualized as a working through of action-oriented impulses in the countertransference, is a necessary component for the actualization of David's inner space.

Actualization, rather than construction, may be a more accurate way of approaching the whole issue of psychic space. Actualization means that something is potentially there. This brings the idea of psychic space into the realm of a general ego function—like the symbolic process. They are not independent concepts. It is hard to conceive of one without the other.

Freedman (1998) talks about a relational space or a potential space that is anchored by the therapist's creation of his or her own symbolizing space. I believe this is what I am describing with David. Based on my experience with David I would say that the therapist must do the lion's share of the work that goes into actualizing this relational space. David creates (actualizes) meanings within me and only then is it possible for me to create (actualize) meanings within him. I am describing a reciprocal relationship between patient and therapist that is directly related to incremental gains in symbolization.

## Incremental Gains, Complexity, and the Action of Psychotherapy

David is doing significantly better in all aspects of his life, including our work together. Given the fact that at David's age we would expect an increased capacity for secondary process thinking (Blos 1979), a reasonable question to pose before ending this paper has to do with the efficacy of psychotherapy. Are we seeing advances in symbolic functioning that are part of the developmental process and relatively independent of our psychotherapeutic endeavors? Of course there are major advances in cognitive functioning at David's age. But David has spent nearly half his life in psychotherapy. Psychotherapy is an integral part of the complex system that *is* David's life. We know that duration of therapy is associated with incremental gains in symbolic functioning and in the capacity for a more meaningful psychotherapeutic relationship (Freedman et al. 1999b). In a system composed of many variables in interaction we would expect incremental gains (or small changes) to have potentially profound effects (cf. Moran 1991). The question of whether psychotherapy "caused" the shifts in David's life implies a linear relationship between cause and effect, which is not the case in complex systems. Something has happened in David's psychotherapy. We have "survived" each other and reached a point where for extended periods of time the work takes on the quality of two symbolizers in dialogue. That this is happening in David's life as well enhances the potential for his continued success. To say that psychotherapy caused these shifts to occur is like saying that David's mother's increased (and now extraordinary) capacity to be a true symbolizer in the presence of her often desymbolized, aggressive, and physically threatening son, caused the shifts in psychotherapy. This argument does not diminish the importance of our psychotherapeutic efforts at all. We hope it gives us pause to think about the complexity of people's lives and the potential for impact that we really do have.

Right before our summer break David missed his last session. I called him and he said, "Oh my God. I forgot. I'm sorry." Here David is able to express an awareness of self in relation to another. That is to say, *I* did this to *you* and *I* have a *feeling* about it. David is able to connect his feeling of being sorry with an action. He is more reflective and can see the event from a different perspective than before. In the past David might have denied that we had a session, or said that I had simply forgotten that we had cancelled. Now he can be less than perfect and not feel obliterated. He can go beyond the immediacy of the moment.

## Summary and Conclusions

In this paper I have emphasized the therapist's capacity to experience in the transference/countertransference matrix aspects of the patient's feeling states without losing the capacity to remain in a relative state of secondary process/symbolization. It is this capacity that is constantly lost and regained throughout the analytic endeavor that can act as an agent that transforms the patient's potential for symbolization into an actuality. A concrete example of this was presented in the nonverbalized internal dialogue of the therapist's sense of worthlessness actualized through David's projective mechanisms. It is the ongoing process of the therapist working through these emotional storms that represents the symbolized countertransference.

As analysts we have certain expectations about our work. We expect to be able to make interpretations, and we expect that patients will be able, to a greater or lesser extent, to make use of these interpretations. This is basically how I began this paper. The bulk of the paper, however, has been devoted to a discussion of a patient who, by and large, could not do this for a number of years. David's ability to do this even now is still limited.

Some of the issues around David's capacity to self-reflect are confounded by his age. Although adolescence is a time of movement toward more secondary process thinking, the narcissistic vulnerabilities of this period make it a less than optimal time for self-reflection (A. Freud 1958). I believe it is David's heightened narcissistic vulnerabilities and the accompanying defenses that contribute the lion's share to his desymbolized experience in the transference. These narcissistic difficulties are readily generalized to many of our adult patients whose capacity for self-reflection is also less than optimal. This presents the analyst with a dilemma: How do we continue to feel like analysts if we cannot make interpretations? Are we doing psychoanalysis when the bulk of our work is similar to what I have been describing with David? Even though David is not in an analysis, a variation of these questions play an important role in how I feel about myself and how I feel about David. These issues go to the very core of our work with all patients at one time or another and, for some patients, for an extended period of time.

Freedman (1998) tells us that an expected part of the analytic process consists of the analyst's being (feeling) marginalized and disregarded, and then at some point becoming the focus of the patient's experience. Suppose the analyst does not become the center of the patient's experience? Suppose, in other words, the patient is not able to experience the transference and/or talk about it?

Here I believe the concept of incremental gain is crucial. Using my work with David as an example, I felt less marginalized and better able to be emotionally available to him when I became aware of how a small change could have significant implications. At some point in our work together David could lose a game of "Spit" without throwing the cards at me. Incremental gains in David's capacity for symbolization allow the game of "Spit," or a touch football game, to be a game, rather than a castrating humiliation of his budding manhood. These examples demonstrate the shift in the relationship of wishes and defenses and David's increased investment in reality. His narcissistic vulnerabilities do not have to be so energetically defended through aggressive grandiosity. This allows him to actively place himself in situations where he can be less than perfect and still feel good about himself.

Incremental gains in psychotherapy can have profound consequences in a person's life. In this paper these gains were viewed along the continuum of the symbolic process and David's capacity to form a meaningful relationship with the therapist.

## *References*

Blos, P. (1979). The second individuation process of adolescence. In *The Adolescent Passage* (pp. 141-170). Madison, CT: International Universities Press.

Freedman, N. (1994). More on transformation: Enactments in psychoanalytic space. In A. K. Richards & A. D. Richards (Eds.), *The spectrum of psychoanalysis: Essays in honor of Martin S. Bergmann* (pp. 93-110). Madison, CT: International Universities Press.

———(1998). Psychoanalysis and symbolization: Legacy or heresy? In C. Ellman, S. Grand, M. Silvan & S. J. Ellman (Eds.), *The Modern Freudians: Contemporary psychoanalytic technique* (pp. 79-97). Northvale, NJ: Jason Aronson.

Freedman, N., Berzofsky, M. & DeMichele, A. (1999a). On transformation cycles: The symbolization of a frozen constellation. Paper presented at the Annual Meeting, Division 39 of the American Psychological Association, New York, April.

Freedman, N., Hoffenberg, J., Vorus, N. & Frosch, A. (1999b). The effectiveness of psychoanalytic psychotherapy: The role of treatment duration, frequency of sessions, and the therapeutic relationship. *Journal of the American Psychoanalytic Association*, 47:741–772.

———& Karliner, R. (1999). On incremental symbolization: Clinical and empirical definition. Paper presented at the Annual Meeting, Division 39 of the American Psychological Association, New York, April.

———& Lavender, J. (1997). On receiving the patient's transference: The symbolizing and desymbolizing countertransference. *Journal of the American Psychoanalytic Association*, 45:79-103.

Freud, A. (1958). Adolescence. *Psychoanalytic Study of the Child*, 13:255–277.

Freud, S. (1912). The dynamics of transference. *Standard Edition*, 12:97–108.

———(1917): Introductory lectures on psychoanalysis, Part III. *Standard Edition*, 16:243–496.

———(1937). *Moses and monotheism*. New York: Vantage, 1969.

Frosch, A. (1995). The preconceptual organization of emotion. *Journal of the American Psychoanalytic Association*, 43:423–447.

———(1998). Narcissistic injury and sadomasochistic compensation in a latency-age boy. In P. Beren (Ed.), *Narcissistic disorders in children and adolescents: Diagnosis and treatment* (pp. 263–280). Northvale, NJ: Jason Aronson.

Herzog, J. (1996). The therapeutic action of play in the curative process. In L. Lifson (Ed.), *Understanding Therapeutic action: Psychodynamic concepts of cure* (pp. 187–200). Hillsdale, NJ: Analytic Press.

Klein, M. (1932). *The psycho-analysis of children* (3rd ed.). London: Hogarth.

Moran, M. (1991). Chaos and psychoanalysis: The fluidic nature of mind. *International Review of Psychoanalysis,* 18:211–221.

Rycroft, C. (1956). Symbolism and its relationship to the primary and secondary processes. *International Journal of Psycho-Analysis,* 37:137–146.

Schafer, R. (1985). The interpretation of psychic reality, developmental influences, and unconscious communication. *Journal of the American Psychoanalytic Association,* 33:537–554.

Segal, H. (1957). Notes on symbol formation. *International Journal of Psycho-Analysis,* 38:39–44.

Steirtgart, I. (1995). *A thing apart.* Northvale, NJ: Jason Aronson.

Winnicott, D. W. (1971). The use of an object and relating through identification. In *Playing and reality* (pp. 86–94). London: Routledge.

# SECTION III

# *Deconstructing Analyzability*

The three papers in this section, all written in 2006, address the subject of who is analyzable and how that is determined. In the first article, "The Culture of Psychoanalysis and the Concept of Analyzability," Frosch takes us from a historical perspective of how Freud's own wishes and defenses helped shape psychoanalytic technique to some contemporary theorists who see the patient rather than technique as the focus of treatment. MaryBeth Cresci, in her illuminating discussion, shows us how Frosch turns back to Freud and the beginnings of psychoanalysis as a way to anchor his thesis about how the individual analyst's ideas and the psychoanalytic culture are greater determinants of analyzability than the makeup of the patient. An analyst's abiding interest in the patient may be the best determinant of the patient's analyzability. Frosch illustrates this by contrasting Freud's loss of interest in his patient Dora when she proves not to be the "good" patient he wanted her to be to confirm his theoretical ideas with a candidate's successful struggle to engage a troubled and difficult patient in analytic treatment despite the patient's provocative acting-out behavior.

The second paper, entitled simply "Analyzability," also points to the analyst as the more important determinant for analyzability but focuses as well on the "fit" of the two members of the dyad. Frosch cautions against "theory-driven countertransference" that can be used to blame the patient for the analyst's discomfort or "resistance" to analyzability.

Janet Fisher helps orient the reader to the Frosch paper in her cogent essay in which she discusses symbolization, once seen as critical to a patient's ability to benefit from analytic treatment. More pertinent now is whether there is a good enough match between analyst and patient and whether the analyst is able to weather the cycles of symbolization and desymbolization in an ongoing treatment while trying to understand the other ways in which the patient is communicating.

In the last of these papers, "Control Cases and Institutional Responsibility: A Creative or Coercive Process," the concept of analyzability is looked at in the context of training. Frosch posits that all those who are in positions of institutional responsibility should be well versed with the analytic literature so that they can help guide the candidates in the selection of control patients and not restrict the pool of patients available because of "theory-driven countertransference." Richard B. Grose describes Frosch's discussion as "a powerful but gentle polemic against institutional representatives coercing candidates." Grose's thoughtful remarks are a wonderful introduction to the article that follows.

# CHAPTER 6

# The Culture of Psychoanalysis and the Concept of Analyzability

### Reflections on "The Culture of Psychoanalysis and the Concept of Analyzability"

*MaryBeth M. Cresci*

In this essay Frosch takes an important question, how to determine the analyzability of the patient, and turns the question on its head. He suggests that we can best answer it by looking at the analyst herself and at the culture of psychoanalysis more so than looking at the patient. Just as stunning, he contrasts Freud's clinical work with that of a candidate in analytic training—certainly two ends of the spectrum with regard to levels of experience and theoretical acumen—and finds much that is commendable in the analytic candidate's ability to contend with a difficult patient.

Frosch suggests that the most important criterion in determining a prospective patient's analyzability is the analyst's ability to maintain an interest in the patient. He quotes passages to indicate that Freud too felt it was essential to take an interest in one's patient. Then Frosch considers Freud's work with his patients, particularly his patient Dora, and cites several possible reasons for Freud's lack of interest in her. One may have been her hysterical symptoms which Freud acknowledged are not easy for a physician to accept in comparison to a patient with actual physical distress. Another may have been Freud's disappointment that Dora was not a cooperative patient and did not indulge Freud's wish to be a conquistador or conqueror who can unlock the secrets of the patient's unconscious and overcome the patient's resistance. Dora asserted her independence from him by prematurely ending the treatment. He (Freud, 1953/1905) refers to her termination of treatment as "an unmistakable act of vengeance" (p. 109). He even speculates that he might have been able to keep her in treatment if he had "exaggerated the importance to me of her staying on, and had shown a warm personal interest in her" (p. 109). He leaves the impression that his primary interest in Dora was in obtaining confirmation of his theories of infantile sexuality, not in helping her deal with a complex set of disturbing relationships with the adults in her life. When Dora decides to return to treatment, he summarily rejects her as a patient, thus turning the tables on her.

Freud also tells us that he belatedly realized that an underlying issue was Dora's pre-oedipal dependent and homoerotic longings for Frau K. Frosch suggests that Dora's pre-oedipal dependence on a maternal figure came too close to Freud's own fears of loss and abandonment by his mother and nursemaid during his early years. He proposes that some of Freud's more abstract theories, such as the concept of the death instinct and significance of the primordial father, were actually a means for Freud to avoid his unresolved feelings of loss and abandonment by his pre-oedipal mother. Thus, given his unwillingness to address his own pre-oedipal fears, Dora's love for Frau K may have been particularly difficult for Freud to uncover and interpret in a way that would help Dora resolve these feelings.

Frosch suggests that the transference-countertransference enactments engaged in between Freud and Dora could have been the precursor to a successful treatment if Freud had been able to recognize his negative countertransference and use it in the treatment. Instead, the culture of psychoanalysis that he espoused expected the patient to be cooperative (i.e., analyzable) and the analyst to have solved any personal dilemmas that would have induced countertransference reactions to the patient. This sort of idealized analytic treatment allowed both parties to focus on intellectual interpretations instead of dealing with difficult, uncomfortable feelings that might surface between the analyst and the patient.

In contrast, Frosch presents a case conducted by an analytic candidate in which the patient and analyst have remarkably dissimilar cultural and ethnic backgrounds. The factor that keeps this treatment on course is the analyst's considerable interest in her patient. By the time this treatment was conducted, the culture of psychoanalysis had changed. Countertransference was now seen as a useful tool to help the analyst better understand herself and the patient. Enactment was now an accepted part of the treatment whereby the desymbolized actions of the analyst and patient could be viewed as the initial steps in moving toward symbolization and understanding of the patient's underlying dynamics.

Thus, in this essay Frosch brings us from the early culture of psychoanalysis to a much more contemporary version that sees analyst and patient working through resistance and transference-countertransference dilemmas to a position of trust and mutuality. In this psychoanalytic culture, the question of the patient's analyzability becomes the responsibility of both patient and analyst.

## References

Freud, S. (1905). Fragment of an analysis of a case of hysteria. *Standard Edition*, 7:1–122.

*     *     *

# The Culture of Psychoanalysis
# and the Concept of Analyzability

## Allan Frosch[1]

*The author discusses the subjective nature of the concept of analyzability. The argument is made that the analyst's idea about psychoanalysis is an essential variable that contributes to the decision as to whether a person is or is not analyzable. We organize clinical material according to our theoretical beliefs that, by definition, are always affected by our desires. Some of Freud's thinking about the relationship between culture and psychoanalytic theory is presented as well as the author's ideas about how Freud's wishes and defenses influenced his notion of analyzability. Clinical material is included.*

When Freud wrote about culture or civilization, he said that our beliefs or cultural values were organized around wishes and defenses designed to keep our fears in check (1961a/1927; 1961b/1929). These fears were related to the forces of nature, the uncertainties of life such as death and disease, as well as to the "passions that rage as they do in our souls" (1961a/1927, p. 16) as we struggle to live and work together. And he cautioned us against accepting these beliefs as some preordained road to perfection (1961b/1929, p. 16). This same cautionary note was raised in regard to our scientific theories, which are also organized around wishes and defenses to reduce anxiety or unpleasure. Nothing, said Freud, should stop us from looking at ourselves as we construct our theories of mind (1961a/1927, p. 34; 1950b/1913, pp. 210–211). In a recent article Mitchell Wilson (2003) provides a contemporary rendering of some of Freud's ideas when he says that "The analyst's deeply held and deeply personal desires . . . become clothed in essentialist notions of the psychoanalytic process" (p. 73). Wilson highlights Freud's point that since our theories are always constructed around our desires they are always self-serving (pp. 75–77, see also Almond, 2003).

---

[1] I thank Albert Brok, Joseph Cancelmo, MaryBeth Cresci, Richard Lasky, Betsy Lawrence, Ruth Oscharoff and Neal Vorus for their input into this article.

In this paper I will look at the culture of psychoanalysis and show how it has shaped our ideas about who is or is not "analyzable" or, on a more visceral level, who is a "good" patient and who is a difficult or "bad" patient. By the culture of psychoanalysis, I mean Freud's culture of psychoanalysis, that is, how Freud's wishes and struggles to contain his passions influenced psychoanalysis. I will also argue that the contemporary culture of psychoanalysis, our conscious and unconscious fantasies, organizes the data of psychoanalysis today just as Freud's did a century ago, and that our ideas about who is analyzable, or what is a psychoanalytic process, are always subjectively constructed. In other words, in addressing the question of analyzability, my focus will be on variables associated with the analyst rather than the patient.

I will view psychoanalytic theory as a compromise formation that, like all compromise formations, has wishful, defensive, adaptive, and maladaptive aspects to it with the overall goal being to maximize pleasure and minimize unpleasure or discomfort. This brings us to the question of what gave Freud pleasure and what produced discomfort in him which I will discuss in the first half of this paper. In the second half, I will present and discuss some clinical material from the standpoint of analyzability.

I think it gave Freud great pleasure when he thought of himself as a "conquistador"—someone who through the exercise of his intellect conquers the mysteries of the mind. "Such people," said Freud, "are customarily esteemed if they have really discovered something, otherwise they are dropped by the wayside" (Masson, 1985, p. 398). As a counterpoint to Freud's wish to be the conqueror, I believe his impulses and feelings in relation to the mother of his early childhood caused him great discomfort.

In this section of the paper, I will talk about how I think the tension between Freud's unresolved issues around dependency and abandonment and his wish to be the great discoverer—the conquistador—influenced his work with Dora as well as his work with patients nearly 20 years later in Beyond the Pleasure Principle.

In a letter to Fleiss dated December 22, 1897, Freud said that he thought of himself as someone who could (almost) say what the mind was, but Fleiss, of course, was someone who could say what life itself was about (Masson, 1985, p. 287); and 7 years later, Freud (1953a/1904) said that the way we understand the mind of another is through our interest in the person. In that same paper, however, he went on to say that some patients were such bad people that he just could not have any interest in them: ". . . if the physician has to deal with a worthless character, he soon loses the interest which makes it possible for him to enter profoundly into the patient's mental life" (p. 254). Freud said that a patient's intelligence and ethical development were two areas of consideration for the physician's interest. One might say, therefore, that he is beginning to set certain parameters for analyzability. There is, however, a personal tone to the discussion that argues against a purely cerebral or objective construct of analyzability.

This more personal tone is reinforced when we consider some of Freud's comments in his paper "On Psychotherapy" (1953b/1905; 1957a/1910). In his paper "On Psychotherapy," Freud said that in order to effect a cure, patients must have an expectation colored by faith (p. 258), and it is the personality of the physician (i.e., therapist) which induces such faith. In the first Clark lecture, he pointed out the difference in a physician's attitude toward hysterical patients as compared to patients who have organic diseases: He (referring to the physician) does not have the same sympathy for the former as for the latter . . . (p. 11). Very often, Freud said, a physician's training "leaves him in the lurch when he is confronted by the details of hysterical phenomena. He regards [such patients] as people who are transgressing the laws of his science—like heretics in the eyes of the orthodox. He attributes every kind of wickedness to them, accuses them of exaggeration, of deliberate deceit, of malingering. And he punishes them by withdrawing his interest from them" (p. 12). I think it is reasonable to assume that a great deal of what Freud (1953c/1905) said referred to his work with Dora. In her book *Freud, Dora, and Vienna, 1900*, Hannah Decker describes Freud as being unconsciously exploitative of Dora whom he used to support his theoretical positions (1991, p. 199). Here we see Freud the conqueror and Dora the object of his desire who must provide him with the spoils of his intellectual war. Decker argues that Freud's overall negative attitude toward

Dora reflected the cultural bias of his time (p. 204). I think Freud gives us another important insight into his "overdriven striving" to conquer Dora: "A man," said Freud, "who has been the indisputable favorite of his mother keeps for life the feeling of a conqueror, that confidence of success that often induces real success" (Jones, 1953, p. 5). It is certainly true that Freud was his mother's favorite, and he was, in fact, possessed of great confidence in himself. At the same time, however, he was not always his mother's favorite. When Freud was about 8 months old, his mother became pregnant with Julius who died 6 months after he was born, and 8.5 months later when Freud was about 2.5 years old, his sister Anna was born. During this period of time, as well as the time when his mother was grieving for Julius, Freud was in the care of a nursemaid whom he seemed to love very much (Gay, 1988, p. 7) When Freud was 3, this woman was put in jail by Freud's older brother Philipp because of some petty pilfering of money from the Freud household. In effect, Freud lost 2 mothers in the course of 2 years, and a number of authors (Jones, 1953; Gay, 1988; Gedo, 1968) have argued that unconscious fantasies related to Freud's preoedipal and oedipal relationship to his mother were a constant source of pressure that led to the impossibility of Freud ever mastering separation conflicts (Gedo, 1968, p. 111). If this is so, we would expect to find reflections of it in his work. Freud provides some help for us in the postscript to Dora where he acknowledges that he failed to understand Dora's love for Frau K—a mother figure. Blos (1979) picks up on this and argues (like Freud [1953c/1905, p. 63]) that we often miss the preoedipal issues because of what he calls the oedipal defense, that is, heterosexuality pushed to the forefront of the mind that aids in the repression of preoedipal longings (pp. 489–490). I am suggesting that Freud's wish to be the oedipal winner, the hero or conqueror, helped to conceal his unconscious wishes and defenses in relation to Dora and ultimately his own mother. If Dora was a "good" analytic patient, that is, if she accepted Freud's interpretations and got better, she could be the good mother who made Freud feel he was conquering the mysteries of hysteria. He certainly would not have punished her by a withdrawal of interest and a refusal to work with her again when Dora came back to ask for his help 15 months after she had left treatment: " . . . but I promised to forgive her for having deprived me of the satisfaction of affording her a more radical cure for her troubles" (p. 122). Freud is stuck and can see the situation from one, and only one, perspective. Dora left and deprived him of something that he desperately needed. Now he turns passive into active and rather than the needy child Freud becomes the rejecting mother. He leaves Dora. In today's terminology, this could be thought of as a transference-countertransference enactment and, for many, a potential prelude to productive analytic work.

Clearly, my ideas about Freud's early conflicts and what Dora meant to him unconsciously are highly speculative. What is most important, however, is the idea that Freud's wishes and defenses, whatever their source, had an impact on his approach to analyzing her. Thus his wish to be the conqueror and his discomfort with Dora, both of which are in my opinion fairly clear in his writing about the case, contributed to the enacted dimension (Katz, 1998) of the treatment, and affected his perceptions of Dora, himself, and, of course, the psychoanalytic process. I am not so willing, however, to beg off my position about the influence of Freud's unresolved issues with his mother. I certainly think the progression from the central importance of the mother that Freud articulated a few years later in his paper on Leonardo quickly followed by a shift to the father of our prehistoric past (hinted at in the Leonardo paper [1957b/1910, p. 88; see also, Freud, 1950a/1912, p. 99]) and developed more fully in "Totem and Taboo" (1953d/1913), can be seen as a defensively tinged shift away from the "organic impression" of the infant at the mother's breast (1957a/1910, p. 87) to the more abstract father of our phylogenetic past.

I also think that we can see the influence of Freud's early conflicts in one of his most important papers, "Beyond the Pleasure Principle" (1959/1920), a paper that, I believe, had a significant impact on the concept of analyzability. Here is what Freud had to say about his observation that patients repeated unpleasant experiences: "Patient's revive these unwanted situations and painful emotions with the greatest ingenuity. They seek to bring about the interruption of treatment; they contrive once more to feel themselves scorned, to oblige the physician to speak severely to them and treat them coldly" (p. 21). Freud's tone is accusatory and sounds very similar to the therapist's withdrawal of interest as a punishment to patients who did not behave as he wanted them to. It is hard to be a conqueror when the enemy does not cooperate. I believe, however, that there was another factor that led Freud to view the repetition compulsion as a resistance and a representative of the death drive. Patients, said Freud, did not want to leave treatment: "This same compulsion to repeat frequently meets us as an obstacle to our treatment when at the end of an analysis we try to induce the patient to detach himself completely from the physician" (p. 36). He goes on to say that when people " . . . feel an obscure fear—a dread of rousing something that, so they feel, is better left sleeping . . . they are afraid of this compulsion with its hint of 'daemonic' power" (p. 36). In the very next paragraph, Freud tells us that we may have come upon a universal attribute of instincts and perhaps of organic life in general (p. 36). The repetition compulsion is an urge inherent in organic life to return to an earlier state: "The aim of all life is death . . ." (p. 38). Freud moves from the emotionally charged issue in the heat of the transference when he wanted to end treatment and patients did not, to the more abstract realm of the meaning of life conceptualized as a battle between life and death. Harry Slochower (1975) argued that Freud felt threatened about uncovering his own curiosity about one of his buried desires: "to see and be united with his own sources, his preoedipal and oedipal mother . . ." (p. 2), and Slochower went on to say that the Thanatos theory " . . .may be seen as a wish to return to the sexual mother and the womb at the beginning of time . . ." (pp. 2–3). In his paper "The Theme of The Three Caskets" (1950c/1913), Freud said that it was Mother Earth . . . the "Goddess of Death that will take an old man into her arms" (p. 301). Freud was 57 when he wrote this paper and quite convinced that he would die at 62 (Gay, 1988, p. 58).

Here then is my fantasy/theory of the interpenetration of wishes and defenses as compromise formation: Freud moves from wishes and defenses organized around his unresolved loss of 2 mothers, his countertransferentially induced dependence which in his mind is better off left alone, and defends against these repressed issues by a theoretical/ philosophical tour de force that culminates in the meaning of life itself. Now Freud has truly become the oedipal victor. It is no longer Fleiss who knows the meaning of life. Freud has articulated the essence of life itself: A struggle between Eros and Thanatos. The aim of life is death. I believe there is a defensive component to this shift that moved Freud away from his unresolved and unconscious issues of dependency and fears of abandonment—as he put it, being dropped by the wayside if one does not make an important discovery. Like all compromise formations, this defensively skewed movement toward death also contained a wish, so that death unconsciously represents a reunion with mother.

Freud's idiosyncratic organization of wishes and defenses led to a view of the repetition compulsion as a manifestation of the death instinct and an ultimate obstacle to successful treatment because patients' repetition of their early dependency need made it too difficult for them to separate from the analyst (cf. Frosch, 2006). I think that Freud fell into a trap that he warned us about in a short but important paper "On Psycho-Analysis": scientific arguments can support emotional resistances (1950c/1913, pp. 210–211). Freud's intolerance of his own feelings (particularly those around separation and loss) influenced his perception of repetition in analysis, even though he was well aware that such repetitions were an attempt to master overwhelming affect (1959/1920; 1964/1914).

In the context of this discussion about the analyst's subjectivity, I think it is important to add that although I do think that some of Freud's recommendations regarding treatment came from his own countertransferentially induced discomfort (as well as his discomfort in relation to the behavior of some of his most trusted colleagues [see Haynal & Falzeder, 1993]), these subjective factors need not negate the value of many of his recommendations. The use of the couch, for example, may have reduced Freud's discomfort about being looked at but, in my opinion, is an integral part of the analytic process. I do think, however, that the subjective factors I have discussed in the Dora case and in "Beyond the Pleasure Principle" have contributed to an "historical prejudice" (Stone, 1961, pp. 31–32, cited by Gehrie, 1993, p. 1099) that tends to idealize technique and, by extension, psychoanalysis. Eissler's seminal paper on parameters (1953) and, in particular, his discussion of Freud's "normal ego" is another case in point. Contemporary authors, such as Bach, 1985; Modell, 1988; Rothstein, 1998 and Stone, 1954, favor an approach that places the patient, rather than an idealized technique/process, as the focus of treatment.

When we move away from a more idealized way of doing things, we enter an area where so called tried and true psychoanalytic concepts such as interpretation or resistance can have multiple context-dependent meanings (Sandler, 1983). A rigid adherence to one meaning for example, the standard or idealized meaning, can reflect "theory driven countertransference" (Frosch, 2006). This subjective distortion of the analytic process can play a major role in shaping our ideas about analyzability.

With specific reference to some of Freud's ideas about analyzability in "Beyond the Pleasure Principle," a contemporary analyst like Betty Joseph (1959) is more apt to view the dynamic aspects of repetition as wishes and defenses "likely to be repeated whenever problems [a]round dependence are activated" (p. 221). In other words, the repetition compulsion is seen as a vital part of the analytic process. Along these lines, Joseph (1985) has argued that much of our understanding of the inner world of our patients comes through our understanding of how they act on us to feel things for many varied reasons; how they try to draw us into their defensive systems; how they unconsciously act out with us in the transference, trying to get us to act out with them; how they convey aspects of their inner world built up from infancy . . . experiences often beyond the use of words . . . (p. 447). These nonverbal, other than symbolic, experiences (Bucci, 2002; Segal, 2003) set an affective orientation in place that can be affected by psychoanalysis, and it may be that psychoanalysis is the only treatment that can have a significant impact on this most basic emotional organization of one's world (Clyman, 1991; Eagle, 2003; Frosch, 2003). I believe that Freud understood these issues very well, although he did not discuss them in the terms I am using. "In Remembering, Repeating and Working Through" (1964/1914), for example, he made it clear that he knew certain complexes or psychological issues had to be acted out as opposed to being remembered. At times, he said, an analyst will feel that all is lost, that there is nowhere to go and treatment is at an end. Not so, said Freud, this is the treatment. The analyst needs to help the patient "work through" these issues. "It is a trial of patience for the analyst" (p. 155). I think Ellman's (1991) description of a "trial by fire" (p. 164) is more to the point. At any rate, to use Freud's language: What happened to his patience in 1920? I am suggesting that what happened to Freud is what happens, or certainly can happen, to all of us when we feel threatened. He eliminated or devalued the source of his discomfort—the patient who remembered through repetition and action the nonverbal, other-than-symbolic wishes and defenses associated with the early, dependency-laden mother-infant relationship. A century of analytic dialogue has led to a greater appreciation of the complexity of the analytic situation so that in today's analytic culture there is a greater emphasis on the analyst's thoughts and feelings and, ultimately, a more questioning attitude about the psychoanalytic process itself. It is in this context that I present the work of Nora and Dr. C.

Nora was referred for treatment through the clinical center of an analytic institute which offered reduced fees. She was 29 when she entered treatment with Dr. C, a candidate at the institute, and I was the supervisor. Nora is a dark-skinned Latin woman who was living on the edge of poverty. Dr. C is a blond, blue-eyed woman with children Nora's age who saw Nora in her fashionable private office on Park Avenue. Nora was born in Puerto Rico and came to New York with her family when she was 6 years old. She is the oldest of 4 children. Nora described her home life as unhappy. Her parents divorced when Nora was 13, and both parents returned to Puerto Rico. At that point Nora was in a special school for creative children and decided to stay in New York to continue her education. She lived with relatives, and when Nora was 16, she was raped by an older cousin and shortly thereafter made a suicide attempt for which she was hospitalized. Nora continued to do well in school, however, and was the first member of her family to attend college. She has a master's degree in fine arts, majoring in theater with a minor in comparative literature.

Nora sought out treatment because she was unhappy and feeling desperate about her life. She was not working as an actress, was not going to auditions on any sort of a regular basis, and barely paid her rent through intermittent substitute teaching. Nora did have a wide circle of friends but rarely saw them. She spent many hours each day alone in her apartment lost in a world of fantasy. She was sexually promiscuous and engaged in unsafe sex.

Nora began a twice weekly treatment that was characterized by explosive outbursts, declarations of disgust and contempt for Dr. C, and a hopeless despair that anything good could come through talking about herself. Nora frequently missed sessions. Dr. C stayed very close to what Nora said, and her comments were mainly designed to clarify and explain rather than "interpret." On those occasions when she did try and explore why Nora had missed a session or had not paid her bill on time, Nora would get furious and withdraw. Nora paid for all missed sessions, and by the middle of the 2nd year of treatment, she had begun to attend on a more regular basis and was up-to-date in her payments. She started to go to auditions, had a nice role in a play off-Broadway, and organized her work life so that she was not feeling quite so desperate financially. She also was feeling less comfortable about "booty calls," that is, sexual favors for men.

An incident occurred in the middle of the 2nd year of treatment when Dr. C forgot something that Nora had told her. Nora missed both of her sessions the following week. When she did come back, Dr. C said that she had been thinking about their discussion: "You know I did forget that you told me that and I am sorry. I thought that when you missed your sessions last week it might have . . . ." At this point, Nora angrily cut her off and said, "No! You always think you are so fucking important in my life. I missed because I was too busy to come. Do you get that?" Over time Dr. C and I came to understand that Dr. C's initial attempt to explore the missed sessions before some basic sense of analytic trust was reestablished was probably experienced by Nora as Dr. C treating her as if she did not exist and an extension of what she might have felt when Dr. C forgot what Nora had told her. At this point I thought Nora began to treat Dr. C as if she did not exist. For the next four months, Nora averaged less than one session a week, although she kept both of her hours. And she stopped paying for her sessions.

It might have happened that Nora's behavior could have led Dr. C, to use Freud's language, to speak sharply to or withdraw interest from Nora. Or perhaps Dr. C might not want to work with her anymore. This did not happen, and over the course of this 4 month period, Dr. C was able to talk with Nora about how hurt and angry she thought Nora might be about her failure to remember her. Most of the time, however, Dr. C's construction of the analytic situation was internal, and her actual comments to Nora were few and far between. A great deal of Dr. C's internal dialogue had to do with being able to understand her own thoughts and feelings in relation to what Nora eventually came to call, her "angry tirades." Over time Dr. C came to see these tirades and accompanying action as a necessary part of the treatment. She thought they were Nora's attempt to put herself forcibly in Dr. C's mind. It was certain that Dr. C would not forget Nora while she waited for Nora to come to sessions. As long as Dr. C thought about her, Nora existed. Over time Dr. C was able to talk about Nora's withholding of money as an expression of her feelings of hurt and anger, but also Nora's desire to see if Dr. C cared for her even if she weren't paid.

I think it is quite likely that many analysts today and certainly a great many during Freud's lifetime might think that Nora's propensity to act would rule out psychoanalysis. Of course another way of looking at the situation is to view action as communication so that the analytic process is tied to how Dr. C responds to and understands the action, and analyzability is seen as a function of the process of treatment (Bach, 1985, pp. 219–236). From this latter perspective, Dr. C's attention to what was going on in her own mind—her wish for this to be a control case, her ideas about an analytic process and of course her reactions to Nora's action prone emotionally laden sequences was essential to the ongoing development of the work. Such attention to one's internal state enhances the potential for the therapist to have, what Arnold Rothstein (1994) considers the most essential aspect of analytic technique, a positive and optimistic attitude toward the patient (p. 685). I think this must be what Freud meant by the analyst's interest in the patient or what a contemporary theorist like Ted Jacobs (2002) means when he talks about the analyst's investment so that the patient feels truly cared about (cf. Frosch, 2003) By the 3rd year of treatment, Nora was attending her sessions and paying her bills. Nora felt better and continued to show improvement in all areas of her life. Dr. C wanted to use this as a control case and thought 4x weekly work would be helpful for Nora. Nora agreed and a schedule of 4 sessions a week was established. I will now present some clinical material that took place right before a one-week vacation that Dr. C was taking. In the weeks prior to this session, Nora said repeatedly that the only thing the vacation meant to her was that she would save money.

Nora began the session by saying she had nothing to say and quickly added she didn't think Dr. C had anything meaningful to say either. Whenever the analyst did try and speak, not necessarily about the vacation, Nora cut her off and angrily dismissed her. Dr. C said she had an image of hiding behind the couch so she could avoid being hit by the next barrage of rage. The rage felt relentless, and Dr. C felt dismissed. And the analytic work was skewed toward Dr. C's internal world and her struggle with her countertransference. With about 5 minutes left in the session, Nora angrily said, "You are leaving me . . . I am dependent on you." Here Nora begins to talk about her passive experience of being left by someone she feels so dependent on. I believe the 1st part of the session can, in my theoretical language, be thought of as a desymbolized experience for Nora and, to a lesser extent, Dr. C as well. A number of authors (Freedman, 1994; Frosch, 2002; Lasky, 2002; Schimek, 2002) have talked about desymbolization as an active destruction of meaning that is a necessary prelude to more symbolized or introspective work. For Nora the idea that a vacation from the analysis only meant a saving of money may have helped her cope with the potential consequences of considering the possibility that she was emotionally affected by the vacation. Along similar lines I believe Dr. C's attention to her desymbolized countertransference, where she initially felt like hiding behind the couch to avoid Nora's anger, was an essential part of the analytic process. When Dr. C was able to see her reaction to Nora's anger in a different light, she was better able to help Nora to move toward a more symbolized position. In the analytic situation, a subtle shift in the analyst's internal state affects what she does or does not say, tone of voice, body language, and the like. And all of this has a profound effect on the other.

In the sessions that immediately followed the vacation, Nora began to talk about her skin color, and how stupid, crude, and primitive she felt. She did not like being a Latin woman and felt she didn't fit in any-where. She also considered some new ways of looking at things: She could make mistakes and not necessarily think of herself as stupid. And she could tolerate the mistakes of others without writing them off. She felt better about herself and said it was important that she allow herself to appreciate how much it meant to feel "affirmed" by her analyst. Nora also continued to have long periods in the analysis where she felt Dr. C was a "stupid pain in the ass." And that, Nora said, was reality.

And it was absolute reality that she felt too dependent on Dr. C and had to reduce her sessions. This angry declaration followed a weekend break in treatment where, in my opinion, Nora felt that she was being abandoned and on the verge of losing control. It wouldn't be surprising if the therapist had a similar struggle so that she must attend both to Nora and her own worries that her control case may leave. Maybe she wants Nora to leave? Is Dr. C tired of Nora's endless repetition of a reversal of her fears of abandonment, that is, "I will get rid of you. I will turn passive into active and feel strong, not vulnerable." Truth be told, however, the patient does not leave. She goes on in this session to talk about one of her oldest friends—an African American woman who is having a biopsy for a suspicious growth. Nora hates and distrusts doctors, but she is on Dr. C's couch. We have called out the demon from the unconscious—Nora's fears of being left, of feeling alone and helpless: this dark-skinned Latin woman with a white doctor and Nora's dark-skinned friend with her white doctor. Nora hates doctors because she feels they are prejudiced, hate her, and will not take care of her. And she has good reason for such fears. And sometimes she does not have good reasons. If she brings all of these fears and anger to her sessions, will Dr. C also feel prejudiced, hate her, and want to get rid of her? Here is the trial by fire. It is not a question of patience. I think our countertransfer-ence in these situations is tied to and an integral part of our representation—our conceptualization—of the analytic process. If we really understand, and believe on a visceral level, that some things cannot be remembered and must be repeated—again and again—then we can see that Nora is talking to Dr. C through action. The words are vehicles to convey fear and rage: "I love you and need you . . . you don't love me or need me and you leave me on weekends, you go on vacation and who takes care of me?"

In a recent article Jacobs (2001) argued that the strain of working with patients who evoke feelings of frustration and hopelessness, who make us feel discouraged—and may even make us question what it is to be an analyst—may lead us to see these patients as suffering from such bedrock difficulties that they are not analyzable. This may be a sophisticated form of what Arnold Rothstein (1999) called name calling. It is name calling, of course, in the context of a theory that makes us feel better. It is not that the analyst may be missing something, or has some subtle, or not so subtle, countertransference, or views the situation from a perspective that is not helpful. "After all," Dr. C might justifiably say, "if Nora wasn't so traumatized, she wouldn't keep yelling at me. I am not trying to rape her." This is what I would call a desymbolized position for the analyst. It is looking at the situation from one, and only one, perspective; and it pits the analyst against the patient. It is do or die: You are wrong or I am wrong. These positions are not so different from the difficulties that Freud struggled with. What is different is the analytic milieu that forms the context for our wishes and defenses so that countertransference can become an important piece of analytic data. There is something about the ongoing therapeutic process that allows the people we work with to move from desymbolized moments—I have to leave because that is reality—to moments organized on a more introspective level. I believe the "something" refers to the analyst's movement from being caught in the moment where there is only one way of looking at things to a more secondary process or symbolized way of functioning that allows for multiple perspectives.

## Summary and Discussion

In this paper I have tried to show how Freud's personality defined psychoanalysis as seen through the concept of analyzability. In looking at how the idiosyncratic organization of Freud's wishes and defenses shaped his ideas, we also need to take into account his genius that gave rise to the richness and complexity of psychoanalytic theory. Freud's wish for a perfect patient to assist him in his quest to conquer the mysteries of the mind led him to develop an analytic approach that helped him to control the passions that arose in his soul, but also has served us very well. For those of us who are not possessed of such genius, however, the attempt to further develop psychoanalysis led to the stultifying notion that one had to possess special attributes to be an analysand (cf. Moskowitz, 1996). As a complement to this idea, the analyst was also seen as (more or less) "purified"—another of Freud's wishes. Analyst and patient were supposedly quite healthy so that when reasonable interpretations were made in a tactful and timely way they would be accepted and therefore changes would occur in an equally timely fashion. It's a pleasant wish—antiseptic and pretty well geared toward the protection of the passions that might come to the surface of the analyst's soul, and perhaps the patient's as well. It's a fiction, an illusion, and Freud knew it (1964/1914)and used it to develop a model of psychoanalysis that we took too literally. Psychoanalysis became a thing to be guarded by its followers. If you wanted to avail yourself of this precious gift, you had to pass the test of analyzability. In the real world, however, purified analysts don't exist, and patients come to us because they are suffering.

In the case vignette of Nora, I have tried to show that the analyst's idea about psychoanalysis is an essential variable that contributes to our concept of analyzability. And the analyst's ideas are always shaped by desire. Wishes and defenses organize our perception of the world, including the world of who is or is not analyzable. In this sense I would say that the analytic process exists in the mind of the analyst. We organize and construct the clinical material according to our theoretical beliefs that, by definition, are always affected by our desire to feel safe and our wish to feel like a competent-potent analyst. I believe that part of this construction refers to the analyst's capacity to trust that a patient wants help, and to the patient's capacity to trust that the analyst wants to help. Analyzability is dependent on the development of a reciprocal relationship that allows for the development of mutual trust (cf. Ellman, 2002). It is this relationship that allows us over time to tell our patient some of our ideas. And we put this into language that the patient understands so that the timing, frequency, and duration of what we say varies from patient to patient and from session to session with the same patient. Somewhere in this process we decide, consciously or unconsciously, whether what we are doing is an analysis or something else. The decisions we arrive at are culturally determined if we can think of the analytic culture as the idiosyncratic organization of wishes and defenses that organize clinical data.

## References

Almond, R. (2003). The holding function of theory. *Journal of the American Psychoanalytic Association,* 51:131–153.

Bach, S. (1985). *Narcissistic states and the therapeutic process.* Northvale, NJ: Jason Aronson.

Bachrach, H. (1998). The analyst's thinking and attitude at the beginning of an analysis. In T. Jacobs & A. Rothstein (Eds.), *Beginning the treatment* (pp. 19–26). New York: International University Press.

Blos, P. (1979). *The adolescent process: Developmental issues.* New York: International University Press.

Bucci, W. (2002). The referential process, consciousness, and the sense of self. *Psychoanalytic Inquiry,* 22:766–793.

Clyman, R. (1991). The procedural organization of emotions: A contribution from cognitive science to the psychoanalytic theory of therapeutic action. *Journal of the American Psychoanalytic Association,* 39:349–382.

Decker, H. (1991). *Freud, Dora, and Vienna.* New York: The Free Press.

Eagle, M. (2003). Clinical implications of attachment theory. *Psychoanalytic Inquiry,* 1:27–53.

Eissler, K. R. (1953). The effect of the structure of the ego on psychoanalytic technique. *Journal of the American Psychoanalytic Association,* 1:104–143.

Ellman, S. (1991). *Freud's technique papers—A contemporary perspective.* Northvale, NJ: Jason Aronson.

———& Carsky, M. (2002). Symbolization and development of interpretable transference. In R. Lasky (Ed.), *Essays in honor of Norbert Freedman: Symbolization and desymbolization* (pp. 280–305). New York: Karnac.

Freedman, N. (1994). More on transformation: Enactments in psychoanalytic space. In A. K. Richards & A. D. Richards (Eds.), *Spectrum of psychoanalysis: Essays in honor of Martin S. Bergman* (pp. 93–110). Madison, CT: International Universities Press.

Freud, S. (1904). Freud's psycho-analytic procedure. *Standard Edition,* 7:249–254.

———(1905) On psychotherapy. *Standard Edition,* 7:257–268.

———(1905). Fragment of an analysis of a case of hysteria. *Standard Edition,* 7:1–122.

———(1910). Five lectures on psycho-analysis. *Standard Edition,* 11:3–55.

———(1910). Leonardo Da Vinci and a memory of his childhood *Standard Edition,* 11:63–137.

———(1912). The dynamics of transference. *Standard Edition,* 12:99–108.

———(1913). On psycho-analysis. *Standard Edition,* 12:205–217.

———(1913). The theme of the three caskets. *Standard Edition,* 12:289–301.

———(1913). Totem and taboo. *Standard Edition,* 13:1–162.

———(1914). Remembering, repeating and working-through. *Standard Edition,* 2:147–156.

———(1920). Beyond the pleasure principle. *Standard Edition,* 18:3–64.

———(1927). The future of an illusion. *Standard Edition,* 21:3–56.

———(1929). Civilization and its discontents. *Standard Edition,* 21:59–145.

Frosch, A. (2002). Survival, symbolization, and psychic space. In R. Lasky (Ed.), *Essays in honor of Norbert Freedman: Symbolization and desymbolization* (pp. 366–386). New York: Karnac.

———(2003). Psychic reality and the analytic relationship. *Psychoanalytic Review,* 90:599–614.

———(2006). Analyzability. *Psychoanalytic Review,* 93:835–843.

Gay, P. (1988). *Freud: A life for our time.* New York: Norton.

Gedo, J. E. (1968). Freud's self-analysis and his scientific ideas. *American Imago,* 25:99–117.

Gehrie, M. J. (1993). Psychoanalytic technique and the development of the capacity to reflect. *Journal of the American Psychoanalytic Association,* 41:1083–1111.

Haynal, A. & Falzeder, E. (1993). Slaying the dragons of the past or cooking the hare in the present: A historical view on affects in the psychoanalytic encounter. *Psychoanalytic Inquiry,* 13:357–371.

Jacobs, T. (2001). Reflections on the goals of psychoanalysis, the psychoanalytic process, and the process of change. *Psychoanalytic Quarterly,* 70:149–181.

———(2002). Secondary revision: On rethinking the analytic process and analytic technique. *Psychoanalytic Inquiry,* 23:3–28.

Jones, E. (1953). *The life and work of Sigmund Freud.* New York: Basic Books, Inc.

Joseph, B. (1959). An aspect of the repetition compulsion. *International Journal of Psycho-Analysis,* 40:213–222.

———(1985). Transference: The total situation. *International Journal of Psycho-Analysis,* 66:447–454.

Katz, G. A. (1998). Where the action is: The enacted dimension of analytic process. *Journal of the American Psychoanalytic Association,* 46:1129–1167.

Lasky, R. (2002). Introduction. In R. Lasky (Ed.), *Essays in honor of Norbert Freedman: Symbolization and desymbolization* (pp. 1–29). New York: Karnac.

Masson, J. (1985). *The complete letters of Sigmund Freud to Wilhelm Fliess 1887–1904.* Cambridge, MA: The Belknap Press of Harvard University Press.

Modell, A. H. (1988). The centrality of the psychoanalytic setting and the changing aims of treatment: Perspective from a theory of object relations. *Psychoanalytic Quarterly,* 57:577–596.

Moskowitz, M. (1996). The end of analyzability. In P. Foster, R. Moskowitz & R. Javier (Eds.), *Reaching across boundaries of culture and class: Widening the scope of psychotherapy* (pp. 179–193). Northvale, NJ: Jason Aronson.

Rothstein, A. (1994). A perspective on doing a consultation and making the recommendation of analysis to a prospective analysand. *Psychoanalytic Quarterly,* 63:680–695.

———(1998). *Psychoanalytic technique and the creation of analytic patients* (2nd ed.). New York: International University Press.

———(1999). Some implications of the analyst feeling disturbed while working with disturbed patients. *Psychoanalytic Quarterly,* 68:541–558.

Sandell, R., Blomberg J., Lazar, A., Carlsson, J., Broberg, J., et al. (2000). Varieties of long-term outcome among patients in psychoanalysis and long-term psychotherapy. *International Journal of Psychoanalysis*, 81:921–942.

Sandler, J. (1983). Reflections on some relations between psychoanalytic concepts and psychoanalytic practice. *International Journal of Psychoanalysis*, 64:34–35.

Schimek, J. (2002). Some thoughts on symbolization and transference. In R. Lasky (Ed.), *Essays in honor of Norbert Freedman: Symbolization and desymbolization* (pp. 257–279). London: Karnac.

Segal, H. (2003). Imagination, play and art (1991). In R. Steiner (Ed.), *Unconscious phantasy* (pp. 211–221). London: Karnac. (Original paper published 1991.)

Slochower, H. (1975). Philosophical principles in Freudian psychoanalytic theory: Ontology and the quest for "matrem." *American Imago*, 32:1–39.

Stone, L. (1954). The widening scope of indications for psychoanalysis. *Journal of the American Psychoanalytic Association*, 2:567–594.

———(1961). *The psychoanalytic situation*. New York: International University Press.

Wilson, M. (2003). The analyst's desire and the problem of narcissistic resistances. *Journal of the American Psychoanalytic Association*, 51:71–99.

## *Appendix*

After a little over a year of her 4 time a week analysis, Nora precipitously ended her treatment. The stated reason was money. In the context of this paper, we need to ask what effect Nora's leave taking has on our understanding of analyzability. Perhaps the most accurate statement we can make is that this patient could not go any further in her analysis with this analyst at this point in their lives. The question whether Nora can be analyzed is, in some ways, beside the point. She was analyzed for a little over 1 year. More to the point, however, is how long Nora can actually stay engaged in an analysis. Although I do believe that Nora benefited from her analysis (and psychotherapy), it is also clear that, from the analyst's and supervisor's points of view, the analysis was incomplete. The premature ending is consistent with some of the research on analyzability(Bachrach, 1998) and psychoanalysis (Sandell, Blomberg, Lazar, Carlsson, Broberg et al. 2000) which indicates that less vulnerable and higher functioning patients will, on average, be better able to collaborate in the analytic endeavor than more vulnerable patients who do not function as well in their lives. One of the factors mentioned by Bachrach and Sandell et al. that impacts on analytic success is the experience level of the analyst. Dr. C was a candidate and therefore lacking in analytic experience. My own sense of the process, however, was that Dr. C's lack of analytic experience was more than balanced out by her positive regard for Nora and her belief in the analytic enterprise.

In my opinion, the kinds of "heroic" efforts that many candidates and analysts make can stretch our concept of analyzability just as an analyst's private beliefs can change our public or standard beliefs about a great many analytic concepts. This was Joseph Sandler's point in a paper written nearly a quarter of a century ago (Sandler, 1983); and Sandler's point is relevant to the concept of analyzability. The ideas generated by analysts working with "less than classical patients" create a tension with our more established (or establishment) ideas about analyzability. And this tension can be a potential life saver for psychoanalysis by stretching our concept of analyzability while retaining its essential meaning. And one aspect of such a "stretch" is the challenge it poses to our own narcissism. I think most, if not all, analysts would acknowledge that the fit between patient and analyst is crucial in any discussion of analyzability. It is one thing to acknowledge this in the abstract, however, and quite another thing to acknowledge it in the heat of the moment when our visceral response might take the form of negating the potential for analysis because of some defect in the other. Any question about the limits of analyzability must include the person of the analyst.

CHAPTER 7

# Analyzability

## Reflections on "Analyzability"

### Janet Fisher

In this condensed and yet far-reaching consideration of previously neglected aspects of the clinical conversation over what kinds of patients can
benefit from analysis, Dr. Frosch addresses both sides of the proverbial
question: that is, does the determination of who is suitable for analytic
treatment rest on the qualities of the prospective patient or on the qualities
of the prospective analyst? He underscores properties of both parties that
allow or interfere with achieving a workable analytic "fit."

Historically, analysts believed that patients who could not participate
in symbolic communication would not profit from analytic treatment
because of an inability to engage in mutual reflection with the analyst.
Frosch observes that, in designating a patient as "pre-symbolic," we risk
a reductive kind of assessment of the patient. First, states of mind, such
as concreteness, action orientation and intense emotionality, developmentally precede symbolization but do not necessarily preclude it, nor
are they necessarily defensively destructive of analytic understanding.
Second, effective analytic treatments often involve cycles of symbolized
and desymbolized states within and between both patient and analyst.
What is more familiarly categorized as the analyst's countertransference,

according to Frosch, actually contains within it a loss of symbolic functioning.

The assessment of analyzability can be influenced by the analyst's expectations of the patient's proper "behavior" in treatment. When the patient acts out or fails to respond to the analyst's interpretive efforts, for example, the analyst may countertransferentially invoke theory to disqualify the patient as an adequate participant in the therapeutic venture, and in so doing fails to bring a desirable curiosity, self-inquiry and receptivity to the puzzle of perceived treatment impasses or glitches.

The analyst is supported, on the other hand, in pursuit of successful treatment with seemingly "unqualified" patients, by several important factors: a personal experience of, and conviction, about the life-enhancing benefits of psychoanalysis; an attitude of acceptance and "positive regard" (p. 838) toward the patient which offsets the impulse to react with intolerance or judgments which can, themselves, be a form of desymbolization on the part of the analyst. That is, an interest in meaning and understanding devolves into labeling, hostile application of clinical theory, or mutual acting out.

What other theorists have called cycles of rupture and repair or symbolization and desymbolization in the analytic work, Frosch describes in the context of "match" between the two parties, a match that depends on the analyst's ability to weather these cycles, attend to the flux in the transference and countertransference with an ongoing capacity to wait, restore reflectiveness, and to appreciate that interpretation is not the only means through which analysis takes place. This requires rethinking our tendencies to treat "resistance" as an unwanted event or a reflection of the patient's unfavorable qualities and to privilege interpretation and transference over other common aspects of analytic work including enactments and apparent loss of meaning. We must maintain an attitude of acceptance toward how any individual analytic treatment unfolds. We may only be able to answer the question of how analysis succeeds one case at a time.

\*     \*     \*

# *Analyzability*

## *Allan Frosch*

Is analyzability a viable concept? I believe it is. In the past the focus was on the patient, the analysand. In this paper my focus will be on the analyst—the notion being that psychoanalysis is a concept that exists in the mind of the analyst, so that who the analyst is and what he or she brings to the analytic situation is crucial in any discussion of analyzability. The shift from a focus on the capacities of the patient to those of the analyst highlights the importance of psychoanalytic training in theories of mind; clinically supervised experience, particularly analytic experience; and the analyst's own personal or training analysis. However, a caveat is appropriate here: Psychoanalysis is a two-person enterprise, after all, so that to exclude the patient can lead to the same oversights that occurred in the past when the analyst was more or less left out of consideration. Therefore, one question that needs to be asked at the outset is whether or not analyzability is contingent on certain capacities in the patient, specifically, the capacity to symbolize?

Norbert Freedman (1998), for one, answers this question in the affirmative: "The quality of thought we call symbolic, in both patient and analyst, is an indispensable part of analytic work" (p. 82). I use the term "symbolization" herein to refer to a process whereby we can meaningfully understand that an event can be looked at from many different perspectives. It is a process where we can view our thoughts as an object of our thoughts. We self-reflect. Furthermore, it is a term that always includes its counterpart: desymbolization, where things are as they appear to be.

There are no other perspectives, at least none that have any emotional significance—that is, meaning. If we do not view desymbolization solely as a rigid defense that destroys meaning, it can be seen as providing some immediacy of concrete, lived experience, which is a necessary building block for symbolization (Frosch, 1995; Schimek, 2002). Stanley Grand (2002), commenting on the action component of desymbolization, has "emphasized the more positive symbolic making processes that are involved in the use of action" (p. 278).

A number of authors have outlined the nonverbal, other than-symbolic, sensorimotor patterns of the infant and very young child that are elaborated by subsequent verbal and pictorial fantasies. This implicit or procedural knowledge (cf. Clyman, 1991), what Hannah Segal (1991) called basic hypotheses about the world encoded in the body, is embedded in our more secondary process elaborations. Jean Schimek (1975), and others, have argued that these desymbolized, action-oriented, and affectively laden experiences must sometimes precede symbolization. In other words, action sometimes comes before insight. This process of movement between symbolization and desymbolization has received both empirical and theoretical support (Britton, 2004; Freedman, Lasky & Hurvich, 2003) and is an integral part of all therapeutic work that we call psychoanalysis. However, I do not believe we can describe a patient's capacity to move between symbolization and desymbolization without including the relationship between the patient and the analyst, and the analyst's capacity to self-reflect.

My focus in discussing the analytic relationship is on what I call "theory-driven countertransference." My frame of reference is that theories are subjective constructions, compromise formations wherein wishful and defensive components are organized to maximize pleasure and minimize unpleasure. This is certainly how Freud (1913) viewed psychoanalytic theory, and he warned us that sometimes we can use theory to defend against uncomfortable emotions. Analysts, like most people, want to feel reasonably safe and secure in what they do. When we do not, we can use our theories to blame patients for not behaving as our theory dictates they should. Freud (1910) certainly knew this, and he said so in the Clark Lectures. Therapists, he said, often punished patients who behaved in ways contrary to the therapist's expectations.

I believe Freud was referring to his own work with Dora (1905a), where he refused to resume treatment when Dora came back to see him a year after she had left, "but I promised to forgive her for having deprived me of the satisfaction of affording her a more radical cure for her troubles" (Freud, 1905a, p.122). If we look at the case of Dora in terms of analyzability, we could say that a patient should listen to the analyst's interpretations and get better, and not act out by leaving treatment before the analyst thinks it was time to do so. Nearly twenty years later, in *Beyond the Pleasure Principle,* Freud (1920) commented that patients repeated unpleasant experiences and did not make the progress that he thought they should because "they contrive once more to feel themselves scorned, to oblige the physician to speak severely to them and treat them coldly" (p. 21). Freud's tone is accusatory and sounds very similar to his earlier discussion of punishing patients who did not behave as he wanted them to. Generally speaking, Freud observed that most patients really did not behave as he wanted them to. Those he was treating in 1920 did not want to leave treatment when he thought the analysis was over. They were clearly under the sway of the death instinct, a limiting factor in analysis. Freud (1920) elaborated these ideas into a metapsychological battle of the giants: Thanatos and Eros: "The aim of all life is death" (p. 38).

This is a brilliant theoretical tour de force whether one buys the theory or not. In my opinion, however, Freud moved from the emotionally charged issue in the heat of the transference when he wanted to end treatment and patients did not, to the more abstract realm of the meaning of life conceptualized as a battle between life and death. Freud's intolerance of his own feelings (particularly those around separation and loss), influenced his perception of repetition and action in analysis, even though he was well aware that they were an attempt to master overwhelming affect (Freud, 1914, 1920; cf. Frosch, 2004).

Analysts today (like Freud) sometimes handle their discomfort by using theory to blame the patient. This behavior cuts across all theoretical persuasions. It is a function of the analyst's discomfort, not of a particular theory. That it can take the form of using theory makes it all the more important that when we discuss analyzability we put it in the context of the analyst's training.

At the heart of all analytic training is one's own analysis, which is indispensable for helping us better understand our defensive use of theory. Another reason why analysts need to have a good personal analysis is because we need to know that the psychoanalytic process is life affirming, often life saving. No amount of formal training in theory and technique can do this. A positive experience in one's own analysis can provide the sense of conviction and hope that both we and our patients need to do this work. But we need it first. Without a sense of conviction and hope about what we do, we have deprived ourselves and our patients of something that is necessary for a successful analysis.

There is a very long literature on the effects of the analyst's interest, thoughts, and feelings on the analytic process. We can go back to Freud's early writings on the need to feel interested in and sympathetic toward patients (Breuer & Freud, 1893; Freud, 1904, 1905b), and the patient's need to have a sense of hope that is directly related to the personality of the therapist, "which induces such faith" (Freud, 1905b, pp. 258-259). In 1949 Adelaide Johnson wrote an extraordinary paper on superego lacunae, wherein she said that children become what we as parents unconsciously think of them or want them to be. She emphasized the shaping role of parents' unconscious fantasies about their children. Johnson extended this into the analytic situation, where she discussed the importance of the analyst's genuine acceptance, his or her positive regard for the other. We see the contemporary presentation of these ideas in some of Fonagy's work (2001) and Fonagy and Target's (2002) work on mentalization and the construction of reality. Shelly Bach (2005), Mark Grunes (1998), Arnold Rothstein (1999), Irving Steingart (1995), and many others have written about the place of love in the analytic relationship. In a recent paper Jessica Benjamin (2004) argued that without the analyst's "compassionate acceptance" of the analysand our observations are apt to be experienced as judgments. This acceptance is easier said than done when the other's implicit and unconscious beliefs about the world lead to actions that make the analyst uncomfortable. We could argue that it is precisely these moments in the heat of the transference where there may be great potential for furthering the analytic process (cf. Bird, 1972). By the same token, of course, it is exactly those moments where our patient's desires and defenses are most pronounced that the analyst's capacity for symbolization can break down.

This breakdown is often what happens, and in order for such ruptures to be repaired the analyst must somehow find his or her way back to a position of symbolization. More often than not there is, in my opinion, a reciprocal process wherein analyst and patient help each other move from affectively charged desymbolized moments of enactment or action to affectively charged moments of symbolization. There are times, however, particularly in the heat of the transference-countertransference scenario, when the analyst must take the lead in this. The analyst must "survive," that is, contain and process his or her own feelings, including feelings for the patient, and allow himself or herself to see the situation from a variety of perspectives.

In using a word like "survive," or ones like "rupture" and "repair," "breakdown" and "build-up," I am saying that something has gone awry: The analytic process has broken down. I believe a more accurate way of putting it is that these are the transformational cycles that define psychoanalysis. This way of looking at it can have a significant impact on the analyst's perceptions, that is, his or her thoughts, feelings, and attitudes toward self and other. It is at these moments, however, that we can also use theory as a defense against our own discomfort, a point I turn to now.

Our theory of mind today, as it was in 1914, is that we often remember through action, not words. This takes on a particular importance when we consider some of the ideas presented earlier about implicit ways of responding, automatic procedures that are nested in later representations. We might think of a person's silence, or not coming to sessions, and its impact on the analyst as part of a communication about early, quite likely traumatic experiences. Of course we could also think of these things as a resistance (it is not one or the other). Resistance is a fine thing if we really do believe that it is part and parcel of how the mind works. There is no reason why a patient's resistance should necessarily take away from his or her analyzability. Yet we hear this all the time. The patient is too resistant—or worse yet—the patient is too disturbed for an analysis. Sometimes when analysts say this it means that the patient is not doing, behaving, thinking, the way we want him to. Or perhaps this behavior makes us feel uncomfortable, angry, impotent, and the like. We might do well at these moments to think of Robert Michel's comment about resistance: "Why do I choose to think of this patient's behavior from the perspective of resistance at this point in the analysis" (Panel, 2004, p. 250). Michel's comment is consistent with an idea presented in a recent paper by Marila Aisenstein (2003) that we reconceptualize our view of resistance in terms of the analyst working through his or her resistance. Is it part of our resistance that we believe patients should limit their propensity toward action? If so, how much?

In the culture of psychoanalysis today, many analysts would view these action representations or enactments as potentially informational and/or of therapeutic value in and of themselves. Like most analytic concepts, however, the quantitative dimension is crucial. At what point does the frequency and duration of these "enacted memories" (Loewald, 1980) lead the analyst to argue against analyzability? When does the analyst become uncomfortable enough with what Gil Katz (1998) called the enacted dimension of psychoanalysis that the self-serving aspect of theory kicks into high gear, and thoughts that "the patient is making me uncomfortable" switch to "the patient is borderline and the resistance so pathological that he (she) cannot be analyzed?"

In other words, analyzability may be determined by a match or mis-match between the patient's transformational cycles—the movement between symbolization and desymbolization—and the analyst's capacity to tolerate them—a capacity I would quickly add that is very much tied to the analyst's own movement between symbolization and desymbolization. In very down-to-earth terms, all of this can be dis-cussed in the context of how comfortable the analyst is with the frequency and duration of the patient's self-reflective moments; this is directly tied to how often the analyst feels he or she has to make an interpretation—leaving aside the ambiguity of that term. Does the analyst define himself or herself or feel competent based on making interpretations?

In a recent paper Steven Ellman and Monica Carsky (2002) make the point that interpretations made in the midst of a patient's desymbolized process (when basic trust is low) can derail the analytic process. The same kind of thinking applies to analysts when they are in the midst of a desymbolized process. Ellman and Carsky's focus is on transference interpretations, and I would include extratransference interpretations as well.

In mentioning transference and extratransference interpretations I have touched on another possible criterion for analyzability. There is a widespread belief that interpretations in the here-and-now of the transference are more mutative than any other. Many analysts hold to this assumption, and, to a great extent, it defines not only analyzability but their sense-of-self as analysts. So what does it mean if work in the transference is not a significant part of a particular analysis? How do we even define what is significant? In a recent article Ted Jacobs (2001) argued that patients who can make us question what it is to be an analyst may lead us to see them as suffering from such bedrock difficulties that they are not analyzable. This can pit the analyst against the patient. It is do or die: You are wrong or I am wrong. These positions are not so different from the difficulties that Freud struggled with.

## *Summary*

In this paper I have tried to show that the analyst's idea about psychoanalysis is an essential variable that contributes to our concept of analyzability. Furthermore, the analyst's ideas are always shaped by desire (Wilson, 2003). Wishes and defenses organize our perception of the world, including the world of who is or is not analyzable. In this sense I would say that the analytic process exists in the mind of the analyst. We organize and construct the clinical material according to our theoretical beliefs that, by definition, are always affected by our desire to feel safe and our wish to feel like a competent/potent analyst (cf. Frosch, 2004, p. 25). Part of this construction refers to the analyst's comfort in entertaining a variety of different perspectives. We can all acknowledge that the world of psychoanalysis is a pluralistic world. It is one thing to acknowledge this and quite another to be reasonably conversant about the different conceptual approaches so that we have the tools to play with theory. The tools do us very little good, however, if we are stuck in some defensively skewed desymbolized position where all meaning is destroyed—treated as useless—except the meaning that makes us feel better. Along these lines I have introduced the term "theory driven countertransference" to account for one aspect of the analyst's resistance to analyzability.

# *References*

Aisenstein, M. (2003). Does the cure come as a byproduct of psychoanalytic treatment? *Psychoanalytic Quarterly*, 72:263–274.

Bach, S. (2006). *Getting from here to there: Analytic love. Analytic process.* Hillsdale, NJ: The Analytic Press.

Benjamin, J. (2004). Beyond doer and done to: An intersubjective view of thirdness. *Psychoanalytic Quarterly*, 73:5–46.

Bird, B. (1972). Notes on transference: Universal phenomenon and hardest part of analysis. *Journal of the American Psychoanalytic Association*, 20:267–301.

Breuer, J. & Freud, S. (1893). Studies on hysteria. In *Standard Edition*, 2:1–335.

Britton, R. (2004). Subjectivity, objectivity, and triangular space. *Psychoanalytic Quarterly*, 73:47–61.

Clyman, R. (1991). The procedural organization of emotions: A contribution from cognitive science to the psychoanalytic theory of therapeutic action. *Journal of the American Psychoanalytic Association*, 39 (Suppl.):349–382.

Ellman, S. & Carsky, M. (2002). Symbolization and development of interpretable transference. In R. Lasky (Ed.), *Essays in honor of Norbert Freedman: Symbolization and desymbolization* (pp. 280–305). London: Karnac.

Fonagy, P. (2001). *Attachment theory and psychoanalysis.* New York: Other Press.

———& Target, M. (2002). Early intervention and the development of self-regulation. *Psychoanalytic Inquiry*, 22:307–335.

Freedman, N. (1998). Psychoanalysis and symbolization: Legacy or heresy? In C. Ellman, S. Grand, M. Silvan & S. Ellman (Eds.), *The modern Freudians: Contemporary psychoanalytic technique* (pp. 79–97). Northvale, NJ: Jason Aronson.

Lasky, R. & Hurvich, M. (2003). Two pathways towards knowing psychoanalytic process. In M. Leuzinger-Bohleber, A. U. Dreher & J. Canestri (Eds.), *Pluaralism and unity? Methods of research in psychoanalysis* (pp. 207–221). London: International Psychoanalysis Library.

Freud, S. (1904). Freud's psychoanalytic procedure. *Standard Edition*, 7:249–254.

———(1905a). Fragment of an analysis of a case of hysteria. *Standard Edition*, 7:1–122.

———(1905b). On psychotherapy. *Standard Edition*, 7:257–268.

———(1910). Five lectures on psycho-analysis. *Standard Edition*, 11:3–55.

———(1913). The claims of psychoanalysis to scientific interest. *Standard Edition*, 13:165–190.

———(1914). Remembering, repeating and working-through. *Standard Edition*, 12:147–156.

———(1920). Beyond the pleasure principle. *Standard Edition*. 18:3–64.

Frosch, A. (1995). The preconceptual organization of emotion. *Journal of the American Psychoanalytic Association*, 43:423–447.

———(2006). The culture of psychoanalysis and the concept of analyzability. *Psychoanalytic Psychology*, 23(1):43–55.

Grand, S. (2002). Action in psychoanalysis: On the symbolization of peremptory discharge. In R. Lasky (Ed.), *Essays in honor of Norbert Freedman: Symbolization and desymbolization* (pp. 262–279). London: Karnac.

Grunes, M. (1998). The therapeutic object relationship, II. In S. Ellman, S. Grand, M. Silvan & S. Ellman (Eds.), *The modern Freudians: Contemporary psychoanalytic technique* (pp. 129–140). Northvale, NJ: Jason Aronson.

Jacobs, T. (2001). Reflections on the goals of psychoanalysis, the psychoanalytic process, and the process of change. *Psychoanalytic Quarterly*, 70:149–181.

Johnson, A. (1949). Sanctions for superego lacunae of adolescents. In K. R. Eisler (Ed.), *Searchlights on delinquency* (pp. 245–265). New York: International Universities Press.

Katz, G. (1998). Where the action is: The enacted dimension of analytic process. *Journal of the American Psychoanalytic Association*, 46:1129–1167.

Loewald, H. (1980). *Papers on psychoanalysis.* New Haven, CT: Yale University Press.

Panel, X. (2004). Resistance in the 21st century *Journal of the American Psychoanalytic Association*, 52: 243–253.

Rothstein, A. (1999). Some implications of the analyst feeling disturbed while working with disturbed patients. *Psychoanalytic Quarterly*, 68:541–558.

Schimek, J. (1975). A critical re-examination of Freud's concept of unconscious mental representation. *International Review of Psycho-Analysis*, 2:171–187.

———(2002). Some thoughts on symbolization and transference. In R. Lasky (Ed.), *Essays in honor of Norbert Freedman: Symbolization and desymbolization* (pp. 257–279). London: Karnac.

Steingart, I. (1995). *A thing apart*. Northvale, NJ: Jason Aronson.

Wilson, M. (2003). The analyst's desire and the problem of narcissistic resistances. *Journal of the American Psychoanalytic Association*, 51:71–99.

CHAPTER 8

# Control Cases and Institutional Responsibility:
# A Creative or Coercive Process

## Reflections on "Control Cases and Institutional Responsibility: A Creative or Coercive Process"

*Richard B. Grose*

In this paper, Allan offers a powerful but gentle polemic against institutional representatives coercing candidates, the coercion seen as causing candidates to limit their choice of control patients to the more classically analyzable ones and as creating in candidates a fear that their work with control patients could be dismissed as only a transference cure.

Taking first the choice of control patients, Allan asserts his view: "...candidates should not have to convince institutional representatives that a case is an analytic control or that a 'valid' analytic process is in effect, but sometimes this is what happens." His contrasting position is clearly that any patient requiring more intensive treatment should be seen at the frequency that is indicated and should also be considered to be potentially as good a control patient as any other. When the criteria for selection are narrower, Allan explains, it may be due to the unfortunate influence of theory on the selection process, which he terms "theory-driven countertransference," or "the analyst's defensive adherence to a particular theoretical perspective."

To highlight this point, he contrasts the ideas of Paul Gray and Sheldon Bach regarding treatment. Gray needs to limit the patient pool to those who can work in the transference—thus his way of working requires a careful preselection of patients. But when that set of ideas is applied to a candidate looking for a control patient, the result is to limit the candidate's choices. Bach, on the other hand, works with patients who cannot handle transference interpretations and is willing to work with them for a long time until they can. His ideas therefore lead to a potentially wider pool of control patients. Although Allan doesn't say this explicitly, he is clearly with Sheldon Bach here.

The second form of coercion would create in candidates the fear that their work with control patients could be dismissed as a transference cure. This is the more serious issue for Allan, as indicated by the space he devotes to it and the different kinds of arguments he marshals against it. He quotes Arnold Cooper, who writes about the odd circumstance that seasoned therapists in analytic training subject their control patients, who are "in a strange position, with a unique form of communication with another human being," to of all things—silence. Allan also discusses the idea of the "unobjectionable positive transference," which was very important to Freud's notion of how treatment functions, implicitly arguing that the charge of "transference cure" risks devaluing this essential (to Freud) part of the patient's experience, the positive feelings for the therapist. He discusses Freud's long and fraught history of struggling with the idea of suggestion, something that he found at once ubiquitous, necessary, as well as dangerous in its implications to the status of psychoanalysis as a science.

He discusses the important distinction between a therapist's public and private theories. This leads perhaps to the core of Allan's argument, because as he puts it, "Candidates, just as the rest of us, must work to help their patients, and this means developing their own implicit, and often unconscious, ideas about what is most useful clinically for a particular patient." Later he discusses Freud's tension between public and private theories: "On a clinical level Freud treated patients in ways that he thought were the most effective. And this included personal influence (suggestion) via the unobjectionable positive transference. In his published writings, however, Freud was driven by concerns that psycho-analysis would be seen as another version of hypnosis—a successful form of treatment based on suggestion, but not as an objective science (1917)." These thoughts indicate what was important for Allan here: when candidates are having their first experience of working analytical-ly, he thought it was very unfortunate if they were supervised in ways that made adherence to rules (watch out for a transference cure!) more important than developing their own sense (a private theory) of what will help the patient.

Allan Frosch was the irreplaceable clinician and writer that he was because he combined a tremendous passion for psychoanalysis with a tremendous self-control that was founded on a respect for others. Here we see both of these elements. The word "coercion" itself points to his passion, to the seriousness with which Allan took his subject. It is a strong word. In other hands, it could easily have been a fighting word. But this paper was also written with the feelings of his opponents in mind. It joins a passionate polemic to a gentle, often indirect presenta-tion that embraces even as it challenges.

\*   \*   \*

# Control Cases and Institutional Responsibility:
## A Creative or Coercive Process

*Allan Frosch[1]*

Analysts are often frightened to do what we are trained to do. This does not, I hope, come as a great surprise to anyone. Psychoanalysis is difficult work, and any analysis puts emotional demands on the analyst, as well as the patient. I have recently used the term "theory-driven countertransference" (Frosch, 2006) to discuss the analyst's resistance to doing an analysis. Theory-driven countertransference refers to the analyst's defensive adherence to a particular theoretical perspective. I see that as a limiting factor in answering the following questions: Is the patient analyzable? When should an analysis begin, and how can it be maintained to an agreed-upon termination? I think of theory-driven countertransference as part and parcel of the analyst's desire to feel safe, secure, competent, and knowledgeable in a situation that is not designed to provide such comfortable feelings. But there is more to it than that. The more refers to our knowledge of theory and, in particular, to the evolution (or revolution, see Aron, 2005) of psychoanalytic concepts.

In this paper I will emphasize the responsibility of representatives of training institutes to have a "good enough" command of theory so that a creative space can exist between a candidate and the institutional representative regarding the question of analyzability. I will organize my thinking around what many contemporary analysts refer to as a "transference cure" or what Freud thought of as a cure through suggestion. The idea of a transference cure is rooted in Freud's fear that psychoanalysis would be seen as another version of hypnosis; were that the case, psychoanalysis would be ruled out as a serious (scientific) endeavor.

---

[1] I would like to add my thanks to Donna Bassin and Ruth Oscharoff for their input to this paper.

## *Transference and Hypnosis*

I suspect that most contemporary analysts would agree that it is an oversimplification to think that transference is purely a one-person event. This harkens back to Freud's early view of transference as a false connection and is very much related to his support of Charcot and the notion of autosuggestion (where something "real" exists in the patient) as opposed to Bernheim's idea that hypnosis (and by extension transference) is more of an interpersonal event. For Sigmund Freud at the turn of the twentieth century this would have made hypnosis and psychoanalysis distinctly unscientific. George Makari (1992) has discussed this in some detail and has shown how Freud's early ideas about transference, and therefore psychoanalysis, were so much a part of the debate (also known as the Hypnotic War) between Charcot and Bernheim.

To understand key psychoanalytic concepts, I think we need to be immersed in the world of psychoanalysis, meaning we have to have an investment in learning—devouring, incorporating—the history of the unfolding of theories of mind and of theories and practice of technique. Having said this, I would like to return to the idea expressed above— that it is an oversimplification to think that transference is purely a one-person event and point the reader to the articles cited below which take up this topic. Unfortunately, some therapists have not had the good fortune of knowing about Makari's work, or for that matter about the work of Levy and Inderbetzin on suggestion (2000), or Lew Aron on a two-person process (1990), or Mark Gehrie on the development of self-reflection (1993), or Steven Mitchell on Freud's influence (1996). All of these papers, which directly or indirectly bear on the concept of transference, would be of particular value to analytic candidates, the very clinicians who are unlikely to have read these articles simply because they are new to the field and inundated with so much reading material. It is candidates, after all, who need control cases and who are faced with the following anticipatory ideas (1917, p. 452) that act as a stimulant to the patient's own nascent ideas. "Suggestion pushes open the doors which are in fact slowly opening of themselves for autosuggestion" (1883, p. 83). This formulation allowed Freud to preserve the objective nature of psychoanalysis along with the analyst's influence. It is Freud's compromise between Charcot and Bernheim that helped him to move away from hypnosis without leaving it completely. Suggestive rapport, said Freud, is the "complete prototype of what we call transference today (1914, p. 12; 1926a, p. 268).

This rapport between patient and analyst does not mean that the patient suggests whatever he pleases: "We guide his [auto] suggestions so far as he is in any way accessible to its influence" (1917, p. 452), which is not the same as unscientific "hackwork" (1917, p. 449) of direct or prohibitive suggestion that characterizes hypnosis. It is true that analysts make use of this particularly large suggestive influence, but not to force the patient to give up his/her symptoms. The analyst's personal influence via the unobjectionable positive transference is used as a "motive force to induce the patient to overcome his resistances" (1926b, p. 225). Ultimately we protect the patient from a cure through suggestion by analyzing the transference (1925, p. 43). Through this formulation Freud was able to use the unobjectionable positive transference to accomplish what he considered an essential task of psychoanalysis—and one which differentiated it from hypnosis—the patient's work with his/her "internal resistances," including the resistance in the transference. If suggestion is a demon, then a cure by suggestion (i.e., a transference cure) is the devil incarnate.

## Transference Cure

Transference cure refers to the idea that change occurs through the relationship to the analyst without any conscious, verbally mediated insight. These changes are assumed to be dependent on the continued relationship with the analyst and are "permanent" only as long as the relationship exists. A complete resolution of the transference was another weapon (along with anonymity, neutrality and abstinence, cf. Levy and Inderbetzin, 2000) employed to separate psychoanalysis from hypnosis; so that at the end of an analytic treatment the transference must be "dissected in all the shapes in which it appears" (Freud, 1917, p. 453). But, we could add, not quite all the shapes. Freud did not advocate "dissecting" the unobjectionable positive transference. He always saw this as a necessary condition for the patient to "persevere" when, so to speak, the going got tough (Ellman, 1991, esp. p. 87). That is to say, when a patient's passionate feelings "either negative or positive" entered into the analysis as a resistance, it was the unobjectionable positive transference that allowed the patient to resolve these transference resistances and move toward a resolution of core conflicts: "and if success is then obtained or continues, it rests, not on suggestions, but on the achievement by its means of an overcoming of internal resistances, on the internal change that has been brought about in the patient" (1917, p. 453).

## Contemporary Theory and Control Cases

In terms of contemporary theory and its impact on candidates we can look at Paul Gray's work where he advocates interpretation of transference fantasies "either intimidating, or inhibiting, on the one hand, or forgiving and approving on the other" (1988, p. 48) "from the beginnings of the work with patients" (p. 45). Gray argues against any use of the unobjectionable positive transference in an analysis and acknowledges that in his approach the "treatment situation narrows" (p. 45). Where Paul Gray treats the patient through his focus on the analysis of the transference, Sheldon Bach (1985) permits and encourages the patient to "treat himself" in the presence of the analyst: ". . . the treatment belongs to the patient, at least until the time he is able and willing to share it with us" (pp. 224-225). For Bach this is a necessary step in order for many patients to develop a sense of trust in the analyst and the analytic process so that interpretive work (eventually in the transference) is not experienced as a trauma. And when the transference cannot be analyzed, "there is always the countertransference to be privately mined for clues, to the extent that we are able to admit that we are participants in the unfolding drama" (p. 229).

Where Gray sees certain ego strengths as necessary for analytic work, Bach sees the development of these capacities as part and parcel of psychoanalysis: "Although one may refer to this as a "preparatory phase," I do not consider this as a preparatory phase before the analysis begins;

this *is* the analysis, conducted in another way" (p. 224, italics in the original). For analysts who hold views similar to Bach's, the population of potential analysands is more inclusive than would be the case if one were coming from a perspective advocated by Gray. To put it differently as a way of returning more directly to the central issue of this paper: If one holds to a point of view along the lines of Sheldon Bach, then "good-enough" analysts are practitioners who can allow themselves to be used subjectively so that more objective use can be made of the analyst at a later time (p. 73). In other words, the patient's positive fantasies are seen as an important condition for treatment to progress. Not so for Paul Gray whose emphasis is on the defensively motivated aspects of such fantasies and the importance of analyzing them early on in treatment. Patients who are unable to do this are considered better suited for psychotherapy (p. 44). Depending on the candidate and the institutional representative's understanding of theory, the population of control cases is narrowed or expanded.

## Freud's Private and Public Theories

In his paper on "Constructions in Analysis" (1937), written a year before his death, Freud argued that the "danger of our leading a patient astray by suggestion, by persuading him to accept things which we ourselves believe but which he ought not to, has certainly been exaggerated" (p. 262). Freud quickly added "that such an abuse of suggestion has never occurred in my practice" (p. 262). I think that Freud's defensiveness around his use of suggestion may be an example of his struggle between private and public theory. On a clinical level Freud treated patients in ways that he thought were the most effective. And this included personal influence (suggestion) via the unobjectionable positive transference. In his published writings, however, Freud was driven by concern that psychoanalysis would be seen as another version of hypnosis—successful form of treatment based on suggestion, but not as an objective science (1917).

Given such an array of ideas, what is a candidate to do? Candidates, just as the rest of us, must work to help their patients, and this means developing their own implicit, and often unconscious, ideas about what is most useful clinically for a particular patient. In order to develop private theories, there has to be some flexibility in one's "analytic super-ego." Training analyses are indispensable for this. Also very helpful are supervisors and teachers, i.e., representatives of the institutional establishment who can contextualize theory.

## Concluding Comments

Most analysts would probably agree that for patients to use interpretive work, particularly in the transference, they must have the capacity to view things from multiple perspectives. From my own point of view, a patient's ability to "play," i.e., to move between different constructions of the world, is not independent of the analyst's capacity to do the same. I have argued that for a creative process to emerge between candidate and institutional representative, there must be an openness to a certain kind of play. And this play takes the form of moving between different theoretical perspectives. Theory-driven countertransference interferes with this process. I believe that representatives of training institutes must take primary responsibility to make sure that a rigid adherence to theory does not stifle the creative interchange, or space, that can develop when candidates present their control cases.

In this paper I have shown how the concept of transference cure was shaped by Freud's relationship to hypnosis. Contextualizing this concept may destigmatize it sufficiently for us to be able to consider whether it refers to "something more" (Boston Change Process Group, 2005; Rosegrant, 2005) or something other than insight in terms of its contribution to therapeutic success. The notion of a transference cure is only one of any number of possible concerns about the psychoanalytic process. For example, if part (or all) of the analytic work is conducted on the telephone, can we call the treatment an analysis? More specifically are we comfortable accepting telephone work as a control analysis? A recent issue of this newsletter (Summer, 2005) helped "stretch" the concept of the analytic frame vis-à-vis phone sessions. My own thinking is that most patients benefit from multiple sessions per week so that phone contact and/or morning and evening sessions on the same day would, other things being equal, be preferable to fewer sessions per week.

One of the ways we can stretch some of our cherished psychoanalytic concepts (be it the frame, technique, or theory of mind) is in the space between candidate and institutional representative around control cases. I have argued that it is the institute representative's responsibility in this endeavor to have a passion for psychoanalysis, i.e., an intense interest in theories of mind and technique. Anything less shortchanges our candidates, psychoanalysis and, most importantly, the patients that seek out our help. The elasticity of concepts, i.e., adding new meanings to some of our basic beliefs about psychoanalysis, is an invaluable endeavor only when we come to it via an informed place about theory. We are at a point in psychoanalysis where there are many well-established—can I say "classical"—theories, and we have very little empirical support for one over the other, or for the validity of some of our most "hallowed" concepts. Until such support is more in evidence, it is probably a pretty good bet to argue that our ideas, whatever our theoretical orientation may be, are organized around fantasies designed to keep us from feeling too insecure. The defensive use of theory cuts across all theoretical perspectives. We are all more similar than different.

## References

Aron, L. (2005). Acceptance, compassion, and affirmative analytic attitude in both intersubjectivity and compromise formation theory: Commentary on paper by Arnold Rothstein. *Psychoanalytic Dialogues*, 15: 443-446.

———(1990). One person and two person psychologies and the method of psychoanalysis. *Psychoanalytic Psychology*, 7: 475-485.

Bach, S. (1985). Narcissistic states and the therapeutic process. Northvale, NJ: Jason Aronson.

Boston Change Process Group (2005). The "something more" than interpretation revisited: Sloppiness and co-creativity in the psychoanalytic encounter. *Journal of the American Psychoanalytic Association*, 53: 673-729.

Cooper, A. M. (1985). Difficulties in beginning the candidate's first analytic case. *Contemporary Psychoanalysis,* 21:143-149

Ellman, S. (1991). *Freud's technique papers: A contemporary perspective.* Northvale NJ: Jason Aronson.

Freud, S. (1888). Preface to the translation of Bernheim's suggestion. *Standard Edition,* 1:73-85

———(1905). On psychotherapy. *Standard Edition,* 7:257-268.

———(1914). On the history of the psychoanalytic movement. *Standard Edition,* 14:7-66.

———(1917). Introductory lectures on psychoanalysis (Part III). General theory of the neuroses. *Standard Edition,* 16.

———(1923). A seventeenth century demonological neurosis. *Standard Edition,* 19:72-105.

———(1925). An autobiographical study. *Standard Edition,* 20:7-74.

———(1926a). Psychoanalysis. *Standard Edition,* 20:263-270.

———(1926b). The question of lay analysis. *Standard Edition,* 20:183-258.

———(1937). Constructions in psychoanalysis. *Standard Edition,* 23:257-269.

Frosch, A. (2006). Analyzability. *Psychoanalytic Psychology,* 93:835-843.

———(2006). The culture of psychoanalysis and the concept of analyzability. *Psychoanalytic Review,* 23:43-55.

Gehrie, M. J. (1993). Psychoanalytic technique and the development of the capacity to reflect. *Journal of the American Psychoanalytic Association,* 41:1083-1111.

Gray, P. (1988). On the significance of influence and insight in the spectrum of psychoanalytic psychotherapies. In A. Rothstein (Ed.), *How does treatment help? On the modes of therapeutic action of psychoanalytic psychotherapy* (pp. 41-50). Madison, CT: International Universities Press.

Levy, S. T. & Inderbitzin, L. B. (2000). Suggestion and psychoanalytic technique. *Journal of the American Psychoanalytic Association,* 48:739-758.

Makari, G. J. (1992). A history of Freud's first concept of transference. *International Review of Psychoanalysis,* 19:415-432.

Masson, J. (1985). The complete letters of Sigmund Freud to Wilhelm Fliess 1887-1904. Cambridge, MA, and London, England: The Belknap Press of Harvard University.

Mitchell, S. (1996). When interpretations fail: A new look at the therapeutic action of psychoanalysis. In L. Lifson (Ed.), *Understanding therapeutic action* (pp. 165-186). Hillsdale, NJ: The Analytic Press.

Rosegrant, J. (2005). The therapeutic effects of the free associative state of consciousness. The *Psychoanalytic Quarterly*, *74*: 737-766.

Sandler, J. (1983). Reflections on some relations between psychoanalytic concepts and psychoanalytic practice. *International Journal of Psychoanalysis*, 64:35-45.

*The Round Robin*. (2005). Vol. 20, No. 2.

# Empirical Psychoanalytic Inquiry

It is the word "inquiry" which we feel best fits Allan Frosch's orientation to "research." According to Merriam-Webster, an inquiry is an "examination into facts," a "request for information," or a "systematic investigation often of a matter of public interest."

The development of Allan's psychoanalytic ideas has always been in the service of inquiry—a delving into the unknown to discover (more than uncover) and to facilitate progression in the analytic dyad. This comes through from his earliest clinical paper on "Narcissistic Injury and Sadomasochistic Compensation." Not content to merely report a clinical vignette and discuss its relevance to the literature, he was always oriented to a question —an inherent posture toward research as deep inquiry.

Joan Hoffenberg underscores this well in describing how Allan became involved in research, first, in the IPTAR Clinical Center's research project on the "Effectiveness of Psychoanalytic Psychotherapy." The research team turned to him because of his clinical sensitivity and belief in the power of psychoanalytic treatment, and in turn, the research team became immersed in that work.

Always the developmentalist at heart, he then formed his own research team to explore the ways in which changes in parents' perceptions of their children during their treatment could have transformative power over time, as described by Anthony Mazzella in his essay on Allan's paper, "Psychoanalytic Treatment and Patients' Lives." This research, while unpublished, showed what Rena Greenblatt (a member of the Child Research Team) described as tracking the synergistic, intersubjective process between a child's growth in treatment and positive shifts in parents' self and object representations—their view of themselves as parents and in turn, of their children. Again, the idea of Freudian co-construction of reality comes through, a riff that became elaborated and deepened over time in subsequent clinical researches.

Phyllis F. Hopkins brings these points home in her essay on "The Effect of Frequency and Duration on Psychoanalytic Outcome." While Allan described himself as simply reporting on existing research findings that supported the psychoanalytic frame and treatment edifice, she notes his elaboration of and passionate argument for an open-systems orientation to our work. Here he inquires through the rubric of frequency and duration about an area of much contemporary interest to us as psychoanalysts: how to orient ourselves more deeply to the essence of analytic process, beyond the concreteness of the standard frame and rules of engagement in terms of frequency that can become restrictive and counter-analytic.

# CHAPTER 9

# The Effectiveness of Psychoanalytic Psychotherapy:
## The Role of Treatment Duration, Frequency of Sessions, and the Therapeutic Relationship

## Reflections on "The Effectiveness of Psychoanalytic Psychotherapy: The Role of Treatment Duration, Frequency of Sessions, and the Therapeutic Relationship"

*Joan D. Hoffenberg*

Not knowing where to begin this essay, I thought a chronological reconstruction of how this paper got written and how Allan came to be involved might be interesting.

In 1995 *Consumer Reports* (CR) published a study: "Mental Health: Does Therapy Help?" In this study individuals completed a questionnaire describing their experiences in therapy. There was a high rate of satisfaction, with satisfaction increasing when an individual was in treatment longer. This intrigued me, and I brought it to the attention of my then supervisor, Dr. Norbert Freedman. We considered how to apply this study to the newly founded IPTAR Clinical Center (ICC) to consider how patients seen at the Center assessed the treatment they received there. Adapting the instrument from CR, we used the scores from our patients' questionnaires to assess the effectiveness of the treatment we were offering. We had an advantage over the CR study in that unlike the original study, all of our patients were treated using psychoanalysis or psychoanalytic psychotherapy; and all the therapists were trained or training to be psychoanalysts.

It was not long before Bert and I realized that the statistical needs of the study were beyond our abilities, and we asked Dr. Neal Vorus to join us, at first to help with the statistics, but shortly to become a necessary part of our expanding study. Our goals were to look at *how* time in treatment and session frequency affected a person's perception of treatment outcomes. Creating an Effectiveness Score from the original questionnaire, we found a significant range of people's satisfaction with their treatment and that satisfaction generally increased with greater frequency of sessions and longer time in treatment. Although we had ostensibly accomplished our goals, we became intrigued with matters that were increasingly clinical and dynamic in nature; e.g., the relationship between clinical syndrome and treatment conditions and perceptions of the therapist, all of which led to audio-recorded *interviews of therapy remembered* with selected patient/respondents. These interviews were conducted by Neal Vorus.

And this is where Allan enters the picture. We were always interested in bridging the gap between the theoretical and the clinical and were trying to understand what it was/is in the clinical encounter that accounts for satisfaction and change. We wanted someone to listen to these interviews and discern what about these people makes for a difference in their attitudes about the treatment they received. Why Allan? There were several reasons: he was one of the directors of the clinical center; he was already known as someone who could think about analysis and translate it into words that resonated with people; he was someone we knew and liked. Allan listened to the first interviews and wrote "Two Pathways towards Internalization: Ms. A and Ms. B," a sophisticated synthesis of two different kinds of internalizations. Ms A reported that she "does not think about her therapist on a conscious level because she is available to her on an unconscious level." This is an object relationship that is always with her in contrast to Ms. B. for whom " it was not the intensity of the analytic relationship but its continuity" that "provided a much-needed structure." Allan returned to this theme in his 2012 paper.

Allan's interest in Effectiveness Research continued in a study of children and adolescents he and others conducted at the ICC and in his

2012 paper, "The Effect of Frequency and Duration on Psychoanalytic Outcome: A Moment in Time." In this paper he wrote " my institutional affiliations and experience from both sides of the couch, as well as my own research on frequency and duration and outcome (Freedman, et al., 1999) lead me to believe that the combination of high frequency and longer duration (open-ended) treatment is the most effective form of psychoanalysis" (p. 11); and "I view frequency and duration in the context of determining the optimal psychoanalytic treatment, rather than defining characteristics of the process itself" (p. 12). He continues: "that those who receive high intensity treatment internalized the therapeutic relationship as a soothing and helpful inner presence and that this and longer duration encourages a helpful internalization that continues well after the analysis has ended."

Allan was someone whose views about analysis developed over time. It pleases me to think that his work on this early project contributed somehow to his thinking. His view that psychoanalysis and a psychoanalytic attitude were relevant for all our clinical work permeated his thinking and teaching. He saw psychoanalysis along a continuum rather than making a hard distinction between psychoanalytic psychotherapy and psychoanalysis. This belief has touched the lives of his many students, analysands and supervisees.

\* \* \*

# The Effectiveness of Psychoanalytic Psychotherapy: The Role of Treatment Duration, Frequency of Sessions, and the Therapeutic Relationship

*Norbert Freedman, Joan D. Hoffenberg, Neal Vorus and Allan Frosch[1]*

*This is an effectiveness study of treatment outcome that relies on patients' perception of their mental health during and after psychoanalytic psychotherapy. Ninety-nine outpatients attending the IPTAR Clinical Center (ICC) responded to the Effectiveness Questionnaire (EQ) adapted from that developed by* Consumer Reports. *Effectiveness is studied from various perspectives. Findings indicated (1) an incremental gain in effectiveness scores from six to over twenty-four months of therapy; (2) an incremental gain with greater session frequency from one to two or three weekly sessions; (3) facilitation of effectiveness by the experience of a positive relationship with the therapist; (4) an interplay between clinical syndrome and treatment conditions. A method giving clinical validity to the quantitative findings is described. Brief summaries of two recorded interviews reveal differential reconstruction of events that had occurred during treatment. The findings are discussed from the vantage point of two hypotheses: cognitive dissonance and internalization of therapeutic experience.*

Psychoanalysis today finds itself not in a situation of crisis, but surely in one of reorganization. Within such a climate, the objective documentation of our clinical enterprise should be accorded high priority. This is true not only from the vantage point of our public image in a world increasingly

[1] This is a revised version of a paper presented at the annual meeting of the Division of Psychoanalysis (Division 39) of the American Psychological Association, April 26, 1998, Boston. The authors wish to acknowledge the generous funding provided by the Van Ameringen Foundation, which made this research possible. The continuation of this research is being supported by the Research Advisory Board of the International Psychoanalytical Association. The authors want to acknowledge the valuable contribution of Audrey Siegel, Richard Lasky, and Marvin Hurvich from the IPTAR Research Committee; Steven Ellman, Reuben Margolis, and Peter Meiland for statistical consultation; and Annette DeMichele for thoughtful editorial work.

dominated by managed care, but also in terms of our own satisfaction as practicing analysts and our investment in the morale of the next generation of analysts. And yet, the history of analytically oriented outcome research has been a varied one. It is not possible to offer here an adequate review of outcome research relevant to psychoanalysis or psychoanalytic therapy. The interested reader is referred to excellent comprehensive reviews by Bachrach et al. (1991), Doidge (1997), and Kantrowitz (1997). Here we will only sketch out some selected historical highlights.

The historical beginnings of systematic psychoanalytic research can be found in Fenichel's statistical report (1930) on the therapeutic activities of the Berlin Psychoanalytic Institute from 1920 to 1930. Not only were there impressively high rates of substantially improved and cured patients, but the very definition of cure reflected the optimism of the era. Cure was seen in the "strictest" terms, and results included not only symptom relief, but completely rational and understandable character changes that were identified retrospectively.

Fenichel's work set the stage for the systematic evaluation of the efficacy of psychoanalysis within the confines of a given institute. Decades later in the United States, beginning in the 1950s and 1960s, we find the projects of the Columbia University Psychoanalytic Clinic, the Boston Psychoanalytic Institute, and the New York Psychoanalytic Institute (Bachrach et al. 1991, Doidge 1997). These studies were based predominantly on the work of analytic candidates. Moreover, they were based largely on clinic records, and while in some instances patient ratings or independent ratings of the clinical record were used, these studies relied most heavily on the treating analysts' judgment. These projects reported treatment effects on substantial samples of patients and yielded impressive improvement rates, from 60 to 90 percent (Bachrach et al. 1991). However, there were serious methodological limitations inherent in these studies, as recently summarized by Kantrowitz (1997).

The field of treatment evaluation was shaken in the 1950s by the very critical report of Eysenck (1952). This virulent attack has since been effectively refuted (Doidge 1997), but the impact of Eysenck's challenge led to a new wave of methodologically sophisticated research. From the late 1950s onward, two efforts stand out.

First was a project at the University of Chicago culminating in the volume *Psychotherapy and Personality Change* (Rogers and Dymond 1954). Indeed, this study remains an exemplar of systematic treatment research based on a known population, a common theoretical framework, a known set of interventions, specification of independent and control conditions, and a host of innovative evaluative methods including wire recordings of sessions, independent coding of process, application of the Q-sort method, and evaluation of outcome at termination as well as at post-termination follow-up points.

The seminal study of more specifically psychoanalytic treatments during this period was the comprehensive evaluation of both psychoanalysis and psychoanalytic psychotherapy at the Menninger Clinic. It too resulted in a host of novel and imaginative methods of assessment, and an extensive literature has emerged from it. Highlights of its findings were presented in Wallerstein's *Forty-two Lives in Treatment* (1986).

Both the Chicago and the Menninger projects were guided by the belief that every bit of good process is also a good outcome. Such studies led to a wealth of new assessment procedures—PERT (Gill and Hoffman 1982), FRAMES (Dahl 1988), CCRT (Luborsky and Crits-Christoph 1990), and Referential Activity (Bucci 1997), to cite just a few—with each method reflecting a belief as to what matters most in effective treatment. This work has crystallized in the ongoing efforts of the Collaborative Analytic Multisite Project (CAMP), headed by Wallerstein, which sets itself the task of applying multiple process measures to a common database of audiorecorded analytic sessions. In addition, decades of work have culminated in Luborsky's current efforts to apply the CCRT and other methods of coding text to more than fifteen recorded and completed psychoanalyses, with the outcome of each case evaluated using the Health-Sickness Ratio as a measure of change (Luborsky, personal communication).

What is largely missing from these evaluations is the study of the role of conditions of treatment exposure as an independent source of variance. If we reject the notion of random assignment of cases to treatment or no treatment (as is the practice in psychopharmacological research that relies on a placebo vs. active drug comparison), then we must find some other condition that captures variation in treatment intensity.

Duration and session frequency are obvious conditions crucial to analytic work.

Systematic observations on the quantitative aspects, length and intensity of treatment exposure, have been relatively sparse. The studies from the Columbia, Boston, and New York Institutes consistently report better treatment outcomes for patients in psychoanalysis with greater treatment lengths. The greater efficacy rates for patients treated with analysis, as against those for psychotherapy, may reflect a relationship between session frequency and outcome. However, because the two groups also differ systematically in analyzability and in form of treatment, it is difficult to assess the relative impact of intensity of treatment exposure as against that of subject differences or form of treatment proffered.

Howard et al. (1986), in their introduction of the "dosage" model, made an important methodological advance. The concept of treatment dose has also been examined by Kächele in Germany. Howard initially reported a twenty-six-session optimal dose effect and a plateau thereafter. A later, more rigorous study from the same research group noted an optimal psychotherapy effect at fifty-eight sessions (Kopta et al. 1994). Congruent findings of a duration effect for patients with personality disorders in dynamic psychotherapy lasting up to one year were reported by Hogland (1993) in Norway; this effect was also noted two years and four after termination. A major objective of the present report is to corroborate these findings of a "duration" effect and to go beyond them.

More recently, a new round of outcome research has been undertaken in Europe, giving rise to studies with particular bearing on the evaluation of the impact of session frequency. A stellar effort is the Stockholm Psychotherapy and Psychoanalysis Project (Sandell 1996; Sandell, Bromberg, and Lazar 1999), which relies on methodology never before used. The researchers studied large groups of patients in psychoanalysis conducted four or five times per week, or in once-or twice-a-week psychotherapy. Patients were evaluated at various points in treatment, at termination, and at post-termination, using objective assessments (SCL-90, Scale of the Sense of Self-Cohesion, and a scale of social adaptation). Comparisons were made with a "normative" control population. Results indicated that in both treatment groups there was a similar reduction in symptomatology. Differences did emerge after successive follow-ups. At three years post-termination, there was a substantial relationship between treatment dose (both duration and frequency) and outcome.

Congruent findings have been obtained by Target and Fonagy (1994) in a retrospective study conducted at the Anna Freud Centre, as well as by Heinicke and Ramsey-Klee (1986), but these studies deal exclusively with child and adolescent patients. To our knowledge, only the Swedish studies provide persuasive support for the role of session frequency in the treatment of adults.[2] This issue frames the second major objective of the present paper.

Outcome research has a Rashomon quality, in that it can be viewed from several perspectives: that of the analyst observer, that of the independent researcher, and that of the patient's direct experience. Much previous work has focused on the first two. Now attention must be given to the patient as consumer, satisfied or not. Does the patient feel that therapy or analysis has made a difference in his or her life?

This is the notion of effectiveness, as distinct from efficacy, as proposed by Seligman (1995). This effectiveness model has injected a new perspective into outcome research and, with it, the direct participation of the patient as a unique source of evaluation. This approach found application in the recent *Consumer Reports* study (Seligman 1995, 1996) a nationwide survey in which forty-two hundred respondents who had received some form of individual psychotherapy completed a questionnaire about their

---

[2] It may be added that projects similar to the Swedish studies are under way in countries that have the benefit of national health insurance and that provide a context that makes such research possible. We in the United States, with the emphasis on privatization and the impact of managed care, are not as fortunate; here the burden falls on individual psychoanalytic societies. IPTAR, the Institute for Psychoanalytic Training and Research, has allocated its resources to create a section that pursues a comprehensive program of research encompassing three spheres of empirical investigation: (1) outcome studies of the effectiveness of psychoanalytic psychotherapy; (2) studies of the therapy process; and (3) studies of recorded psychoanalyses. The present paper is the first in a series reporting this research.

treatment experience. Not only was the rate of satisfaction high, but there was a progressive increment with length of treatment exposure. We shall build on this report.

We were fortunate to receive from *Consumer Reports* not only the items of their questionnaire, but their scoring methodology (M. Kotkin, personal communication). What is presented here is in part a replication of the *Consumer Reports* study on a new, independently drawn sample of patients. Moreover, in this study all patients were treated with specifically psychoanalytic psychotherapy by therapists with analytic training. Going beyond a replication effort, we will treat the data in a manner specifically responsive to issues of special concern to psychoanalysts and to patients in psychoanalytic treatment.

In addition, we have a methodological advantage over the *Consumer Reports* study in that we are dealing with a known population from a single clinical center, with a known group of therapists, all with similar analytic training. Because we are in a position to compare the attributes of responders to those of the clinic population overall, we can evaluate a treatment modality within a single psychoanalytic community, as did Rogers and Dymond over four decades ago.

It is in this context that we present an empirical study of treatment outcome. It is an effectiveness study that relies on patients' perceptions of their mental health during and after psychoanalytic psychotherapy. Our approach was guided by a series of questions: (1) What is the impact of treatment exposure (i.e., duration) on treatment outcome? (2) What is the impact of session frequency on treatment outcome? (3) What is the role of both duration and frequency on the evolving treatment relationship? (4) Is there an interaction among clinical syndrome, duration, frequency, and outcome?

## Treatment Setting, Patients, and Research Methodology

### Treatment Setting

The research was conducted under the auspices of the IPTAR Clinical Center (ICC), a component of the IPTAR Society. The ICC was established in 1993 to serve a population that is in need but cannot afford ongoing psychological services. It is a community-oriented mental health center whose goal is to maintain the treatment of every patient accepted to its natural completion without regard to financial considerations. Patients are seen in the private offices of clinic therapists or, if necessary, at the IPTAR offices. The ICC is a low-cost facility, and most treatment is paid for out of pocket, without third-party payments. The ICC is a freestanding clinical center whose forty-five therapists are either in training or are members of the IPTAR Society. Under the supervision of IPTAR members, which is provided free, ICC therapists see on average a hundred patients annually in over six thousand hours of psychoanalytic psychotherapy.

### Data Collection

Work on this project began in September 1996. All patients, past and current, were contacted by letter and asked to participate in a study of the effectiveness of the psychotherapy they had received at the ICC. They completed the Effectiveness Questionnaire (EQ), which was adapted from the questionnaire used in the national sample by *Consumer Reports* (1995). Two hundred forty questionnaires were sent out and 99 returned, a rate of 41 percent. This return rate should be evaluated in light of the fact that (1) we followed *Consumer Reports* procedures and (2) ICC therapists were not involved in the data collection and did nothing to encourage compliance. Within that context, 41 percent is a satisfactory rate of return; Seligman (1995) reports a return rate of only 13 percent for the *Consumer Reports* study.

All aspects of our study were designed not to intrude on the privacy of the treatment relationship. The IPTAR Research Committee notified the therapists of the intent of the project, but they played no part in implementing patient compliance. Recall Validation, described below, begins only *after* the patient has terminated, thus yielding "retrospective reconstructions" of what has happened in the course of therapy.

### Sample Description

The sample for this study was drawn from the total patient population of the Clinical Center. Comparisons were made between the demographic profile of the clinic patient census for 1996. Clinic samples are presented in Tables 1A and 1B.

*Table 1A: Demographic Characteristics: Research Sample and Clinic Population*

|  |  | N=99 Sample |  | 1996 Clinic Statistics |
|---|---|---|---|---|
| Gender | Female | 67% |  | 69% |
|  | Male | 33% |  | 31% |
| Age | <35 | 63% | <2 | 2% |
|  | 35–44 | 20% | 13–19 | 1% |
|  | 45–54 | 14% | 20–29 | 41% |
|  | 55–64 | 2% | 30–39 | 36% |
|  | >65 | 1% | >50 | 7% |
| Marital | Single | 74% |  | 72% |
|  | Divorced | 13% |  | 9% |
|  | Married | 11.7% |  | 17.8% |
|  | Widowed | 1.3% |  |  |
| Education |  |  |  |  |
|  | HS | 5.2% |  | 7% |
|  | in College | 16.9% |  | 15% |
|  | BA/BS | 18.2% |  | 32% |
|  | Grad Schl | 29.2% |  | 32% |
|  | Post-MA | 22.1% |  | 25% |
| Primary Language |  |  |  |  |
|  | English | 75.3% |  | 77% |
|  | Spanish | 3.9% |  | 10% |
|  | French | 2.6% |  |  |
|  | Other | 3.9% |  | 13% |
|  | Unspecified | 14.3% |  |  |

Ethnicity

|  | | | |
|---|---|---|---|
| | White | 58.4% | 65% |
| | Afr. Amer. | 13% | 14% |
| | Hispanic | 7% | 10% |
| | Asian | 5.2% | 7% |
| | Unspecified | 16.4% | 4% |
| Medication | | (27.4%) | (31%) |
| | Antidepressants | 15 patients | 25 patients |
| | Antianxiety | 5 | 2 |
| | Mood Stabilizer | 0 | 2 |
| | Antipsychotic | 1 | 1 |

*Table 1B: Demographic Characteristics: Research Sample and Clinic Population*

|  | N=99 Sample | 1996 Clinic Statistics |
|---|---|---|
| Previous Treatment | | |
| | 66% | 40% |
| Previously Hospitalized | | |
| | 8% | 4% |
| Frequency of Sessions | | |
| 1/week | 55% | 52% |
| 2/week | 32% | 38% |
| 3/week | 8% | 8% |
| 4/week | 2% | — |
| missing | 3% | 2% |
| | | |
| Duration of Treatment | | 1997 Data |
| <1 month | 1.1% | 3.5% |
| 1–3 months | 6.4% | 15% |
| 4–6 months | 13.8% | 6% |

| | | |
|---|---|---|
| 7–11 months | 19.1% | 10.5% |
| 1–2 years | 38.2% | 30.5% |
| 2+ years | 21.3% | 34% |

Diagnostic Features at Intake

| | | |
|---|---|---|
| Depressive Reaction | 58.2% | 3.5% |
| Anxiety Reaction | 16.9% | 15% |
| Personality Disorder | 11.7% | 6% |
| Adjustment Reaction | 3.9% | 10.5% |
| Schizophrenia | 2.6% | 30.5% |
| Bipolar Disorder | 1.3% | 34% |
| Eating Disorder | 1.3% | 34% |
| Somatoform Disorder | 1.3% | 34% |
| Substance Related | 1.3% | 34% |
| Unspecified | 1.2% | 34% |

The demographic data for the Responder Group, our research sample (n=99) can be seen in Tables 1A and 1B. There are considerable similarities between the 1996 clinical center sample and the research sample. The demographic profile from the research sample reveals that it, too, was predominantly female, young (under thirty-five), single, college-educated, and English-speaking. Duration of treatment exposure ranged from one month to over two years, with 38 percent in treatment for from one to two years and 21 percent over two years. Again, similar to the total patient population, 55 percent of the sample is being seen once a week, with 32 percent going twice and 8 percent three times. Diagnostically, too, the sample is similar to the overall patient population. Initial diagnostic impressions include dysthymic reactions, anxiety reactions, and adjustment and personality disorders, as well as substance abuse problems and, in small numbers, more severe pathology. Twenty-eight percent of Responder Group patients were on psychopharmacological medication, largely antidepressants.

### Instruments

The Effectiveness Questionnaire (EQ) consists of twenty-eight items asking patients in simple language to identify the problems that brought them into treatment; qualities of the treatment setting (frequency and duration); attitudes toward their therapist; and perceptions of the outcome of their treatment. The EQ is a shortened version of the questionnaire developed by *Consumer Reports* and is used with their permission and their scoring system.

### Measures

Measures for several variables were used to evaluate patients' responses.

*Effectiveness Score (ES).* The major outcome variable is the Effectiveness Score (see Table 2). This score comprises three parts, each derived from separate questions on the EQ, and is identical to the outcome measure used by *Consumer Reports.* The first part is *specific improvement,* how much the treatment helped the respondent with "the problems that led me to therapy." The six-point scale was transformed into a 0–100 scale, with "made things a lot better" as 100, "somewhat better" as 80, etc. This measure is also known as Focal Symptomatic Gains. The second part is *satisfaction* with one's therapist. The six-point scale was converted by the same transformation into a 0–100 scale. Third is *global improvement,* how respondents felt at the time of the survey, compared with how they felt when they began treatment. A similar transformation to a 0–100 scale was made by comparing the earlier and later scores. Thus, a person who improved from "very poor" to "very good" would score 100, while a person regressing from "very good" to "very poor" would score 0.

### Table 2: Effectiveness Score and Its Components

The following items are converted to a 100-point scale and added together for a possible 300 points.

1. How much do you feel your therapy helped with the specific problem that led you to therapy?
1 = made things a lot better
2 = made things somewhat better

3 = made no difference
4 = made things somewhat worse
5 = made things a lot worse
6 = not sure

2. Overall, how satisfied are you with your therapist's treatment of your problems?
1 = completely satisfied
2 = very satisfied
3 = fairly well satisfied
4 = somewhat dissatisfied
5 = very dissatisfied
6 = completely dissatisfied

3. Emotional state at beginning of treatment subtracted from current emotional state.
1 = Very poor: I barely manage to deal with things.
2 = Fairly poor: Life usually is pretty tough for me.
3 = So-so: I have my ups and downs.
4 = Quite good: I have no serious complaints.
5 = Very good: Life is much the way I like it to be.

| | |
|---|---|
| Possible points = 300 | Range = 190 |
| Mean = 209 | Minimum = 97.5 |
| Std. Dev. = 42 | Maximum = 287.5 |

The three parts of the score are added together to create the Effectiveness Score, which can range from 0 to 300. For our patient sample, ES scores ranged from 97 to 287, with a mean of 209. Seligman (1995) wrote that the aim of this multivariate measure was to provide a single estimate of effectiveness based on these three items, as it was felt that no single measure of therapy effectiveness would do.

*Adaptive Life Gains.* We developed a second outcome variable from items on the EQ to assess gains in concrete aspects of living. We call this the Index of Adaptive Life Gains.

*Table 3: Prevalence of Patient Concerns and Clinical Syndrome:*
*Factor Analysis*

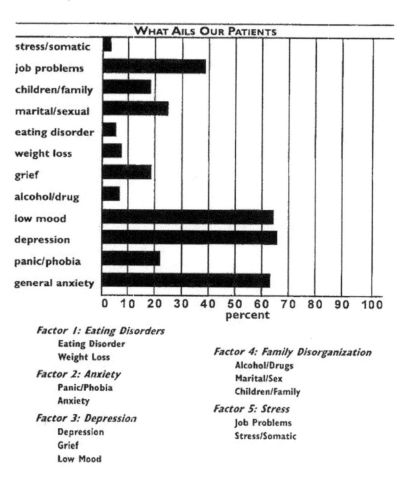

Factor 1: Eating Disorders
   Eating Disorder
   Weight Loss

Factor 2: Anxiety
   Panic/Phobia
   Anxiety

Factor 3: Depression
   Depression
   Grief
   Low Mood

Factor 4: Family Disorganization
   Alcohol/Drugs
   Marital/Sex
   Children/Family

Factor 5: Stress
   Job Problems
   Stress/Somatic

Here a patient rates changes in ability to relate to others; being productive at work; coping with everyday stress; enjoying life more; personal growth and insight; self-esteem and confidence; and alleviating low moods. Each choice could be scored from 1 (made things a lot better) to 5 (made things a lot worse).

*Profile of Clinical Constellations.* In order to describe our treatment sample in terms of clinically meaningful constellations, patients' responses to the first question of the EQ were tabulated. Question 1 asks responders to check any of twelve problems for which they "sought help from [their] therapist." Table 3 shows the distribution of problems checked by our respondents. As can be noted, there is a wide spectrum of concerns and problems identified, with low mood, depression, and anxiety having the greatest frequency.

In order to form clinically meaningful groups from the symptoms checked, we carried out a factor analysis. Using orthogonal rotation, five factors were extracted, and these were labeled based on the cluster of complaints with the highest loading for each. The factors are (1) eating disorders (including weight loss and anorexia and bulimia); (2) anxiety (including general anxiety, panic attacks, and phobias); (3) depression (including depression, frequent low moods, and grief); (4) family disorganization (including alcohol and drug problems, marital or sexual problems, and problems with children or other family members); and (5) stress (including job problems and stress-related problems). Patients were assigned factor scores based on their loading on each of the five factors and were placed in homogenous groups with respect to their highest factor score.[3]

## Relationship Indices (PRI, NRI, ORI)

The relationship indices are calculated from items within the EQ descriptive of patients' perception of and experience with their therapist. These items are different from those used to calculate the ES.

In the Positive Relationship Index (PRI) the patient appraises his or her experience of the therapist as supportive, responsive, empathic, and/or insightful. Items making up this index ask the patient whether the therapist was "easy to confide in," "generally reassuring," etc.

In the Negative Relationship Index (NRI) the patient's critical assessment of the therapist as judgmental, rude, controlling,

---

[3] As should be clear from our description, these clinical groups are based purely on a statistical analysis of questionnaire responses dealing with self-reported presenting complaint, and are not meant to represent diagnoses according to DSM-IV or any other formal diagnostic system.

condescending, defensive, and/or discouraging is described. Here, for example, patients are asked whether the therapist was "too judgmental or controlling," "condescending or rude," etc.

These two indices combined, and weighted equally, create the Optimal Relationship Index (ORI).

## *Effectiveness, Treatment Duration, and Session Frequency*

In the contemporary array of multimodel psychoanalytic perspectives there is a range of presumed psychic experiences that unfold during psychotherapy. We may ask, to paraphrase a current title, "What do therapists really want?" (Sandler and Dreher 1996). The answer is to facilitate the reworking of pathological compromise formations, to help find a good or good-enough object, to define boundaries and recognize defenses, to provide a stable frame of safety for the development of a cohesive self, to arrive at insight, to recognize that symptoms are symbols, and to create a sense of meaning in the context of a therapeutic relationship. Each of these diverse modes of therapeutic action requires time and sustained treatment exposure if it is to be effective, and herein lies part of the common ground of all psychoanalytic psychotherapies (Wallerstein 1992).

The issue of treatment duration and session frequency is not simply a matter of clinical theory, economics, or social reality, but is a crucial consideration in the evaluation of the process itself. It introduces the notion of incremental treatment effectiveness. It deals not simply with "before and after," or "treatment versus no treatment," but instead with how much more effort yields how much more result. Because time and intensity have particular methodological implications, we would reject a study that introduces a "wait" or "no treatment" control condition. We would also be critical of a design that assigns patients randomly to two treatment conditions, say minimal or maximal frequency, because random assignment introduces an element of artificiality by ignoring the fact that duration and frequency are choices that emerge out of clinical considerations negotiated within the therapeutic couple. It is our view (along with Seligman 1995) that such choices are integral to the therapeutic process and therefore cannot be decided extraneously without distorting the treatment method. Instead, we favor examination of the issue of time and frequency within an ongoing treatment setting, with minimal intrusion of research demands on the clinical process.

Thus, the ideal method for studying the cumulative effect of duration and frequency on treatment effectiveness would involve a naturalistic, open-ended clinical setting in which one can observe patients at various points in treatment. Such observations can be quite systematic: one can evaluate successive groups of patients having varying levels of treatment exposure, and can conduct follow-up studies in which patients' retrospective appraisal of their terminated treatment can be noted. In our research we follow both paths and ask questions concerning the effects of duration and frequency, and the combined effects of both on outcome.

### Duration

Our evaluation of the impact of duration proceeded in successive phases. The overall impact of treatment exposure was first considered, and then specific time periods in the course of therapy. It was possible to study different treatment durations because patients who responded to the questionnaire had been in treatment for varying lengths of time, ranging from those just beginning therapy to others who had been in treatment for over two years. Patients were thus assigned to groups based on whether they had been in therapy for less than one month, one to six months, seven to eleven months, one to two years, or over two years. Our choice of these treatment increments was determined by the original *Consumer Reports* study.

The overall impact of treatment exposure on effectiveness was noted by a correlation of .28(p<.005), indicating increasing Effectiveness Scores with increasing treatment durations from one month to over thirty-two months. Next we delineated the impact of varying lengths of time in treatment on Effectiveness Scores: first six months, then seven to eleven months, then twelve to twenty-four months, and finally twenty-five months and beyond. The results are depicted in Table 4. Using Analysis of Variance (ANOVA), a procedure for assessing the statistical significance of differences between multiple groups, we found that these duration increments differed significantly. Multiple-range tests yielded the following differential treatment effects: mean Effectiveness Scores for patients receiving up to six months of psychotherapy compared with patients receiving seven to eleven months revealed no significant differences between the groups; however, significant differences were found in mean Effectiveness Scores between patients receiving up to six months of psychotherapy and twelve to twenty-four months and then again for patients receiving up to six months and over twenty-five months.

*Table 4: Time in Treatment and Mean Effectiveness Score: Analysis of Variance (N=86)*

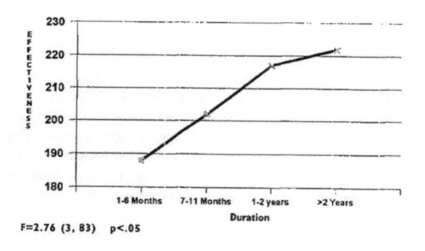

F=2.76 (3, 83)   p<.05

*Table 5: Frequency and Mean Effectiveness Score: Analysis of Variance (N=84)*

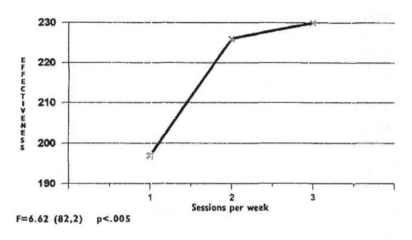

F=6.62 (82,2)   p<.005

These findings of the relationship between duration of treatment and patients' perception of an effective clinical course are consistent with the hypothesis of an incremental treatment effect. It is also a finding of Seligman's earlier report and thus constitutes a replication of that study, now on an independently drawn sample of patients. All other analyses of data in this study go beyond the Seligman report and are directly inspired by specific concerns raised in the appraisal of psychoanalytic psychotherapy.

*Session Frequency.* What is the impact of session frequency regardless of duration? In Table 5 we note mean Effectiveness Scores for patients receiving varying levels of treatment frequency. The Effectiveness Scores respectively are: for once per week (195.3), twice per week (225.4), and three times per week (230.4). Analysis of variance showed these groups to differ significantly (F=6.62; p<.005). Further, multiple-range tests demonstrated significant differences between once-a-week sessions compared to both twice and three times a week, but not between two and three sessions weekly.

To test the limit of the impact of session frequency on Effectiveness Scores, the focus is on patients who have had a meaningful treatment exposure, here defined as a duration of seven months or more. An identical analysis of variance was carried out. Mean Effectiveness Scores for once, twice, and thrice weekly sessions for patients in treatment seven months or longer paralleled the effect noted in the sample as a whole (F=5.10; p<.01). The choice of the restricted range of treatment exposure was guided by clinical reasons, in that the first six months are often a turbulent period with more frequent dropouts, whereas after seven months the treatment relationship tends to become more stable. Findings support the idea that under these more stable conditions added frequency yields incremental gain. Thus, we can conclude that increased sessions make a difference, a finding with specific relevance to psychoanalytic psychotherapy.

## Joint Effect of Frequency and Duration

To further assess the relation of treatment parameters to outcome we used linear multiple regression, which allowed us to construct a model using frequency and duration together as predictors of effectiveness. We found the combined predictive power of frequency and duration to be quite significant (F=6.71; p<.005). Further, by partialing out the linear relation between duration and frequency, we determined that these variables account for separate portions of the variance in effectiveness. Thus, we can conclude that in the sample as a whole, frequency and duration contribute to outcome in qualitatively different ways.

## Duration, Frequency, and Quality of Effectiveness

In order to complete the analysis of a potential incremental trajectory, qualities of the patient's perception of clinical change were examined. It will be recalled that the Effectiveness Score has three components: specific improvement (how much the treatment helped with the problem that led the patient to therapy); satisfaction with the therapist's treatment of the problem; and global improvement (how respondents felt at the time of the survey compared to when they began treatment).

Duration was not significantly related to global improvement or to symptomatic gain, but there was a significant relationship between

216

duration and the patient's satisfaction with the therapist's treatment of his/her problems (F=2.42; p<.05). In contrast, frequency was significantly related to specific symptomatic gain (F=5.05; p<.01) and to satisfaction with the treatment received (F=4.29; p<.05). Once more we find that duration and frequency are associated with distinct aspects of effectiveness.

## Final Note

The finding of a substantial relationship between treatment conditions and Effectiveness Scores supports the hypothesis that the experience of a sustained therapeutic presence has an incremental impact on the patient's experience of clinical improvement. This is supported further by the observations of patients in treatment beyond seven months. At that point a stable treatment frame had been established, and added session frequency appeared to augment effectiveness. In addition, there is a linear progression in patients' description of their therapist's helpfulness up to thirty-two months of treatment. This last observation introduces the facilitating role of the treatment relationship in perceived effectiveness—a topic we turn to next.

## The Treatment Relationship: Promise and Challenge

The effect of objective treatment conditions has been our organizing variable as we traced the impact of frequency and duration on the patient's perception of effectiveness. Our findings support the notion that, in general, more intensity yields greater gain. However, we would now like to look at the situation from a psychoanalytic perspective. Treatment conditions and the act of attending sessions are in a sense physical facts. But they also create a psychological reality; they create the possibility for the experience of an object relationship. As analysts we hold that an object relationship, if it is to be therapeutic, has to be internalized.

A variety of otherwise divergent analytic perspectives share the view that the patient's affective involvement in treatment facilitates effectiveness. Such involvement is mediated through specific forms of investment in the relationship with the therapist, whether this is conceptualized in terms of transference, the real relationship, or points in between. Clinical phenomena bearing on such issues as therapeutic alliance, treatment relationship, and the patient's experience of the therapist have been identified as crucial conditions favoring a positive treatment response (see, e.g., Orlinsky and Howard 1986). More recently, Luborsky (1996) listed the therapeutic alliance and its correlates as a principal factor in successful outcome. We hope next to confirm the idea that the experienced treatment relationship is important in facilitating a positive clinical response. We will take the additional step of studying the quality of the treatment relationship, as a facilitating condition, and its influence on treatment outcome regardless of frequency and duration—that is, as an independent source of variance.

## Empirical Observations

The Positive Relationship Index (PRI), the Negative Relationship Index (NRI), and the Optimal Relationship Index (ORI) are our principal relationship indices. Each of these indices revealed substantial correlations with overall effectiveness: PRI ($r=.56$; $p<.001$); NRI ($r=.26$; $p<.01$); ORI ($r=.47$; $p<.001$). As the PRI is the most robust of these correlations, it is used as our primary indicator of the therapeutic relationship. Thus, we found the patient's experience of a positive relationship with the therapist to be significantly correlated with effectiveness, indicating that patients who most experience their therapist as reassuring, supportive, and insightful are also those most likely to report positive outcomes.

More crucial for our purposes is to determine whether the PRI contributes to outcome independently of our two other predictor variables, duration and frequency. For this purpose we used multiple regression analysis to predict effectiveness.

We constructed a model to predict effectiveness from duration, frequency, and the quality of the therapeutic relationship. Two variables, frequency and PRI, were found to be highly significant predictors of effectiveness ($F=23.11$; $p<.0001$), and to account for over a third of the variance in effectiveness ($R2=.36$). In our model, both frequency and

PRI were statistically significant; duration was not. The data also indicate that frequency and the therapeutic relationship are independent sources of variance in effectiveness, a finding that further supports the idea that frequency and duration (and its correlate, the treatment relationship) are related to qualitatively different aspects of therapeutic outcome.

## A Matter of Interpretation

The findings reported above point to the strong connection between duration of treatment and the quality of the treatment relationship as it shapes outcome. Further, session frequency may now be seen as an independent source of therapeutic gain, and the cumulative impact of frequency and positive therapeutic relationship becomes a powerful predictor of treatment outcome.

It has been our belief that increased therapeutic exposure (frequency and duration) contributes to the experience of greater affective intensity in treatment, and that such intensity facilitates a perception of the therapist as optimally responsive to the patient. Further, we believe these conditions to be particularly important because of their role in facilitating a process of internalization that in turn supports the development of a relatively enduring internal relationship with the supportive and growth-enhancing aspects of the therapist.

However, several alternative arguments should be considered. First, it could be argued that instead of the positive treatment relationship functioning as a vehicle of therapeutic change in its own right, it merely indicates positive feelings that may have facilitated a patient's compliance with other treatment conditions that themselves function as agents of change. For example, one could argue that specific therapeutic interventions make the difference once patients are induced to stay in treatment by positive feelings for the therapist. While different from our view—that psychic change takes place through a process of internalization—this view would be consistent with Freud's early view of the role of the unobjectionable positive transference (1912), which brings about the successful result in psychoanalysis, largely by providing the incentive for the patient to work analytically toward the achievement of insight. Others have widened this idea, with concepts such as the "working alliance" (Greenson 1967) and "analytic trust" (Ellman 1991), to include, as aspects of the optimal positive relationship, conditions that the patient might need simply for the analytic relationship to be tolerable. Once these conditions are met, it is the various interventions aimed at insight or integration or other such goals that are ultimately mutative. In our view, this is one possible interpretation of the data, and while it shifts the emphasis somewhat as regards the function of the therapeutic relationship, it does not dispute the importance of an optimal treatment relation as a condition of therapeutic change.

A second argument against our interpretation of the data is more problematic, namely, that what we have observed is merely the effect of "cognitive dissonance" (Festinger 1957). Simply put, it could be asserted that the idea that one has changed, the belief that one's therapist is benevolent and supportive, and the awareness that one has spent considerable time and expense in therapy are cognitively consistent with one another. To avoid an experience of internal dissonance, patients who have spent much time in treatment will tend to construct for themselves ideas about the relative benefits of therapy and the good qualities of their therapist. These perceptions then serve to justify actions the patient has taken, rather than reflect anything more meaningful about what has actually transpired in treatment or how it has helped. Clearly, this is an argument that undercuts the very rationale of this study, namely, that patients' subjective perception about their treatment is a useful indicator of its effectiveness.

In our view, the complexity of our data may well challenge the cognitive dissonance argument. When patients evaluate their treatment as effective, we believe, changes have indeed taken place in their life, changes that can be attributed to what was offered during the treatment. This is not an easy thing to show. Yet several aspects of our study might constitute a response to the cognitive dissonance hypothesis: namely, the complex interactions between frequency, duration, and, as we will show, patients' clinical syndrome and perceived outcome.

The notion of cognitive dissonance assumes a singular motivation for the perception of improvement: the need for consistency between actions and attitudes. In challenging this view, we look for conditions of differential response; i.e., we look to see whether the treatment conditions of frequency and duration are related to differential patterns of treatment response. Indeed, we are now ready to consider revising our earlier statement, that more input or effort yields more results, because our analysis indicates that frequency and duration serve different functions. Along these lines we now ask two additional questions:

1. Is it not true that selective and differential responsiveness due to patient characteristics challenges the cognitive dissonance hypothesis? If patients with different clinical constellations respond more to one treatment condition than to another, then surely something other than dissonance avoidance must be taking place.

2. If there are differential observations of effectiveness anchored outside the clinical situation and elaborated in specific detail, would not the thesis of cognitive dissonance then be qualified? Thus, under conditions of post-termination recall, if a patient can specify positive and negative events in his or her life and relate these to particular aspects of the treatment, would this not also challenge the dissonance hypothesis? Indeed such a finding might prove relevant to our hypothesis of an internalization process at work in effective psychotherapy. Preliminary observations on these two questions are sketched out below.

## Effectiveness, Treatment Conditions, and Clinical Syndrome: An Exploratory Study

We now turn to an exploration of the selective impact of treatment conditions on effectiveness when the patient sample is divided according to clinical syndrome. Having established that duration and frequency are significantly related to the perceived effectiveness of treatment outcome, our attention naturally turns to whether this is true across clinical groups.[4]

---

[4] Because of the size of our current sample (n=99), this analysis is merely preliminary and exploratory; rigorous testing of our hypothesis of variable treatment effects according to clinical syndrome requires a discriminant function analysis. Such an analysis

### Identifying Clinical Conditions

As noted earlier, five factors were created from patients' responses to Question 1 of the Effectiveness Questionnaire: (1) eating disorders (including weight loss and anorexia and bulimia); (2) anxiety (including general anxiety, panic attacks, and phobias); (3) depression (including depression, frequent low moods, and grief); (4) family disorganization (including alcohol and drug problems, marital or sexual problems, and problems with children or other family members); and (5) stress (including job problems and stress-related problems).

## Evaluating the Selective Role of the Clinical Syndrome

To reexamine the impact of frequency and duration on distinct clinical constellations, the correlation between effectiveness, frequency, and duration was computed for each of the five factor groups. As indicated by Table 6, correlations between treatment conditions and effectiveness begin to suggest certain trends when clinical groups are considered separately.

*Table 6: Relationship between Frequency, Duration, and Effectiveness by Clinical Syndrome*

| Effect by Factor | Frequency | Duration |
|---|---|---|
| Overall | r=.29*** | r=.28*** |
| 1. Eating Disorders | r=.51* | r=.09 |
| 2. Anxiety | r=.57** | r=.14 |
| 3. Depression | r=.25 | r=.22 |
| 4. Family Disorganization | r=.17 | r=.44* |
| 5. Stress | r=.07 | r=.49** |
| | *=p<.05; | **=p<.01; ***=p<.005 |

awaits a larger sample size in order to reach a significant distribution of subjects into groups.

Significance is reached only for patients in the anxiety factor group (r=.57; p<.006) and those in the eating disorder factor group (r=.51; p<.03) when correlated with increasing number of sessions. That is, as intensity of treatment increases, individuals who are in these groups experience more effective treatment outcomes. Specifically, we can say that when patients describe themselves as primarily anxious or concerned about eating disorders, higher frequency of sessions is associated with greater treatment effectiveness; whereas among patients having comparable syndromes who receive lower session frequency, the same positive treatment response is not found.

Similarly, duration was found to be selectively correlated with effectiveness, depending on the clinical group. Here significant correlations are found between duration and effectiveness for patients in the family disorganization group (r=.44; p<.04) and the stress group (r=.49; p<.01). That is, patients in these two groups who receive longer treatment duration (regardless of session frequency) perceive their therapy as more effective. Thus, increased exposure to psychoanalytic psychotherapy over time increases perception of treatment effectiveness in these groups.

In summary, four of the five clinical groups appear to show a selective response to the two parameters of treatment condition (i.e., duration and frequency). These preliminary observations are consistent with the notion that when the clinical syndrome is one of acute disturbance, frequency (i.e., higher intensity of contact) is more salient; and that when the clinical syndrome is more chronic, increased time spent in treatment seems more influential

These findings confront us with an additional surprising observation: no significant relationship between either frequency or duration and effectiveness was found when subjects in the depression group are considered separately. Yet depression, as an individual complaint, was the most prevalent symptom. This most puzzling outcome of our research effort provoked further inquiry.

## Grief Depression and Anxious Depression

These findings led to a closer examination of the depression factor. To be included in the depression group, patients had to have checked depression, grief, and low mood on the symptom checklist. This group included only sixteen patients. Yet sixty of the total ninety-nine respondents had checked depression as a major reason for coming to treatment. Thus, the depression group did not include forty-four patients who nonetheless were troubled by depression. Inspection of these forty-four indicated that they had checked both low mood and depression (accompanied by other symptoms, notably anxiety), but not grief. On the basis of our data, then, it made both empirical and clinical sense to recognize a second group of depressed patients, which we have called the Anxious Depression Cluster. Thus, we identified two depression syndromes: *depression with grief* (n=16) and *depression with anxiety* (n=22).

With these two groups identified, the relationship of each to duration and frequency could be studied. But as patients in the two groups differ in the symptoms checked, it is also likely that they differ in the way they respond to treatment or how they recognize change in their symptomatology. Until this point, outcome had been measured by the ES. Now we moved to measure outcome in a somewhat different manner. We compared one component of the ES, Specific Improvement, where patients indicate the extent to which they were helped with the specific symptom that brought them to treatment, and the new outcome variable, Adaptive Life Gains, where patients assess the extent to which concrete aspects of their life have been changed. Now the issue of the differential impact of duration and frequency on the perceived effectiveness of the treatment of those with depressive affect could be studied anew.

The results are presented in Table 7. This table presents a pattern of correlations: by clinical group (anxious depressed/depression with grief), by clinical condition (frequency/duration), and quality of clinical outcome (Focal Symptomatic Gains/Adaptive Life Gains).

*Table 7: Anxious Depression and Grief Depression: Correlations between Treatment Conditions, Symptomatic Improvement, and Adaptive Life Gains*

Anxious Depression

|  | Frequency | Duration |
| --- | --- | --- |
| Focal Symptomatic Gains | .39* | .35 |
| Adaptive Life Gains | −.32 | −.52** |

Grief/Depression

|  | Frequency | Duration |
| --- | --- | --- |
| Focal Symptomatic Gains | .13 | .08 |
| Adaptive Life Gains | −.23 | −.51* |

*=p<.05;

**=p<.01; ***=p<.005

When perceived change is measured by Focal Symptomatic Gains, the two groups differed, with the anxious depressed group tending to show a positive response to both duration and frequency, and the grief depression group not. In other words, when asked to assess the effectiveness of their treatment in bringing about changes in the particular symptom of depression, the anxious depressed group measured themselves as having received more help than did the grief with depression group. However, when outcome was assessed by Adaptive Life Gains, patients in both groups showed a response to duration but not to frequency. In the grief depression group, for the first time, we saw that duration of treatment is strongly related to perceived effectiveness of treatment, now measured by changes in their life situation.

We seem to be dealing with two constellations of depression. One group, the anxious depressed, can name and recognize changes in their symptomatology (i.e., can symbolize their distress) and can benefit from increased treatment exposure. The other, the depression with grief group, though unable to recognize symptomatic change, does acknowledge changes in their lives brought about by treatment over an extended period of time (duration).

The effect of psychoactive medication was studied for its effects on both depression groups and on the sample as a whole. Through the use of partial correlation, we determined that for all cases the previously reported findings on the impact of duration and frequency on clinical syndrome were not altered when the role of psychopharmacological treatment was partialed out.

## Perspectives on Clinical Validity

We now wish to provide clinical validity to what up to now have been statistically reliable findings. Through qualitative interviews conducted after termination, we hope to illustrate how the patients experienced their treatment, and its impact on the quality of their life and on their current state of emotional health. To this end we shall briefly describe our method of "recall validation."

This method was guided by two additional objectives. The first is to give clinical validity to the concept of effectiveness (Seligman 1995, 1996), the idea that a perceived alteration within the patient's life situation has indeed taken place. The second is more exploratory; we wish to discover some of the mediating conditions that account for the perceived treatment effects. The focus is on the internalization of the events of therapy, on the therapist as a person, and on the therapeutic process. In general, we hold that this is a method of retrospective reconstruction of therapy that provides a fruitful database for the identification of mediating mechanisms.

The centerpiece of recall validation is an audio-recorded interview of therapy remembered. The interview includes an associative narrative, patient description of the affective quality of the treatment relationship, salient events during treatment, dreams recalled, and an assessment of current life situation. This hour-long interview is supplemented by selected objective indices of internalization, therapeutic alliance, reflective functioning, attachment, and major symptom clusters.

This endeavor to develop an archive of therapy remembered is the next phase of our research. So far eight patients have participated in the recall study. They represent a range of EQ scores and afford us an opportunity to obtain an account of just how therapy is represented after termination. In order to give the reader an impression of the qualities of the therapy experienced, we present selected material and clinical observations from two patients participating in this phase of the study.

## Two Pathways toward Internalization: Ms. A and Ms. B

Ms. A came to treatment with symptoms of depression and low mood, and concerns over her weight and job situation. During the treatment, which lasted approximately two years, Ms. A came two and three times a week. She had an EQ score of 255 (in the High Effectiveness range).

When she began treatment, Ms. A felt depressed and suicidal and said that she needed "extensive therapy" to make changes in her life. Her organization of the world had a decidedly sadomasochistic quality: "I got shit every day. I was a hard-core punk kid with a chip on my shoulder." The severity of her superego can be inferred from her statement that "prior to therapy everything was always my fault. I always blamed myself." Ms. A had a very strong emotional connection to her therapist, whom she saw as warm, kindly, strong, and nonjudgmental. "She took criticism really well. She didn't flinch. I could say anything and be anything and I felt she would accept me. I feel better about myself. It was scary to feel so dependent on this stranger. She was like a lifeline."

The paradoxical statement expressed by Ms. A, that she does not think about her therapist but at the same time her therapist is not someone she does not think about reflects the internalizations that had been proffered in treatment. From a psychoanalytic perspective the paradox is transparent: I do not think about my therapist on a conscious level because she is available to me on an unconscious level. Ms. A's capacity to feel good, happy, and productive about her life—her self-representation—is directly related to this object representation that is with her always and is experienced as an understanding inner voice that has helped her have "different expectations. I have a right to expect people to treat me well." Throughout the interview Ms. A talked about how her therapist opened a whole new world for her. Ms. A was more able to see things from the perspective of another and had an increased capacity to view self- and object representations from multiple perspectives. In structural terms this represents an advance in the ego and a shift in experienced reality. The changes in Ms. A's life have been profound. "I feel happy. I'm not depressed anymore. Now I can tolerate being alone."

Ms. B came to treatment with symptoms of depression, sexual concerns and job problems. She came once a week for less than two years and noted improvements in Adaptive Life Gains (concrete aspects of her life) but did not recognize changes in her depression. She did say that friends said she was less depressed. Ms. B's EQ score of 202.5 is an average score.

Ms. B began treatment because she felt depressed and said she wanted to be able to put her emotions into words. Ms. B did not talk about her therapist very much, and when she did it was in terms of a distance she experienced between them. Words did not feel like they had "healing" power. She felt tense and uncomfortable and told her therapist that she should have toy blocks. Clearly words could not be used to convey this woman's emotional state, nor could they, when used by the therapist, be used by Ms. B as sources of communication about the nature of self- and object representations. Ms. B spoke about her therapist in physically descriptive terms—the color of her hair and clothes, her tone of voice, body weight, how she looked sitting in the chair, the color of her shoes, and how attractive she was. In short, Ms. B's organization of the world was skewed toward the world of perception and appearances. She could not free herself from the preoedipal world of perception and move into the more mature world of conception. Why then did she stay in therapy for nearly two years? We believe it was because the therapeutic situation provided a much-needed structure. It was not the intensity of the relationship but its continuity—the sense of coming and going, the temporal quality of the relationship.

Ms. B told us that there was something indefinable about the therapeutic relationship that was helpful. She sometimes left sessions feeling more alive, more connected to her body, and better able to put her feelings into words. Her friends said she was less depressed. While she agreed, and thought it must be related to her treatment, she could not say how talking with her therapist actually helped. But Ms. B felt better.

These two cases illustrate not only different pathways of clinical change, but also distinct mediating conditions. Supported by our earlier quantitative findings, the retrospective reconstructions presented above allow us to pursue the qualitative dimension of change.

## Concluding Comments

Psychoanalysis as a mode of treatment finds itself today in a constant state of challenge. In the public domain we encounter a continuous barrage of attacks from the media, the pharmacological industry, insurance companies, academics, and, most notably, managed care. Many of these criticisms focus not so much on the effectiveness of treatment as on its *cost* effectiveness, since psychoanalysis demands time and intensity of contact. Yet the notion of sustained exposure, the intensive interchange in a two-person encounter, is an essential ingredient that lies at the heart of all the psychoanalytic psychotherapies—regardless of particular theoretical persuasion.

Our empirical observations, viewed in the context of new and cumulative knowledge, provide a direct response to these criticisms. Admittedly, there are many sources of therapeutic gain other than those defined by sheer exposure to treatment. But these quantitative considerations, time and frequency, have come under ever sharper scrutiny. Early systematic clinical studies have already pointed in that direction. Now, metaanalytic studies have shown an optimal dose effect up to twelve months, much beyond that acknowledged most often by managed care. Further, our present data reveal a positive incremental effect up to thirty-two months of treatment. As to session frequency, studies in England and Scandinavia have indicated that increased session frequency exerts a persistent and even long-term impact on patients' mental health. Our observations confirm that this is so and move beyond these studies, demonstrating that increased session frequency has a specifiable and differential impact on perceived effectiveness of psychotherapy. With increased duration over the first three years, and with increased sessions per week, there were notable gains in patients' perception of their psychological well-being.

Finally, there is the persuasive criterion of effectiveness as a guide to treatment outcome. It involves the patient as consumer, judging that his or her life situation has been altered in a positive direction. This criterion has to be viewed within the burgeoning literature of empirical psychoanalytic research. The method of retrospective reconstruction may serve to elucidate the clinical conditions that mediate outcome. In the study of recorded analyses we are increasingly in a position to identify the events in sessions that define an optimal psychoanalytic process. But it is the study of effectiveness that enables us to determine that quality of life has been enhanced and, further, that duration and frequency contribute to this end. Our empirical findings, together with those in the evolving literature, establish this as a clinical fact.

## References

Bachrach, H. M., Galatzer-Levy, R., Skolnikoff, A. & Waldron, S., Jr. (1991). On the efficacy of Psychoanalysis. *Journal of the American Psychoanalytic Association,* 39:871–916.

Bucci, W. (1997). *Psychoanalysis and cognitive science: A multiple code theory.* New York: Guilford Press.

Consumer Reports (1995). *Mental health: Does therapy help?* November, pp. 734–739.

Dahl, H. (1988). Frames of mind. In H. Dahl, H. Kächele & H. Thomä (Eds.), *Psychoanalytic process research strategies* (pp. 51-66). New York: Springer-Verlag.

Doidge, N. (1997). Empirical evidence for the efficacy of psychoanalytic psychotherapies and psychoanalysis: An overview. *Psychoanalytic Inquiry,* (suppl.):102–150.

Ellman, S. (1991). *Freud's technique papers.* Northvale, NJ: Jason Aronson.

Eysenck, H. J. (1952). The effects of psychotherapy: An evaluation. *Journal of Consulting Psychology,* 16:319–323.

Fenichel, O. (1930). Statistisher Bericht uber die therapeutische Tatigkeit 1920–1930. In *Zehn Jahre Berliner Psychoanalytische Institut* (pp.13-19). Vienna: International Psychoanalytische Verla.

Festinger, L. (1957). *A theory of cognitive dissonance.* Evanston, IL: Row, Peterson.

Freud, S. (1912). The dynamics of transference. *Standard Edition,* 12:97–108.

Gill, M. M. & Hoffman, I. Z. (1982). A method for studying the analysis of aspects of the patient's experience of the relationship in psychoanalysis and psychotherapy. *Journal of the American Psychoanalytic Association,* 30:137–167.

Greenson, R. R. (1967). *The technique and practice of psychoanalysis: Vol. I.* New York: International Universities Press.

Heinicke, C. M. & Ramsey-Klee, D. M. (1986). Outcome of child psychotherapy as a function of frequency of session. *Journal of the American Academy Child Psychiatry,* 25:247–253.

Hogland, P. (1993). Personality disorders and long-term outcome after brief dynamic psychotherapy. *Journal of Personality Disorders,* 7:168–181.

Howard, K., Kopta, S., Krause, M. & Orlinsky, D. (1986). The dose-effect relationship in psychotherapy. *American Psychologist,* 41:159–164.

Kächele, H. (1994). Remarks on the relationship of frequency and length of treatment of psychoanalytic psychotherapy. *Forschung Psychoanalytische,* 10:252–255.

Kantrowitz, J. L. (1997). A brief review of psychoanalytic outcome research. *Psychoanalytic Inquiry,* (suppl.):87–101.

Kopta, S. M., Howard, K. I., Lowry, J. L. & Beutler, L. E. (1994). Patterns of symptomatic recovery in psychotherapy. *Journal of Consulting and Clinical Psychology,* 62:1009–1016.

Luborsky, L. (1996). Theories of cure in psychoanalytic psychotherapies and the evidence for them. *Psychoanalytic Inquiry,* 16:257–264.

———& Crits-Christoph, P. (1990). *Understanding transference: The core conflictual relationship theme method.* New York: Basic Books.

Main, M. & Goldwyn, R. (1990). Adult attachment rating and classification system. In M. Main (Ed.), *A typology of human attachment organization assessed in discourse, drawings, and interviews.* New York: Cambridge University Press.

Orlinsky, D. E. & Howard, K. I. (1986). Process and outcome in psycho-therapy. In S. L. Garfield & A. E. Berger (Eds.), *Handbook of psychotherapy and behavioral change* (3rd ed.). New York: Wiley.

Rogers, C. & Dymond, R. F. (1954). *Psychotherapy and personality change.* Chicago: University of Chicago Press.

Sandell, R. (1996). Long-term effects of psychotherapy and psychoanalysis. Paper presented to the Deutsche Psychoanalytische Vereinigung, Wiesbaden, November.

———Blomberg, J. & Lazar, A. (1999). Time matters: Long-term follow-up of psychoanalysis and long-term psychotherapy. Paper presented to American Psychological Association, Division 39 (Psychoanalysis), New York City, April.

Sandler, J. & Dreher, A. U. (1996). *What do psychoanalysts want?* London: Routledge.

Seligman, M. E. P. (1995). The effectiveness of psychotherapy: The Consumer Reports study. *American Psychologist,* 50:965–974.

———(1996). A creditable beginning. *American Psychologist,* 51:1086–1087.

Target, M. & Fonagy, P. (1994). The efficacy of psychoanalysis for children: Prediction of outcome in a developmental context. *Journal of the American Academy of Child and Adolescent Psychiatry,* 33:1134–1144.

Wallerstein, R. (1986). *Forty-two lives in treatment: A study of psychoanalysis and psychotherapy.* New York: Guilford Press.

———(1992). *The common ground of psychoanalysis.* Northvale, NJ: Jason Aronson.

# CHAPTER 10

# Psychoanalytic Treatment and Patients' Lives

## Reflections on "Psychoanalytic Treatment and Patients' Lives"

*Anthony Mazzella*

In his paper, "Psychoanalytic Treatment and Patients' Lives," Dr. Frosch gives us an overview of an exploratory, empirically based, psychoanalytically informed child outcome study. For about three years I worked closely with Allan as part of the research team (also including Joseph Cancelmo, Rena Greenblatt, Laura Kleinerman, Maribeth Rourke, and Elizabeth Tingley) on data collection, analysis and the presentation of findings of this study to psychoanalytic colleagues. The primary goal of his paper, which preceded the actual implementation of the study described, was to explore the effectiveness of child psychotherapy treatment. I would like to demonstrate, however, that Allan's interest did not stop there. If treatment was found to be effective, Allan wanted to explain "how" and "why" this happened. It was true that we used well established standardized measures to closely understand how parents felt about themselves as parents and how they saw and thought about their children. It was also true that the research method was based on a time-series design that could demonstrate change by comparing the baseline and follow-up data. This, however, would not explain *how* change occurred.

Closer examination of Allan's paper reveals that he was grappling with how to understand and articulate the mutative effects of treatment. Allan initially considered the idea of incremental gain over time as an inherent part of the psychoanalytic process. He then talks about the need to establish more "adaptive compromise formations" to determine if change was correlated with gains or losses in the child's school work or object relations. He goes on to consider the effect of "transformations in the transference/countertransference matrix as it evolves over the course of treatment" because he wants to better understand the impact of the therapeutic relationship. Finally, he discloses his wish to create a scale to measure symbolization/desymbolization processes. This line of thinking, I believe, brought him closer to what may have been his real interest at this time; it had to do with the extent to which the therapist could maintain a "symbolized or more secondary-process orientation" and when necessary, to be able to "regress with the patient" and remain reliable and consistent, surviving the patient's desymbolized moments and experiences" (p. 72 ).

Implicit in this model was Allan's belief that if the parent/therapist can use his interest or "love" (as he calls it in his 2003 paper on the Analytic Relationship) to enter into the child's/patient's mind, this is what produces change. When he presented our final research results, he told us that "how we think of the other effects how the other thinks about him/herself." In fact, much to Allan's delight, one of our major findings suggested that as parents' perceptions of themselves shifted from anxious to less anxious, their perception of their child's internal state also shifted; and they saw their child as complaining less and as less anxious, depressed and withdrawn. Since these two factors were found to be strongly correlated, another way to understand this relationship is that a shift in the child over the course of treatment led to changes in the parents' perception of themselves and their children. No matter how we tend to interpret it, I imagine that Allan would say that it is important to survive the patient's/child's desymbolized moments and experiences and maintain an "emotional involvement" (2003, p. 608). During this period it seems to me that Allan was thinking that this kind of involvement, this "love" for the patient, was the key to a successful analysis.

# Psychoanalytic Treatment and Patients' Lives

## Allan Frosch

The present study is best understood in the context of our comprehensive research program at IPTAR and in the context of the IPTAR Clinical Center (ICC) where the study will actually take place. The overall thrust of IPTAR'S research program is a concern with the place of psychoanalytic treatment as this may shape patients' lives. Does psychoanalytic treatment leave its mark not only during treatment but after termination as well? Does treatment affect mental health in the narrow sense but also in the quality of a person's life many years after treatment? With IPTAR'S new Child Therapy program we expect to see more and more children at the ICC. Therefore the important research questions initially posed with our adult patients have now been formulated with regard to our child and adolescent population of patients. The research that I will discuss has been conceptualized by the Child Research team (Cancelmo, Frosch, Greenblatt, Kleinerman & Rourke, Coordinator Hushion and statistician E. Greenblatt). The design of the study as well as its day-to-day implementation is the responsibility of the research team. The IPA grant proposal which we submitted in February and the paper I am presenting today are the products of our collaborative efforts.

This is an empirical study of treatment outcome in children and adolescents. Simply put: we want to know if what we do benefits the child. Does treatment work? If it does, then can we say how? This is a psychoanalytically informed child therapy outcome study that is designed to view the child from a variety of perspectives using a number of measures that have previously been used in outcome research with children as well as adults. In this initial project we are interested in replicating previous findings of child therapy outcome research. Our overarching goal is to create a database whereby we can begin to extend some of the work of our research colleagues. In the present study we make an initial foray in that direction by modifying the Effectiveness Questionnaire which was used so successfully in our adult research

(Freedman, et al., 1999) to tap into the patient's experience of psychoanalytic psychotherapy. In our study we look at 1) the differential effects of frequency and duration; 2) sketch out the temporal dimensions of treatment; 3) consider outcome from a variety of perspectives; 4) obtain post-termination measures as well as recall validation interviews; 5) create a data base that can be used to look at different aspects of the therapeutic process with children; 6) Integrate process and outcome variables in the context of incremental gain. In terms of process we pay particular attention to the transference/countertransference matrix and its transformations over time.

Before going into the details of our work let me give you a little background of child research and some of the important issues that are relevant in all psychotherapy research whether we are looking at children or adults.

In a 1999 IPA review of psychoanalytic outcome studies, over eighty studies were reported and slightly less than 10% were child studies. While there is clearly a paucity of data concerning the effectiveness of psychoanalytically informed psychotherapy with children, the data that has been gathered indicates that frequency and duration are related in complex ways to outcome and these effects seem to extend beyond the termination phase (Fonagy & Target, 1996).

Any discussion of outcome studies immediately raises the question of what we mean by outcome. Is it a score on a personality measure, some point along the continuum of a health-sickness scale? Or perhaps it is a measure of how well the person is functioning now as compared to how well he/she functioned before treatment. With children this could mean how well the child does in school, or some measure of social behavior in school or at home. If all of this seems simple enough let me complicate it for a moment by referring to the results of our adult study where we found some patients who said that they felt the same, but friends and family thought the patient was functioning better. With a little imagination we can see how wonderfully complicated this could be with children. Most children typically say there is nothing wrong to begin with so where do you go from there. A teacher might say the child is actually doing better in school but the parents might say that little Susie has become a holy terror at home. The therapist, of course, might say that certain pathological inhibitions have been modified. At the risk of going on ad infinitum I will stop here and say that our approach to outcome is multidimensional. We do not believe that any single measure can give an accurate picture of how a patient has fared in psychotherapy. All measures are value laden and reflect a biased point of view. We emphasize the integration of outcome measures from multiple perspectives, i.e., Family, School, Child, and Researcher/ Clinician.

I will not go into the details of all of the measures we are using. Suffice it to say, however, they are all standardized measures that have been used in child and/or adult research. They range from a projective measure like the draw-a-person test, administered before and after treatment to tap into the child's experience of himself, to the WRAT administered before, at termination, and one year after treatment ends to see how the child is faring academically. Ratings of the child along a health-sickness scale by the therapist and ratings by teachers and parents round out our multidimensional approach to outcome.

I would like to use the time remaining to focus in on a particular approach to the data that in many ways goes to the theoretical heart of our study. I am referring to the notion of incremental gain. On the one hand incremental gain refers to the issue of incremental treatment effectiveness. How much more effort yields how much more gain? Is there a time period where we can not measure any gains in treatment as reflected by our outcome measures? This was certainly the case in our adult study where patients did not begin to show significant effects until after six months of therapy. Similar findings were reported by Fonagy and Target who found that 72% of emotionally disordered children treated for at least six months showed significant improvements (1996, p.119). In the present study we continue the work of delineating the temporal parameters of the treatment process. By taking repeated measures over the duration of treatment we hope to delineate periods of A) no treatment response, B) initial treatment response, C) an ongoing period of therapeutic gain beyond the phase of initial treatment gain. As our research sample grows we will be able to test the hypothesis that duration and frequency of treatment are significant variables affecting the outcome of child psychotherapy. (Our expected N over the next two years, 30 patients, will probably not be sufficient to look at frequency but we can begin to test for the differential effects of duration.)

This approach of marking out the temporal parameters of treatment effectiveness is a way of looking at the notion of incremental gain on a more global or macroscopic way. One can also look at incremental gain on a more microscopic level where subtle shifts in therapy are correlated with changes in a person's life. We would like to be able to document such shifts in therapy. We would also like to be able to get a better understanding of what might be going on in the process of psychotherapy that may be related to these shifts. In a moment or two I will describe what we mean by these shifts in therapy or incremental gains and how they may show up in a child's life. And then I will tell you about our approach to studying the therapeutic process. But first let me make a more theoretical statement about this idea of incremental gain.

Incremental gain at a process and outcome level, and the integration of the two, is an organizing focus of our study. We believe moreover, that it is inherent in a psychoanalytic approach. When we talk about the working through of issues in the transference we are, as we see it, talking about making sometimes subtle shifts in how a patient's defenses are organized in relation to the analyst. If we talk about a shift in compromise formations we are, once again, talking about (sometimes) subtle shifts between wishes and defenses that can tip the compromise formation toward a more adaptive position (Brenner, 1982). For a more concrete example of incremental gain let me describe a situation that anyone who has worked with children will probably be familiar with. A patient likes to play cards with the therapist but cannot tolerate losing. He may throw the cards all over the room or refuse to leave until he can win. If this same child can lose a game of cards to his/her therapist without feeling humiliated and can begin to take more chances academically by making an effort to do well in school we can, from a psychoanalytic perspective, think that the two events are related. If we wish to think in terms of structure we can look at the child's risk-taking behavior as a structural change. Structure is as structure does (Friedman) and the child is organizing the world differently. Losing a game of cards or trying hard in class and not being the best may be a disappointment, but it is no longer a humiliation. The quality of this child's life is different.

In the present study we will test these ideas by going through the therapist's chart notes and summaries in an attempt to identify areas where incremental gains (or losses) are observable in the therapeutic work. We want to see whether such shifts are reflected in the child's work (school), social (object relationships), and family areas. We will initially focus on shifts in the patient's affects, cognition, and fantasies. While these areas represent more than reasonable starting points, they are starting points or, hopefully, points of departure. An ongoing goal in the present study is to sensitize the research team to those moments in psychoanalytic therapy with children and adolescents that are not easy to measure but represent incremental shifts in the process between patient and therapist that allows for, as Herzog puts it, 'something to happen.' That something has to do with the availability of the patient's inner world, which can now be presented to the therapist. Here we are outlining an approach to study transformations in the transference/countertransference matrix as it evolves over the course of treatment. We intend to do this in two ways.

## *Relational Index*

In our adult study the patient's perception of the therapist was explored through the Relationship Index. This measure was derived from the Effectiveness Questionnaire (EQ) and we found a significant correlation between the relationship index and positive outcome. We intend to explore the subtleties of the therapeutic relationship from the child's point of view by modifying the Relationship Index so that it will be applicable to children. By taking a reading of this measure at the end of treatment we can get a global picture of the relationship between outcome and the nature of the therapeutic relationship. But this does not really give us an ongoing account of the therapeutic relationship. For that we have developed a very novel approach to how we use the research team.

## Research Team

The research team will explore the therapeutic process by reviewing the therapists' chart notes which are organized to provide at least one narrative of therapist patient interaction. Process variables will be rated along a scale of symbolization/ desymbolization for the therapist as well as the patient. Our assumption is that the more the therapist can maintain a symbolized or more secondary process orientation—the more his/her countertransference falls within workable limits—the more available he/she can be to the patient and the better this will be for the treatment. We do not expect that this will be a nice neat and clean linear relationship. It is possible, for example, that therapists who are able to regress with the patient and then recover can provide a certain kind of therapeutic milieu that is particularly conducive to therapeutic gains with some patients but, perhaps not with others. Here we are dealing with an issue of survival as Winnicott articulated it. Can the therapist remain a reliable object in the face of the patient's desymbolized experience? Or perhaps we could ask whether the patient can maintain a secondary process orientation in the face of the therapist's more desymbolized (i.e., regressed) experience.

In this very brief overview of our research project I hope I have conveyed some of the excitement and optimism that we think this project generates. At the beginning of this discussion I mentioned that we submitted a grant proposal to the IPA. It was funded in July of this year. This money, along with a very generous contribution from the ICC, allows us to project our research efforts into the future. What this means of course is that we can do the kind of research with children and adolescents who are seen in psychoanalytically informed psychotherapy that really has never been done before. The mission of the ICC allows us to see all our patients until treatment reaches some natural conclusion. In other words: children can remain in multiple session long term treatment as long as is necessary. We can provide the kind of treatment that seems to produce the greatest gain. We also have the potential to create a data base with children and adolescents that can be used to investigate the cumulative effects of frequency and duration on outcome, as well as many other aspects of the treatment process. This is consistent with the overall philosophy of the IPTAR research program.

## References

Brenner, C. (1982). The concept of the superego: A reformulation. *Psychoanalytic Quarterly*, 51:501-525.

Fonagy, P. & Target, M. (1996). Playing with reality: II. The development of psychic reality from a theoretical perspective. *International Journal of Psychoanalysis*, 77:459-479.

Freedman, N., Hoffenberg, J., Vorus, N. & Frosch, A. (1999). The effectiveness of psychoanalytic therapy: The role of treatment duration, frequency of sessions and the therapeutic relationship. *Journal of the American Psychoanalytic Association*, 47:741-772.

# CHAPTER 11

# The Effect of Frequency and Duration on Psychoanalytic Outcome: A Moment in Time

## Reflections on "The Effect of Frequency and Duration on Psychoanalytic Outcome: A Moment in Time"

*Phyllis F. Hopkins*

In this important paper, Frosch, with characteristic humility, suggests that he is only reviewing landmark psychoanalytic frequency and duration outcome research from a subjective perspective prevalent "at a moment in time." I would like to suggest, however, that the paper speaks to the reader at a deeper and more broadly timeless level about issues that are at the very heart of our ongoing psychoanalytic discourse. Frosch focuses on the nature of psychoanalysis. He addresses the implications of a more open-systems view of transference and the internalization of the analyst after treatment ends as the theoretical underpinning for more intensive treatment. He speculates about the crucial import that even small perturbations in any one aspect of analytic process has upon the entire process. Further, Frosch shows himself to be a nuanced theoretical guide who by transparently sharing his own open, inclusive and admittedly subjective thinking about one seemingly circumscribed issue subtly draws his reader into more thoughtful, complex considerations about issues and values at the very core of our field. In this article, as in life, Frosch reveals and draws the reader into an open-systems perspective rather than just intellectually describing it.

Frosch emphasizes Loewald's seminal paper "On the Therapeutic Action of Psychoanalysis" as a basis for reflection on questions of duration and frequency. He emphasizes that as psychoanalysis has moved to a more open-systems model (with its more egalitarian view of the analyst-analysand dyad), one result has been an expanded view of transference which today is less frequently viewed as ending when patient and analyst cease meeting for daily sessions or when the analysand has resolved the transference in favor of a more abstract identification with "an analytic function." Rather, from a more open-systems perspective, long after the dyad no longer meets, the analyst may be viewed as continuing to play a significant role in the patient's internal world. This is qualitatively different from identification with an abstract function. Frosch suggests that it may be the patient's internalization of the "integrative experience" with the analyst as a "soothing and helpful inner presence" that is most important. This is a beautiful example of Frosch's capacity to offer a seemingly small distinction that is anything but small. Understanding this subtle point can make a world of difference in how we view our role in psychoanalysis. This paper highlights the potential we have for becoming an abiding presence in the inner worlds of our patients over the many years of a psychoanalysis.

Frosch is transparent in acknowledging that it is his own subjective experience on both sides of the couch, as well as the research he has reviewed, that leads him to the conclusion that it is more intense treatment (3–5 times a week with open duration) that is optimal for most patients. He goes on to suggest that the crisis confronting psychoanalysis in 2011 (and perhaps even more so in 2018) is that analysts so often lack this conviction. In his interest in understanding what leads to lasting internalizations, Frosch's emphasis on the importance of the analytic relationship (and the role of frequency and duration in establishing it) helps analysts confront their own reluctance to recommend more intensive treatment to their patients.

In his concluding remarks, Frosch creatively turns to Lorenz's "butterfly effect" to suggest that even very small differences or perturbations in any complex physical system will have enormous consequences elsewhere in the system. What seem like minor changes in even one circumscribed area of psychoanalysis (such as frequency or duration) will have far-reaching impact across psychoanalysis for generations. Frosch notes that analysts trained in the context of high-intensity work, including their control work but especially their own training analysis, show the greatest conviction about the desirability of conducting high-intensity work, whenever possible. Today, even more so than in 2011, there is growing interest across the International Psychoanalytic Association in a shift to at least greater flexibility toward lower frequency control work and training analysis than in the past. Frosch suggests that while we don't know for sure what the impact of such changes would be, we do know that there will be a lasting impact. As we consider these weighty issues, we could have no better internalized guide for our deliberations than Allan Frosch.

\*　　\*　　\*

# The Effect of Frequency and Duration on Psychoanalytic Outcome: A Moment in Time

*Allan Frosch[1]*

> *The stuff of the world is mind-stuff.*
> *A. S. Eddington, 1928*

History is shaped by politics, and this is certainly true for the history of psychoanalysis. Theoretical and organizational schisms have led to heated debate about what psychoanalysis is, the "best" way to practice it, and the exclusion of those who do not do it the "right" way (cf. Perron, 2002). These issues are particularly important in a paper on session frequency and duration and their relation to outcome. For many of us this topic has a very visceral, or "in-your-face" quality. My institutional affiliations and experience from both sides of the couch, as well as my own research on frequency/duration and outcome (see Freedman, Hoffenberg, Vorus & Frosch, 1999), lead me to believe that the combination of high frequency and longer duration (open-ended) treatment is the most effective form of psychoanalysis. My gathering together of "facts" in this paper is always embedded in this subjective context. This threatens to politicize a topic that is difficult enough in its own right.

In recent years there has been a veritable avalanche of psychoanalytic outcome research (Fonagy, 2002). To approach a paper on session frequency/duration and outcome feels quite overwhelming, even without the ever-present "political issues." On an organizational level my task in writing this paper was made easier because I had access to George Frank's (2011) excellent paper in this issue. I am happy to use his general organization—(1) What is psychoanalysis? (2) The resolution of the transference and its effect on our thinking about session frequency (and

---

[1] I thank Alan Barnett and his anonymous reviewers at *The Psychoanalytic Review* for their very helpful input following the submission of this paper. I also want to thank Batya Monder and Ruth Oscharoff for their valuable suggestions during preparation of this paper.

duration), and (3) The inconclusiveness of outcome research—as a basis for developing my ideas about psychoanalytic outcome research.

## What is Psychoanalysis?

In this paper psychoanalysis refers to a therapeutic process conducted by someone who has formal training in psychoanalysis and understands and attends to the notion of a dynamic unconscious, transference, countertransference, and resistance[2] and, as George Frank notes, takes into account the goals of psychoanalysis, which are different from those of other treatments. A psychoanalytic treatment, said Freud, "is not undertaken for the purpose of getting rid of a single symptom. Its aim is the refashioning and reeducation of the entire person" (cited by Fichtner, 2008, p. 841). I view frequency and duration in the context of determining the optimal psychoanalytic treatment, rather than defining characteristics of the process itself. From this perspective psychoanalysis is seen along a continuum (Rothstein, Arden, 2010), and rather than making a distinction between psychoanalysis and psychoanalytic psychotherapy, which is characteristic for psychoanalytic outcome research, I will refer to more intense and less intense forms of psychoanalysis.[3] "More intense" refers to a frequency of three to five times per week and a duration that is open ended and measured in years.

## Resolution of the Transference

In her book *The Analyst's Analyst Within,* Laura Tessman (2003) takes a close look at the fate of the transference in the internalization of the analytic

---

[2] It is understood that these concepts have different meanings, both theoretically and clinically, depending on the training model and philosophy of the particular analytic institute.

[3] Not all the studies I will discuss can make the claim that treatment was done by people with formal analytic training. This was one of the "confounding variables" in the Sandell et al. (2000) study. We can view this as interfering with the so called conclusiveness of the work or, as I prefer to see it, as highlighting the importance of who the analyst is and what he or she brings to the analysis.

process. In the chapter on analysis ending and unending, Tessman asks what happens when the analysis, "the carrier of extraordinary intimacy," ends—how does the "actuality of the analyst infuse the after experience" (p. 223)? In talking about the analysis as an extraordinarily intimate experience and the actuality of the analyst (who the analyst is and what he or she brings to the analytic situation), Tessman is beginning to highlight some of the differences between open and closed systems. I believe that psychoanalysis has evolved from the model of a (relatively) closed to an open system. The shift in emphasis from a closed to an open system is at the heart of Hans Loewald's (1960) seminal paper on the therapeutic action of psychoanalysis. It is a shift that has a profound effect on how we understand the resolution of the transference, and how we understand the research on frequency and duration.

## Closed and Open Systems: Description, Evolution, and Implications for the Fate of the Analyst

A closed system is one that is isolated from its surrounding environment. The term often refers to an idealized system in which closure is perfect. In reality no system can be completely closed; there are only varying degrees of closure (see Web definitions of closed systems, for example, en.wikipedia.org/wiki/Closed_systems). In contrast to closed systems, which have relatively "hard boundaries through which little information is exchanged," open systems have "porous boundaries" with ongoing feedback (quoted from the Field Guide to Consulting and Organizational Development, at authenticityconsulting.com). Working from the model of a closed system, the analyst's instrumentality is emphasized. That is to say, transference is seen as a fantasy-laden distortion of reality, and the analyst, like a surgeon extirpating a tumor, reaches into the system (i.e., the patient's mind) and corrects these distortions via interpretations. In a closed system the analyst's availability "is seen in terms of his being a screen or mirror onto which the patient projects his transferences, and which reflects them back to him in the form of interpretations. In this view, at the ideal termination point of the analysis no further transference occurs, no projections are thrown on the mirror; the mirror, having nothing now to reflect, can be discarded" (Loewald, 1960, p. 18). This point of view can be traced back to Freud's (1917) proclamation that at the end of an analysis we must "dissect" the transference "in all the shapes in which it appears" (p. 453).

It is worth mentioning, of course, that Freud never advocated dissecting the positive transference, what he called the unobjectionable positive transference. Since transference was so closely related to suggestion, Freud's rather absolute statement is best understood as a political statement designed to differentiate psychoanalysis from the "demon of suggestion" (Levy & Inderbitzin, 2000, p. 839) inherent in hypnosis. Under the rigid orthodoxy of psychoanalysis in this country (cf. Smith, 2007, p. 1050), during the first half of the twentieth century Freud's hyperbole became established fact. The analyst was situated outside the patient's world and acted as a mirror reflecting the patient's unconscious. When the patient's fantasy-laden constructions of the analyst were rectified via interpretations, the analyst could be discarded, "like a piece of shit" (Lacan, 1959, cited by Tessman, 2003, p. 224). The patient was expected to identify with an "analytic function" (i.e., self-analytic function/self-reflection). This identification with a part object was the compromise in a closed system.

In contrast to closed systems where the analyst is not seen as an integral part of the patient's world, in an open system "transference wishes . . . are already altered by the particular *affective presence* of the analyst. . . . the analyst in his or her reality is positioned differently in the transference and at termination" (Tessman, 2003, p. 224, emphasis added). As Martin Bergmann (1988) noted, "What we need to aim at, is not to resolve the transference neurosis but to make sure that it forms a productive inner structure in the life of the former analysand" (p. 151). In an open system the analyst is an actor on the stage of transference (Loewald, 1960), and in a successful analysis the analyst continues to play a role in the patient's internal world that is qualitatively different from the identification with an analytic function.

For Hans Loewald (1960),

. . . the "resolution of the transference" at the termination of an analysis means resolution of the transference neurosis, . . . [and] this includes the recognition of the limited nature of any human relationship and of the specific limitations of the patient-analyst relationship. But the new object-relationship with the analyst, which *is gradually built in the course of the analysis* and constitutes the real relationship between patient and analyst, and which serves as a focal point for the establishment of healthier object-relations in the patient's "real" life, is not devoid of transference ... to the extent to which the patient develops a "positive transference" (not in the sense of transference as resistance, but in the sense of that "transference" which carries the whole process of an analysis) he keeps this potentiality of a new object-relationship alive through all the various stages of resistance. This meaning of positive transference tends to be discredited in modern analytic writing and teaching, although not in treatment itself. (p. 32, emphasis added)[4]

For Loewald (1960), it is the patient's *"internalization of a longed for integrative experience"* (p. 26, emphasis added) that is necessary for the resumption of structural changes (or ego development). In this context it is important to note that Loewald is referring to the internalization of the interaction-process, not simply the internalization of an object (p. 30). And it is a process that takes place in the emotional context of the analyst's love and respect for the patient. "This love and respect represent that counterpart in 'reality,' in interaction with which the organization and reorganization of ego and psychic apparatus take place" (p. 20). In other words, the analyst's love and respect for the patient is the necessary emotional context that allows for meaningful interpretations of the patient's regressive longings vis-à-vis the analyst. For Loewald the internalization of the analytic interaction always refers to an interaction with a differentiated other so that insight (an-*other* way of looking at things) in the context of an emotional relationship is internalized by the patient. Although the term

---

[4] I would add that the attempt to discredit positive transference is a remnant of our adherence to a closed system and a more linear view of the world where the elimination of our subjectivity is associated with an increased ability to view a "reality" that exists independent of the analysis.

"internalization" is used differently in the various studies that I discuss, I believe Loewald's approach provides a common denominator.[5] (This is particularly clear in the Falkenstrom et al. study (2007), where the internalization of insight and self-soothing aspects of the analytic relationship are spelled out by the authors.) From a "Loewaldian" perspective, in order to help the patient achieve this internalization of an integrative experience, "the analyst must be in tune with the patient's productions, that is, he must be able to regress within himself to the level of organization on which the patient is stuck . . . a regression against which there is resistance in the analyst as well as in the patient" (p. 6). In talking about the analyst's resistance, Loewald exemplifies the idea of the reciprocity ("porous boundaries") of an open system.

I think these comments about the resolution of the transference highlight George Frank's reading of Freud's movement from identifying the transference, to the analyst and analysand working on it in the treatment: " . . . resolving transference is inherently difficult, and, hence, is done *in vivo,* that is, in an analysis of the relationship with the analyst (as opposed to talking about these issues in an intellectual manner ...) [and this] make[s] the case for psychoanalytic treatment necessitating frequent sessions per week" (p. 1-10). I also believe that the "working through" of transference fantasies (along with the analyst's attention to his or her countertransference fantasies) in the "heat of the moment" can provide a theoretical basis for more intense treatment. It brings to mind Charlotte Schwartz's (2003) emphasis on frequency as necessary to establish "the coordinates whereby it is possible to gain access to unconscious material more consistently and in greater depth" (p. 182). I think we can add to this that high-intensity treatment can also help the analyst know himself or herself (e.g., the resistance to regress), which is necessary for a successful "resolution" of the transference.

## Introduction to "Formal" Research

In his paper on session frequency in this issue, George Frank (2011) argues that research on the effect of frequency of sessions is inconclusive

---

[5] It is in this sense that I am using "internalization" throughout this paper.

(p. 1-10). This is a reasonable interpretation of the outcome research. I would add, however, that any notion that our research efforts should be conclusive falls into an idealization of science, where conclusiveness is equated with certainty and truth.

The idea that research is decisive and studies are routinely replicated is part of a fantasy that defends against the uncomfortable fact that we live in a world of uncertainty. The world is an open system where boundaries are porous and variables are constantly interacting. Small differences, or "small" perturbations, can have very large effects. This is true for psychoanalytic research as well as research in the "hard sciences" (Leuzinger-Bohleber & Burgin, 2003, p. 9). In my opinion, however, there is a clear pattern of meaning that has emerged from our psychoanalytic outcome research. I say "pattern of meaning" because I believe twenty-first century ("postmodern") science has moved away from the idealized notion of linear cause-and-effect relationships (or absolute truth) promised by logical positivism with its reliance on the deification of numbers (see Faber, 1999a, 1999b; see also Kelley, 2009). In attempting to understand the general features of a system, we are trying to discern (i.e., to come to know or recognize mentally) patterns of meaning (impressions, trends) in the global system of outcome research. We do this by looking at data from the different components of the system, or different levels of observation.

In any complex system, like the global system of psychoanalytic outcome research, we would expect variability on a "local level," that is, between individual studies, as well as variability on a "micro level," for example, differences in quantitative and qualitative findings in the same study (Leuzinger-Bohleber, Stuhrast, Rüger & Beute, 2003; see especially p. 270). Over time, however, and with enough observations, we would also expect to be able to describe an evolving pattern of meaning that characterizes the global system of psychoanalytic research *at a particular point in time.* In other words, the pattern of meaning is not static. Its "shape" is dependent on input from the various levels of observation that constitute the components of the system. In this paper the different levels of observation, the components in the overall system of outcome research, are input from (1) quantitative research—particularly large scale studies, (2) qualitative research—clinical case studies or variations on this theme, (3) theoretical research in the form of ideas on the resolution of the transference, and (4) the individual research that each analyst does in his or her practice daily. The researcher's task is the same as the individual analyst's task as she or he is involved in clinical psychoanalysis. It is one of pattern recognition. Can we recognize, that is, construct, a pattern that emerges from the variable nature of the data? To extend the analogy between research and treatment further, I would say that research is always an interpretive process, and just as we embrace pluralism in clinical work, we do the same in our research efforts. There are many ways of generating data and many potential interpretations of the data. My interpretation of the data from these different levels of observation is, to use Irwin Hoffman's (2009) language, an attempt "to make something," to construct a way of thinking about the data that is "in the ballpark in terms of plausibility" (p. 1048). It is a given, therefore, that the notion of an "emergent pattern of meaning" is embedded in a context of subjectivity. This is as true for research as it is for clinical psychoanalysis.

## Overview

An emergent pattern of meaning from outcome research is that for most people in psychoanalysis, high-intensity treatment leads to a better outcome compared to low-intensity treatment. Sometimes the difference between the two groups increases dramatically following termination of treatment (Sandell et al., 2000). An important difference between the two groups seems to be the internalization of the therapeutic relationship that is experienced as a soothing and helpful inner presence (Falkenstrom, Grant, Broberg & Sandell, 2007; Freedman et al., 1999). This is also a finding associated with more successful analyses (Tessman, 2003). Some investigators relate this process of internalization to the duration of treatment, that is, longer duration leads to a greater chance of internalizing the analyst in a way that is helpful well after the analysis ends (Freedman, et al., 1999). Others, however, including Freedman and colleagues, see the *interaction* of frequency and duration as a more powerful variable affecting outcome, including the internalization of this helpful and soothing inner presence (Sandell et al., 2000; Falkenstrom et al., 2007). Differences in results between studies are influenced by differences in research methodology (e.g., outcome measures, time interval between measurements), the treating clinician, and the patient population, as well as cultural differences, where the same or similar measure in different countries can lead to very different results (Judson, 2010; see also: https://www.wired.com/2009/08/ff-placebo-effect)[6]

I would reiterate, however, that once we move toward a "theory of hypercomplexity" (Green, 2003, p. 43), variability is expected. Certainty or conclusive results should not be considered the *sine qua non* of outcome research. The findings that the internalization of the analyst is more likely to occur in high-intensity treatment has come about through a shift in our research paradigm from an emphasis on quantitative research to qualitative research, and from a shift in our theory about the resolution of the transference (as discussed earlier). In addition to the more general arguments against the absolute truth value of quantitative studies, there are a growing number of analysts/analyst-researchers who question whether the measures used in large-scale studies can do justice to psychoanalytic outcome research. Analysts like Leuzinger-Bohleber et al. (2003) consider such measures nonanalytic and place qualitative measures at the heart of their research designs. Other investigators (e.g., Sandell et al., 2000) use qualitative measures to shed light on their quantitative data. A third group of analysts (e.g., Green, 2003; Perron, 2002) view large-scale quantitative studies as peripheral, at best, to psychoanalytic research (see also, Hoffman, 2009). I do not think it makes sense to throw out data from large-scale quantitative studies any more than the methodological issues (see Fonagy, 2002, pp. 22 and 283) rule out case studies as a legitimate source of psychoanalytic data.

In the next section a number of research studies bearing on frequency/duration and outcome are discussed. The studies are, from my subjective position, the major studies on frequency/duration and outcome of psychoanalysis. A more inclusive review and discussion of this area of

---

[6] My thanks to Jonathan Hale for bringing this site to my attention.

research can be found in Fonagy (2002) and in Levy and Ablon (2009). In keeping with Jonathan Shedler's (2010) very important comment about the difficulties in understanding research, even for experienced researchers, a narrative rather than a quantitative approach is used. In addition, an overview is provided at the beginning of each study.

## Major Studies

Freedman, N., Hoffenberg, J. D., Vorus, N. & Frosch, A. (1999). The effectiveness of psychoanalytic psychotherapy: The role of treatment duration, frequency of sessions, and the therapeutic relationship. *Journal of the American Psychoanalytic Association* 47:741–772.

> Increased frequency and duration is positively related to outcome.
> High-intensity psychoanalysis contributes to greater affective intensity
> in treatment and facilitates the internalization of the supportive and
> growth-enhancing aspects of the therapist. This process continues
> post-termination and makes a significant contribution to a positive
> treatment outcome.

In this study patient self-reports of how treatment affected them (Effectiveness Score) were used to measure outcome. The authors report increasing outcome scores with increasing duration; this reached significance at six-plus months. The same was true for session frequency, where the difference in outcome was significant between one and two sessions per week and between one and three sessions per week. The difference between two and three sessions per week was not statistically significant but continued the trend in the direction of a positive relationship between outcome and session frequency. Once again, the "critical time period" was a treatment duration of seven months: "after seven months the treatment relationship tends to become more stable," and, at this point, "frequency of sessions makes a difference" (p. 757). In this regard it is noteworthy that in a recent article Sidney Blatt and his colleagues (Blatt, Zuroff & Hawley, 2009) argue that the establishment early on in the treatment process of a positive therapeutic relationship is a very strong predictor of positive outcome (p. 394).

Freedman et al. go on to say that the *combined predictive power* of frequency and duration was "quite significant," and, in addition, that each of the variables contributes to outcome in "qualitatively different ways" (p. 758, emphasis added). Frequency was related to symptomatic gains (how much the treatment helped with the problem that led the patient to therapy) and global improvement (how respondents felt at the time of the survey compared to when they began treatment). Duration, with its strong association to the Positive Relationship Index (see p. 753 for details of this index), was more related to the patient's satisfaction with the therapist; Freedman, et al. see this as an indicator for the potential internalization of the therapeutic relationship.

The statistical teasing out of the role(s) of frequency and duration is a valuable contribution to our understanding of the psychoanalytic process. It is worth asking, however, if the differential effect of frequency and duration is an iteration of the historical tension between insight versus the therapeutic relationship as the mutative factor in psychoanalysis (Gray, 1988; Schlesinger, 1988) That is to say, since increased frequency is associated with alleviation of symptomatic behavior and global improvement (e.g., "I have no serious complaints," p. 751), it seems reasonable that the changes can be related to new ideas in the form of the analyst's interventions that lead to new ways of constructing the world (i.e., the world of self- and object-representations). But new ways of constructing the world, even if they lead to changes that are objectively beneficial to a person's life, do not necessarily translate into a basic alteration in the essence of how one feels. "I have no serious complaints" is not the same as "I feel secure, comfortable, life is really worth living." This may be another permutation of Herbert Schlesinger's (1988) prescient statement about the "untidy fact" that insight does not always lead to change (p. 19). I think we can add to this that insight that leads to actual change in one's life does not necessarily translate into a more positive (and more profound) internal state. A shift in one's internal state seems more closely related to the patient's satisfaction with the therapist's treatment of his or her problems (p. 758).

Freedman et al. argue that increased therapeutic exposure (frequency and duration) "contributes to the experience of greater affective intensity in treatment, and that such intensity facilitates a perception of the therapist as optimally responsive to the patient. Further, we believe these conditions to be particularly important because of their role in facilitating a process of internalization that in turn supports the development of a relatively enduring internal relationship with the supportive and growth-enhancing aspects of the therapist" (p. 760). It is the patient's exposure to "a sustained therapeutic presence [that] has an incremental impact on his or her *experience* of clinical improvement" (p. 758, emphasis added). This was clearly the case in the two patients who were interviewed post-termination, where high frequency in the context of a positive treatment relationship was most predictive of therapeutic success:

Ms. A. came two and three times a week for approximately two years. During the post-termination interview Ms. A. made the paradoxical statement that she does not think about her therapist, but at the same time her therapist is not someone she does not think about. From a psychoanalytic perspective the paradox is transparent: I do not think about my therapist on a conscious level because she is available to me on an unconscious level. Ms. A.'s capacity to feel good, happy, and productive about her life seemed directly related to the internalization of her therapist, who was experienced as an understanding inner voice that has helped her have different expectations about herself and the world (p. 767).

In contrast to Ms. A., Ms. B. came once a week for nearly two years. She seemed to be doing better in her life in terms of how she related to others, or functioned at work, and was experienced as less depressed by her friends. Ms. B. thought there was something about the treatment that was helpful but she could not say how talking with her therapist helped. In the post-termination interview she did not say much about her therapist, and when she did, it was in terms of a distance she experienced between them. The therapeutic relationship lacked emotional intensity and evidence of internalization. Ms. B. was "objectively" better following her treatment but did not seem to feel very different about herself. The words of the therapist did not feel like they had "healing power" (p. 768). The development of a relatively enduring internal relationship with the supportive and growth-enhancing aspects of the therapist was not present with Ms. B. as it was for Ms. A.

The interview data is consistent with the findings from the quantitative aspect of this study, as well as the theoretical ideas presented earlier about the resolution of the transference. From the point of view of attachment theory Morris Eagle's (2003) ideas provide an excellent fit with the Freedman et al. data as well. From Eagle's perspective, what changes a person's experience of the world is the internalization of the therapist "as a secure base" (p. 27) and this, he argues, is related to frequency and duration (p.28). In Eagle's scenario, self-understanding (insight) leads to better ego functioning, one index of which is self-reflection. Feeling understood by the analyst is the pathway for an alteration of procedural rules, that is, our basic emotional sense of self in the world. Of course, an accurate, well-timed, tactful, and well-phrased interpretation, particularly in the context of a good therapeutic relationship, can contribute both to self-understanding and feeling understood (p. 45n). This is a point that is essential to our understanding of the concept of internalization. In this context I would like to cite Schlesinger (1988) to the effect that it "is difficult, and perhaps impossible, to distinguish the effects of correct interpretation from the effects of a good therapeutic relationship, for they are not separable in practice, and it is questionable if they are even separable in contemporary analytic theory" (p. 17).

How we understand the fate of the analyst post-termination is very much related to the resolution of the transference. If we understand the resolution of the transference from the perspective of a closed system, the remains of the analytic relationship are to be found in an identification with a function of the analyst, for example, a self-reflective/self-analytical function. From the perspective of an open system, it is the internalization of the relationship with the analyst that is emphasized. It is a shift in emphasis that has a profound effect on how we understand psychoanalysis and how we understand the research on frequency and duration.

Sandell, R., Blomberg, J., Lazar, A., Carlsson, J., Broberg, J. & Schubert, J. (2000). Varieties of long-term outcome among patients in psychoanalysis and long-term psychotherapy: A review of findings in the Stockholm Outcome of Psychoanalysis and Psychotherapy Project (Stoppp). *International Journal of Psycho-Analysis*, 81:921–942.

> Increased frequency and duration was associated with positive out-
> come, and the difference between high- and low-intensity groups
> became significant three years post-termination.

The authors found that increasing frequency depended on duration, and
vice versa. Increasing frequency had a negative effect in therapies of
short duration, and increasing duration had a negative effect in low-
frequency therapies. There was, however, an increasingly positive effect
of increasing frequency the longer the duration, or of increasing duration the higher the session frequency. Thus, long durations and high
frequencies, *in conjunction,* were associated with the most benign treatment outcomes on the SCL-90, a widely used quantitative measure in
outcome research (p. 932).

A significant part of the outcome differences between patients in
high-intensity treatment and low-intensity treatment could be explained
by the adoption, in a large group of therapists, of "orthodox psychoanalytic attitudes" that seemed to be counterproductive in the practice of
low-intensity treatment but not so in high-intensity work (p. 921).
Sandell et al. suggest that this effect may be a negative transfer of the
psychoanalytic stance into less-intensive (what they refer to as psychotherapy) practice and that this may be especially pronounced when the
attitudes are not backed up by psychoanalytic training. Another way of
looking at this is that something went wrong in the relationship between
analyst and patient. This is certainly what George Frank suggests, and it
is a position that Rolf Sandell very much moves toward in a recent
article (Sandell, 2009), where he argues that "researchers—and therapists—so far have tended to underestimate the accountability of the
therapist factor" (p. 361). To my way of thinking, this is a movement
away from technique (instrumentation) toward who the analyst is and
how this affects the analytic dyad. It seems clear that the person of the
analyst is very much part of how he or she uses psychoanalytic concepts
and technique (Frosch, 2006; Wilson, 2003).

The unintended contribution of therapist variables to outcome highlights how "context dependent" (Hoffman, 2009) psychoanalytic
research is: We cannot control for all the variables that impact outcome.

Psychoanalytic research is "messy." In any given population of therapist-patient dyads, some people "get better," some don't, and some may get worse (Sandell, 2009). The ambiguity of these terms takes us well off the mark of certainty. As Freedman et al. note, some people may "get better" in terms of functioning, but do not feel much better at all. And, we can add, some people may get better by not getting worse. This messiness should not cast a pejorative shade to research efforts, nor should it stop us from coming up with some plausible reflections on what might be going on. Sandell et al. go on to say that what they call dosage factors (high/low intensity) does account for a proportion of the outcome difference between the groups: Of particular interest was the finding that "these effects became visible and significant only at the third follow-up, that is, about three years after termination: Before that there were no significant effects at all" (p. 932). They speculate that something is occurring during the more high-intensity treatment that leads to a different post-termination outcome: "When the specific issue of the between-treatments differentiation is concerned, what will be particularly interesting is of course the patients' accounts of the post-treatment process" (p. 938). They put forward the idea that patients in the high-intensity group may have developed a stronger self-analytic attitude than patients in the less-intense form of treatment. "Whatever one's expectations, however, an open mind is the best instrument for discoveries in texts like these" (p. 938).

Leuzinger-Bohleber, M., Stuhrast, U., Rüger, B. & Beute, M. (2003). How to study the "quality of psychoanalytic treatments" and their long-term effects on patients' well-being: A representative, multi-perspective follow-up study. *International Journal of Psycho-Analysis*, 84:263–290.

> When patients in high-intensity and low-intensity psychoanalysis were interviewed six years post-termination the patients in the high-intensity group had internalized the analyst in more extensive and more intensive ways than those of the low-intensity group. The study represents an important shift in emphasis between quantitative and qualitative methods, with precedence going to the latter.

The major aim of the project was to study patients' retrospective (six years post-termination) views of their treatment. Using questionnaires, the investigators found that approximately seventy to eighty percent of all the patients who responded reported positive changes. Based on the quantitative data (questionnaires), however, there was no statistically significant difference between the high-intensity and low-intensity groups regarding their retrospective assessment of impairment before and after treatment (p. 270). The authors' argue that a lack of difference in outcome between the groups based *on the quantitative measures* does not mean that such a difference does not exist. In point of fact, when the patients in both groups were interviewed, there was a clear difference between the groups: The high-intensity group with "good enough" treatment outcomes "had internalized the analytic function in a more extensive and intensive way" (Leuzinger-Boheleber et al., p. 283; see also Fonagy, 2002, pp. 126–131). Therefore their self-reflective functions were rated as "deeper," "more elaborated," and "more differentiated" than those of the low-intensity patients with similar outcomes (Fonagy, 2002, p. 130).

There are a number of important points that I would like to highlight in this study: This is a retrospective study where quantitative (Questionnaire) and qualitative (Interviews) methods were used. The differential findings between the two sets of measures attests to the complexity of the data and, while inconclusive in the sense that we cannot make absolute statements that the high-intensity group did "better" than the low-intensity group, the investigators' focus on internalization allows us to look at the fate of the analyst post-termination across groups.

The authors argue that the former high-intensity patients had developed a creative "inner analyst" and were thus able to continue with the analytic process more effectively in the postanalytic phase than patients in the less-intensive treatment (p. 283). The notion of an inner analyst could refer to what has often been called an identification with an analytic function, that is, a self-analytical attitude. But there is another way of understanding the "inner analyst" that Leuzinger-Bohleber et al. may also allude to when they talk about the analyst and patient's need for an "inner, resonant" dialogue. In "good-enough" treatments the clinicians were particularly successful in showing empathy and adapting flexibly, openly, and professionally to their patients special traits and idiosyncrasies; their technique was oriented toward the patient's needs, not primarily toward their own convictions or beliefs (p. 282). In less successful treatments in the high- and low-intensity groups, some of the clinicians described their painful memory that they were not able to enter into an "inner, resonant" dialogue with the patient over a long period of treatment. Some of the former patients complained about an analogous perception (p. 282). Here I am building a case, so to speak, to interpret the data from the perspective of an internalization of the analyst, rather than an identification with a function of the analyst. This, of course, is *my interpretation* of the findings, not that of Bohleber et al. It seems clear that the investigators in this study viewed the interview data along the lines of an identification with the self-analytical function of the analyst. And this finding, they argue, may "correspond to the results of the Stockholm Study" (p. 283). In other words, the hypothesized difference between the groups in the Sandell et al. (2000) study would lead to the expectation (prediction) that the post-termination difference between the groups would be in the greater identification of the high-intensity patients with the self-analytic function of the analyst in comparison to low-intensity patients.

The next two studies that I discuss do not support this hypothesis at all. What turns out to be a (perhaps *the*) most important difference between high-intensity and low-intensity groups in the Falkenstrom, Grant, Broberg, and Sandell (2007) study is that the high-intensity group has internalized the analyst as a source of insight and a self-soothing presence, whereas this is not the case with the low-intensity group, where there was an identification only with the self-analytic function of the analyst. In Laura Tessman's (2003) work the difference is not between high-intensity and low-intensity groups but between successful and unsuccessful analyses—all at high intensity. The findings in this study consist of lengthy reports by former analysands and are quite dramatic and clear: The people from the more successful analyses had internalized the analyst as a self-soothing presence, and those from less successful analyses did not, or certainly not to the same degree. In my opinion these findings on the "fate of the analyst" post-termination are a very strong indication of an emergent pattern from our psychoanalytic outcome research that is consistent with current theoretical ideas about the resolution of the transference.

Falkenstrom, F., Grant, J., Broberg, J. & Sandell, R. (2007). Self-analysis and post-termination improvement after psychoanalysis and long-term psychotherapy. *Journal of the American Psychoanalytic Association,* 55:629–674

> High-intensity patients interviewed from the Sandell et al. (2000) study spontaneously mentioned various self-supporting strategies, such as the internal presence of the analyst and self-calming strategies associated with insightful moments in the analysis. This was not the case with patients from the low-intensity group. The development of a self-analytic func-tion was the same for both groups.

This study was the qualitative follow up to the Sandell et al. (2000) study. In the latter study, high-intensity and low-intensity patients continued to improve on quantitative measures post-termination. There was a tendency, however, for the high-intensity group to improve more than the low-intensity group, and this reached statistical significance in the third year post-termination (p. 630). The basic research question for the Falkenstrom team was to see if they could discern what might have been going on with the high-intensity group that would account for the greater post-termination improvement in comparison to the low-intensity group. The working hypothesis was that the difference between groups was to be found in the self-analytic function. To explore this the investigators interviewed ten patients from the high-intensity group and ten patients from the low-intensity group. The patients were matched along a number of dimensions, including psychological health at termi-nation. Each participant in the study was interviewed twice: "The interviews were studied qualitatively using a multiple case study design, and categories of different types of post-treatment development were created from these case studies" (p. 629). The expectation that the differentiating factor between the two groups would be along the dimension of a self-analytic function was not, in fact, the case at all. There was no difference in self-analytic function between the two groups (p. 665). Falkenstrom et al. did find that "the most striking" difference between the groups was in various self-supporting strategies described by members of the high-intensity group but not the low-intensity group. "Self-supporting" strategies were further broken down into (1) use of the analyst as an internal supporting presence, for example, "being able to recall the voice of the analyst as a soothing presence in times of stress or to recall the analyst's office as an inner source of support and containment" (p. 644), and (2) self-calming strategies, for example, recalling meaningful insights from the analysis during difficult times of stress (p. 645). "Most patients (seven out of ten) in the high intensity group spontaneously described such strategies, while none of the low intensity patients did so" (p. 665). The authors note that the self-supportive category seems related to introjection and internalization. In this context I would like to mention again Sidney Blatt's work (Blatt et al., 2009), where he argues that what is crucial to the outcome process is a reduction in the patient's vulnerabilities so as to prevent relapse after the termination of treatment. Central to Blatt's argument is the quality of the therapeutic relationship and its eventual internalization by the patient (pp. 280–281). Blatt et al. take the position that "the quality of the therapeutic alliance significantly predicted the reduction in personality vulnerability that in turn significantly predicted symptom reduction" (p. 292). This formulation is consistent with the Freedman et al. (1999) study as well as Eagle's work (2003), discussed earlier. It highlights the crucial role of internalization in a patient's overall improvement. In the Falkenstrom study we can see the internalization of a soothing presence coupled with insight as part and parcel of the process of the internalization of the relationship with the analyst.

My own impression is that concepts like internalization and introjection connate an unconscious process that in this context refers to a sense of the inner presence of the other. This is in contrast to the self-analytic function, which Falkenstrom et al. regard "as an identification more or less conscious" (p. 666) with the clinician. Of particular importance in thinking about this study is the "counterintuitive" finding about the internalization of the analyst as a self-soothing presence that characterizes the high-intensity but not the low-intensity groups. I say counterintuitive because this study was a follow-up of the Sandell et al. (2000) study, where the authors' expectation of an "analytic function"—the self-analytic function—as a differentiating factor between the high-intensity and low-intensity groups was not supported. Sandell and Broberg, of course, are part of the Falkenstrom study, and their caution about keeping an open mind to what we might consider an internal differentiating factor between high-intensity and low-intensity treatment is very relevant to the Falkenstrom et al. study and to research in general.

Tessman, Laura Heims (2003). *The Analyst's Analyst Within*. Hillsdale, N.J.: Analytic Press.

> Patients who have had a successful analysis internalize the positive presence of their analyst to a far greater extent than patients who have had less successful analyses.

In her book, Laura Tessman explores how the analyst is experienced by the analysand "post-termination." I put this in quotes because of the mistaken idea that the analysis ends when the analytic dyad stops meeting. It is clear from the studies reviewed that this is not the case at all. Tessman highlights the importance of studying the post-termination phase because, as she puts it, "post-analytic developments occur in the wake of what the analysis started" (p. 6). Tessman interviewed analysts at the Boston Psychoanalytic Institute about their own analyses and found dramatic differences between those people who experienced their analysis as positive ("deeply satisfying") and those who did not. "Taken in aggregate, the narratives of Participants suggest that the optimal use of the inner presence of the analyst to further positive development after termination is preceded by satisfaction with the analysis" (p. 18). One participant in the deeply satisfying group said that it was a pleasure to have his analyst in his mind: "He's with me every day. . . . My analysis continues to grow" (p. 41). In contrast to more satisfying analyses, analysands who experienced their analyses as unsatisfying more typically described the absence of an affective presence of their analyst: Tessman—"As you practice analysis, where is he in your inner life? Analysand—Nothing of him. I can't think of any ways that I operate similarly except that I'm prompt and he was prompt. I give people the bill and things like that. Tessman—So just the frame remains. Analysand—Just the frame" (p. 59).

I have outlined some of Laura Tessman's theoretical ideas about the resolution of the transference in an earlier section of this paper, and her findings are consistent with these ideas. An obvious criticism of Tessman's work, therefore, is that of bias. The same "criticism" can be made about everyone's work to a greater or lesser extent. The concern about bias is that it will interfere with discovering something "out there." The idea that there is something out there—an absolute, certain, and infallible truth that we can discover to conclusively answer our questions about frequency/duration and outcome is a particular way of thinking about research. Another way of thinking about research, and also about bias, is that there is not something out there but something we construct, and our constructions will always be influenced by our subjectivity. This is the position I have taken throughout this paper, and it is why I believe the most powerful influence upon the meaning we give to outcome research comes from the people who practice clinical psychoanalysis on a daily basis. If the stuff of the world is mind-stuff, then the stuff of our outcome research is also mind-stuff. And the way each of us thinks about psychoanalysis will shape how we view important dimensions of the psychoanalytic process and how we think about the relationship between frequency/duration and outcome. I believe this to be the case whether the analyst actually does formal research or whether the analyst contributes to the theoretical/clinical literature.

## Analysts and Butterflies

In 1961 the physicist Edward Lorenz was using a computer program to create weather patterns. At one point he rounded off a six-place number to three places: "Lorenz had entered the shorter, rounded off numbers, assuming that the difference—one part in a thousand—was inconsequential" (Gleick, 1988, p. 16). To his astonishment, however, the new computer-generated weather pattern was vastly different from the pattern using the six-place number. Lorenz's accidental discovery came to be known as the "butterfly effect," that small differences or perturbations in a complex system could lead to enormous consequences, for example, the beating of butterflies' wings in one part of the world can influence the weather in a very different part of the world.

It seems that many analysts do not believe that they can do psychoanalysis at a high intensity. There are simply not enough people around who want to be in this form of treatment; insurance companies make it difficult; the competing therapies promise more in a shorter amount of time; and the list goes on. It is important to view these "reality factors" in the context of analysts' longstanding resistance to doing psychoanalysis at a high intensity. In more formal (pseudo) "scientific" terms, we have cloaked our discomfort around the concept of analyzability. Analyzability is the analog of the researcher's quest (i.e., fantasy) for certainty. From a so-called objective perspective, it is a judgment about whether someone is healthy enough to be in psychoanalysis. On a narcissistic level to say someone is analyzable probably reflects the clinician's belief that he or she will be successful in analyzing *this particular person* (the myth of the "good" analytic patient) without moving too far out of the comfort zone of his or her own emotional state. In other words, "I am not too frightened to work with this person and I may even be comfortable enough to work at a high intensity." Major steps away from this approach were taken by Leo Stone (1954) in his widening-scope paper and in the work of Arnold Rothstein (1998, 2006) and others (e.g., Grusky, 1999). All of these authors highlight the analyst's discomfort with the intensity of the analytic situation and, especially, how uncomfortable analysts get with certain so called "disturbed patients." Rothstein (1999) in particular makes the point that when we are uncomfortable with a patient we tend to diagnose the patient as disturbed and argue that we cannot work with such a person at a high intensity.

In a paper written nearly seventy years ago Harold Kelman (1945) argued that high-frequency analysis is necessary "in most cases," with the exception of those situations "in which the analyst feels that the limitation of the analysis to once a week is indicated" (p. 18). Kelman goes on to say that once a week analysis is indicated with patients who are very detached and need distance from others: "One should remember that with such patients, your genuine interest and desire to be helpful may not be so regarded, but may be viewed rather as an intrusion and your desire to clutch, involve, and tie them down" (p. 22). Another kind of patient that Kelman feels is more suitable for low-frequency psychoanalysis is the highly aggressive patient who causes the analyst "to defend himself rather than to analyze the patient" (p. 24). Kelman argues that high-intensity psychoanalysis allows such patients to "waste your time and theirs [and] only incurs increasing their contempt" (p. 24). When there is a reduction in the aggression and the patient's attempts to sabotage the analysis, "the number of hours can be increased" (p. 25).

Kelman's ruling out of certain patients for more intense work is no different than what we do today. Sometimes we do it under the artificial guise of analyzability, potentiated in most cases by our uncomfortable reaction to the patient. It seems reasonable, therefore, that the category of "most people" is indexed by the level of comfort/discomfort in the transference/countertransference matrix. If we have the idea that discomfort is something to be analyzed, then the category of most people will be expanded.

Of course, another way of thinking about Kelman's paper is in terms of a collaboration between analyst and patient with the ultimate goal of higher-frequency sessions. This is certainly a point of view that is very much part of the current literature (see Rothstein, 2010; Carrere, 2010). And it is a point of view consistent with the idea of psychoanalysis along a continuum. My emphasis on the analyst's uncertainty or discomfort in recommending high-intensity treatment stems from my belief that the crisis in psychoanalysis today is that analysts are not "armed with the conviction" (Rothstein, 1998, p. xviii) that high-intensity psychoanalysis is the treatment of choice for most people.

Psychoanalysis is difficult work. We are barraged with feelings triggered by our own unconscious and the unconscious of the people we work with.

And in undertaking a high-intensity psychoanalysis we are taking on a huge responsibility for the life of another person. There is an ever-growing literature on the analyst's uncertainty in taking on this work (Ehrlich, 2004, 2010; Panel, 2002), and it seems more than reasonable that in the face of this uncertainty we have to have a passionate belief in what we do. It is only too easy to rule out patients for high-intensity work. Kelman's paper in many ways was ahead of its time. He worked from the model of an open system and saw psychoanalysis along a continuum. And like all of the people I have read who support less-intensive psychoanalysis (e.g., Coopersmith, 2005; Greenberg, 1986) Kelman believed in high-intensity psychoanalysis. Consider, for example, Hyman Spotnitz's position.

Spotnitz (see Meadow, 1999) was very clear about the "job" of the analyst: " . . . to stay in touch with the unconscious of the patient and with our own unconscious. It's a very difficult job" (p. 12). And he was also quite clear about how we accomplish this. Analysts, he said, "should go to five- or six-year, four- or five-times-a-week analysis like I did" (p. 12). Spotnitz spoke quite poignantly about his own psychoanalysis and its relation to Modern Psychoanalysis: "I saw her [his analyst] five and six times a week for five years. She helped me develop Modern Psycho-analysis" (p. 7). I know that followers of Modern Psychoanalysis (includ-ing, and perhaps especially, Spotnitz himself), also argue for less frequent sessions—sometimes less than once a week (see Meadow & Spotnitz, 1976, p. 13; Spotnitz, 1997, p. 39). Support for less-frequent sessions, however, takes place in the context of a belief in high-intensity work. This is also true today. Even those colleagues who are more favor-ably disposed to less-intense work are not, to cite Stern (2009), "after all, recommending abandoning more intensive analysis" (p. 650). In his discussion of Stern's paper, Lewis Aron (2009) makes a similar point: "Frequency in fact can matter a great deal. No one here is arguing against the advantages of frequency in our clinical work" (p. 666). I would say that analysts who were trained in the context of high-intensity work, *including and especially their own analyses,* are quite supportive of high-intensity work. But what about the next generation of analysts, many of whom are not being trained or analyzed in the context of high-intensity psychoanalysis? In New York State the new licensing law for psychoanalysis does not require high-intensity analysis for control cases or for the prospective analyst's own analysis. This is, to use the language of systems for a moment, a "perturbation" to the overall system of psychoanalysis. And any perturbation in a complex system will cascade through the system (Moran, 1991). We cannot predict the ultimate impact on the system, except to say that there will be an impact.

## Conclusion

In this paper I have attempted to synthesize input from various components in the overall system of outcome research. I have emphasized that changes within and between the components influences how we view research on frequency/duration and outcome. When we view the internalization of the positive relationship with the analyst as a crucial aspect of the resolution of the transference we, quite naturally, begin to look for this in our research. This shift in the theory of transference is influenced by (and influences) a shift toward qualitative research, particularly the follow-up of patients post-termination. And this has radically changed our view of psychoanalysis to one where we consider that the analysis does not end when it ends!

Analysts in their daily work come up with new and often innovative ways of thinking about what we do and how to do it. These changes in how analysts think perturb the system. As expected, in an open system every part of the system is affected by every other part. The next generation of analysts who are not trained or analyzed in the context of high-intensity psychoanalysis will influence the overall system of psychoanalysis, including how we view, conduct, and understand outcome research. At the moment, however, from my subjective perspective and using the research described throughout this paper, the most plausible construction that I come up with is that high-intensity psychoanalysis is the optimal treatment with patients that I feel I can work with at that intensity, and who feel they can work with me. I believe that high-intensity psychoanalysis increases the probabilities for therapeutic success, but I do not believe that less-intensive psychoanalysis precludes therapeutic success.

# References

Aron, L. (2009). Day, night, or dawn: Commentary on paper by Steven Stern. *Psychoanalytic Dialogues,* 19:656–668.

Bergmann, M. (1988). On the fate of the intrapsychic image of the psychoanalyst after termination of the analysis. *Psychoanalytic Study of the Child,* 43:137–153.

Blatt, S., Zuroff, D. & Hawley, L. (2009). Factors contributing to sustained therapeutic gain in outpatient treatment of depression. In R. Levy & J. Ablon (Eds.), *Handbook of evidence-based psychodynamic psychotherapy* (pp. 279–301). New York: Humana Press.

Carrere, R. (2010). Psychoanalysis conducted at reduced frequencies. *Psychoanalytic Psychology,* 27:153–163.

Coopersmith, S. (2005). Determinants of licensing in psychoanalysis: Exclusivity and pluralism. *Psychoanalytic Review,* 92:895–905.

Eagle, M. (2003). Clinical implications of attachment theory. *Psychoanalytic Inquiry,* 23:27–53.

Eddington, A. S. (1928). *The nature of the physical world. Cambridge*: Cambridge University Press.

Ehrlich, L. (2004). The analyst's reluctance to begin a new analysis. *Journal of the American Psychoanalytic Association,* 52:1075–1093.

———(2010). The analyst's ambivalence about continuing and deepening an analysis. *Journal of the American Psychoanalytic Association,* 58:515–532.

Faber, M. D. (1999a). Numbers and psychoanalysis: Reflections on the quest for certainty. *Psychoanalytic Review,* 86:63–107.

———(1999b). Numbers and psychoanalysis: Reflections on the quest for certainty, Part 2 of 2. *Psychoanalytic Review,* 86:245–279.

Falkenstrom, F., Grant, J., Broberg, J. & Sandell, R. (2007). Self-analysis and post-termination improvement after psychoanalysis and long-term psychotherapy. *Journal of the American Psychoanalytic Association,* 55:629–674.

Fichtner, G. (2008). From psychical treatment to psychoanalysis: Considerations on the misdating of an early Freud text and on a hitherto overlooked addition to it (here reproduced). *International Journal of Psychoanalysis,* 89:827–843.

[In Koosman, R. & Weiss, J. (Eds.). (1918–1919). *Die gesundheit lhre Erhaltung, ihre Storungen, ihre Wiederherstellung [Health: Its preservation, disturbance, restoration], 2 vols., 2nd ed.* Stuggart: Union Deutsche.]

Fonagy, P. (2002). *An open door review of outcome studies in psychoanalysis* (2nd rev. ed.). London: International Psychoanalytical Association.

Frank, G. (2011). Theoretical and practical aspects of frequency of sessions: The root of the controversy. *Psychoanalytic Review,* 98(1):1–10.

Freedman, N., Hoffenberg, J. D., Vorus, N. & Frosch, A. (1999). The effectiveness of psychoanalytic psychotherapy: The role of treatment duration, frequency of sessions, and the therapeutic relationship. *Journal of the American Psychoanalytic Association,* 47:741–772.

Freud, S. (1917). Introductory Lectures on Psycho-Analysis (Part 3). In J. Strachey, ed. and trans., *The standard edition of the complete psychological works of Sigmund Freud, 24 vols.* London: Hogarth Press, 1953–1974. 16:243–496.

Frosch, A. (2006). Analyzability. *Psychoanalytic Review,* 93:835–843.

Gleick, J. (1987). *Chaos: Making a new science.* New York: Penguin.

Gray, P. (1988). On the significance of influence and insight in the spectrum of psychoanalytic psychotherapies. In A. Rothstein (Ed.), *How does treatment help? On the modes of therapeutic action of psychoanalytic psychotherapy* (pp. 41–50). Madison, CT: International Universities Press.

Green, A. (2003). The pluralism of sciences and psychoanalytic thinking. In M. Leuzinger-Bohleber, A. Dreher & J. Canestri (Eds.), *Pluralism and unity? Methods of research in psychoanalysis* (pp. 26–44). London: The International Psychoanalytical Association.

Greenberg, S. (1986). Analysis once a week. *American Journal of Psychoanalysis,* 46:327–335.

Grusky, Z. (1999). Conviction and conversion: The role of shared fantasies about analysis. *Psychoanalytic Quarterly,* 68:401–430.

Hoffman, I. Z. (2009). Double thinking our way to "scientific" legitimacy: The desiccation of human experience. *Journal of the American Psychoanalytic Association,* 57:1043–1069.

Jordan, L., (2002). (Chair). Panel: The analyst's uncertainty and fear. *Journal of the American Psychoanalytic Association,* 50:989–993.

Judson, O. (2010, May 4) Enhancing the placebo. *New York Times*, p. 31.

Kelley, J. (2009). The perils of p-values: Why statistical significance impede the progress of research. An open letter to psychotherapy researchers. In R. Levy & J. Ablon (Eds.), *Handbook of evidence-based psychodynamic psychotherapy* (pp. 267–377). New York: Humana Press.

Kelman, H. (1945). Analysis once a week. *American Journal of Psychoanalysis*, 5:16–27.

Lacan, J. (1959). *The seminar of Jacques Lacan: Book 7*. In J. Miller (Ed.), *The ethics of psychoanalysis*. New York: Norton.

Leuzinger-Bohleber, M. & Burgin (2003). Pluralism and unity in psychoanalytic research: Some introductory remarks. In *Pluralism and unity? Methods of research in psychoanalysis* (pp. 1–25). London: International Psychoanalytical Association.

———Stuhrast, U., Rüger, B. & Beute, M. (2003). How to study the "quality of psychoanalytic treatments" and their long-term effects on patients' well-being: A representative, multi-perspective follow-up study. *International Journal of Psychoanalysis*, 84:263–290.

Levy, R. & Abalon, J. (Eds.). (2009). *Handbook of evidence-based psychodynamic psychotherapy*. New York: Humana Press.

Levy, S. T. & Inderbitzin, L. B. (2000). Suggestion and psychoanalytic technique. *Journal of the American Psychoanalytic Association*, 48:739–758.

Loewald, H. (1960). On the therapeutic action of psychoanalysis. *International Journal of Psychoanalysis*, 41:16–33.

Meadow, P. W. (1999). The clinical practice of modern psychoanalysis: An interview with Hyman Spotnitz. *Modern Psychoanalysis*, 24:3–20.

Meadow, P. W. & Spotnitz, H. (1976). The origins of Modern Psychoanalysis. *Modern Psychoanalysis*, 1:3–16.

Moran, M. (1991). Chaos theory and psychoanalysis: The fluidic nature of the mind. *International Review of Psycho-Analysis*, 18:211–221.

Perron, R. (2002). Reflections on psychoanalytic research problems—a French-speaking view. In P. Fonagy, (Ed.), *An open door review of outcome studies in psychoanalysis* (2nd rev. ed., pp. 3–10; 30–33). London: International Psychoanalytical Association.

Rothstein, A. (1998). *Psychoanalytic technique and the creation of analytic patients* (2nd ed.). Madison CT: International Universities Press.

———(1999). Some implications of the analyst feeling disturbed while working with disturbed patients. *Psychoanalytic Quarterly,* 68:541–558.

———(2006). Reflections on the concept "Analyzability." *Psychoanalytic Review,* 93:827–833.

———(2010). Psychoanalytic technique and the creation of analytic patients: An addendum. *Psychoanalytic Quarterly,* 79:785–793.

Rothstein, Arden. (2010). Developing psychoanalytic cases and the candidates who will analyze them: An educational initiative. *Journal of the American Psychoanalytic Association,* 58:101–136.

Sandell, R. (2009). A letter to my friend and researcher colleague, Professor Sy Entist. In R. Levy & J. Ablon, (Eds.), *Handbook of evidence-based psychodynamic psychotherapy* (pp. 361–366). New York: Humana Press.

———Blomberg, J., Lazar, A., Carlsson, J., Broberg, J. & Schubert, J. (2000). Varieties of long-term outcome among patients in psychoanalysis and long-term psychotherapy: A review of findings in the Stockholm outcome of psychoanalysis and psychotherapy project (Stoppp). *International Journal of Psychoanalysis,* 81:921–942.

Schlesinger, H. (1988). A historical overview of conceptions of the mode of therapeutic action of psychoanalytic psychotherapy. In A. Rothstein (Ed.), *How does treatment help? On the modes of therapeutic action of psychoanalytic psychotherapy* (pp. 7–27). Madison, CT: International Universities Press.

Schwartz, C. (2003). A brief discussion on frequency of sessions and its impact upon psychoanalytic treatment. *Psychoanalytic Review,* 90:179–191.

Shedler, J. (2010). The efficacy of psychodynamic psychotherapy. *American Psychologist,* 65(2):98–109.

Smith, H. (2007). The voices that changed psychoanalysis in unpredictable ways. *Psychoanalytic Quarterly,* 76:1049–1063.

Spotnitz, H. (1997). The goals of Modern Psychoanalysis: The therapeutic resolution of verbal and preverbal resistances for patient and analyst. *Modern Psychoanalysis,* 22:31–40.

Stern, S. (2009). Session frequency and the definition of psychoanalysis. *Psychoanalytic Dialogues*, 19:639–655.

Stone, L. (1954). The widening scope of indications for psychoanalysis. *Journal of the American Psychoanalytic Association*, 2:567–594.

Tessman, L. (2003). *The analyst's analyst within*. Hillsdale, NJ: Analytic Press.

Wilson, M. (2003). The analyst's desire and the problem of narcissistic resistances. *Journal of the American Psychoanalytic Association*, 51:71–99.

# From the Frame to the Field

Allan's last published papers show an artist fully in command of his medium. Here we see Allan duck in and out of the trees to survey the forest of psychoanalysis as a whole, working from a great distance with a magnifying glass. Together they comprise a joyous recapitulation of Allan's intricate knowledge of theory and decades of deep analytic work. They are generous tributes, both to our oft' disregarded analytic fore-bears and to our living colleagues who have set up tents, sometimes in opposite corners of the playing field.

But more than that, Allan's final tour de force of theory and practice moves away from the established social order (of which Allan is deeply a part) and achieves a contradictory, alienated relationship with it. In these last papers Allan turns, finally, to the sacredness he finds in psychoanalysis, a sacredness that constitutionally, and even in the reception of these papers, entails a new form of exile.

Allan's writing has become frictionless and playful. Who can't, after all, get behind his re-invoking of psychoanalysis' synthetic virtues? Who can't but appreciate Allan's vivid description of an analytic relationship forged in the trenches of edgy discomfort? These papers are beloved by first year analytic candidates and senior analysts alike because, in Goodman's words, they explain and perform the miraculous music of symbolization. But the smoother style of these late papers is slippery. As we see with both Rothstein's and Evert's engagement with them, it is perhaps exactly *because* of their less conflict oriented aim that they are radically provocative. They provoke thought, competition, and a desire for more of Allan. But how do Allan's last papers constitute a very particular form of exile? It goes back to the root of the word 'sacred' which in Hebrew (*quodesh*) and in Greek (*hagios*) has no religious connotation. In both languages, sacred was "a standing apart" or a "separateness" from the daily aspects of life. In the end it is possible that Allan was returning to where his practice began. It was Allan's first supervisor, Irving Steingart, who coined psychoanalysis, as 'A Thing Apart.'

Early on Allan took this thing apart. Then he put it together. By the end, as we can read in these papers, Allan has taken psychoanalysis, enshrined it, and paradoxically, placed it squarely in the center of human life.

# CHAPTER 12

# Warmed by the Fires of the Unconscious
# or Burned to a Crisp

### Reflections on "Warmed by the Fires of the Unconscious or Burned to a Crisp"

*Arnold Rothstein*

Allan and I were not only good friends, but also co-teachers of a continuous case conference at the Institute for Psychoanalytic Education affiliated with NYU School of Medicine. Because Allan knew I loved him, in collegial contexts we felt free to disagree: I could always tell him what I really thought. I will respond to the editors' request to discuss Allan's paper by imagining he is still alive and has sent me a draft of the paper for my comments.

I would have said, Allan, you have actually written two papers. One is an elegant clinical report of your analytic work with a disturbed and disturbing patient. The second is a theoretical paper on the modes of therapeutic action of psychoanalysis that draws heavily on some of Freud's early ideas of primary and secondary process and on Loewald's concept of analytic love.

In his paper "The Unconscious" Freud (1915) distinguishes between primary and secondary process thinking, reflecting his belief that human beings are capable of being objectively realistic and rational. From this perspective, neurotic suffering derived from a failure of mature rational thinking. Allan builds on these ideas to conceptualize his patient's disturbances as derivatives of "an *inability* to establish and/or maintain a symbolic process" (p. 112, emphasis added).

While it is beyond the scope of this discussion to fully present my view of therapeutic action, I believe both Freud's and Allan's conceptualizations reflect unnecessary either/or thinking (that one can make categorical distinctions between thinking that is primary *or* secondary, symbolic *or* concrete). Toward the end of his paper Allan refers to my 2005 paper on the inter-subjective dimension of compromise formations in which I suggest that Arlow's (1969) conception of the "fantasy function" of the mind and Brenner's elaboration of a mind interminably in conflict provide a more accurate view of all perceptions, thoughts and actions as interminably shaped by unconscious fantasies. From this vantage point, all human experience is subjective, and all relationships are intersubjective; objectivity is a myth, as is the ideal of an objectively rational mind.

In contrast, I experience Allan's elaboration of Loewald's (1960) concept of "analytic love," as well as Winnicott's, Modell's and Bion's conceptions of "holding" and "containing" as very useful ways of understanding his elegant work with his disturbed and disturbing patient. Allan's work demonstrates a fundamental aspect of therapeutic action. He welcomed his patient's disturbances. He embraced them and, in the process of "containing" them, he allowed her to gain some momentary distance from the intensity and interminability of her conflicts and the shaping influences of childhood experiences on her unconscious fantasies.

I wish Allan were still with us. If he were, I'm sure we could have had the pleasure of discussing our different views of the value of Freud's early ideas. He is greatly missed.

## References

Arlow, J. (1969). Unconscious fantasy and disturbances of conscious experience. In *On psychoanalytic theory and practice.* (pp. 155-175). Madison, CT: International Universities Press.

Brenner, C. (1982). *The mind in conflict*. New York: International Universities Press.

Freud, S. (1915). The unconscious. *Standard Edition,* 14:159–215.

Loewald, H. (1960). On the therapeutic action of psychoanalysis. *International Journal of Psychoanalysis,* 41:16–33.

Rothstein, A. (2005). Compromise formation theory: An intersubjective dimension. *Psychoanalytic Dialogues,* 15:415–431.

\*     \*     \*

# Warmed by the Fires of the Unconscious or Burned to a Crisp

*Allan Frosch*

*In this paper I talk about the relationship or link between unconscious and conscious material. When the link is optimal we are warmed by the fires of the unconscious so that what we say and do has meaning—it is alive. When the link between conscious and unconscious is too close we are in danger of being burned to a crisp. The present is the past and the world of consensual reality pales in comparison to the emotionally charged unconscious fantasy pressing for discharge. An extended case vignette is used to illustrate the links between past and present as they unfold in a patient's life and between analyst and patient.*

## Introduction

In this paper I am going to talk about the relationship or link between unconscious and conscious material. Using Freud's (1915a) terminology, the unconscious material will be referred to as "things" or thing presentations—early experiences organized around fantasies that have a raw, driven or primary process quality. Conscious material refers to what Freud called word presentations (i.e., mental representations that stand for the unconscious thing presentations). When the link between thing

281

and word is optimal the word is warmed by the fires of the unconscious (as Loewald, 1978, put it) so that what we say and do has meaning—it is alive. When the link between conscious and unconscious is too close we are overwhelmed (or burned to a crisp) by the unconscious things so that the past is the present; the word is the thing and the multi-dimensional structure of meaning has collapsed. We are in the present moment of the past (Eliot, 1919) and the world of consensual reality pales in comparison to the emotionally charged unconscious fantasy pressing for discharge. And this is what I will be talking about as it occurs in a patient's life including, of course, her life in analysis.

In the next section I will discuss some of Freud's early ideas about memory that inform my thinking about the movement from concrete things to mental representations that stand for things. Following this a case vignette will be presented.

## *The Retranscription of Memories*

On December 6, 1896, Freud wrote to his friend and confidante Wilhelm Fleiss that he had discovered the secret of the neuroses. And it had to do with how memories were encoded:

> As you know I am working on the assumption that our psychic mechanism has come into being by a process of stratification: the material present in the form of memory traces being subjected from time to time to a rearrangement in accordance with fresh circumstances—to a retranscription (Masson, 1985, p. 206).

Freud argued that these retranscriptions represent the psychic achievement of successive developmental epochs. "At the boundary between two such epochs a translation of the psychic material must take place (p. 208)." Psychopathology comes about because "of a failure of translation—(and) this is what is known clinically as repression ( p. 208)."

I believe that a consequence of a failure of translation is an inability to establish and or maintain a symbolic process. This follows directly from Freud's argument that every later transcript inhibits its predecessor and drains the excitatory process from it. "If a later transcript is lacking, the excitation is dealt with in accordance with the psychological laws in force in the earlier psychic period and along the paths open at that time (Masson, 1985, p. 208)." In other words the repressed material is organized along the lines of (what eventually came to be called) primary process thought. Thus, said Freud, an anachronism persists; and here he uses the Spanish word "*fueros*" (Masson, 1985, p. 208) which refers to a province being governed by ancient laws while the rest of the country is in the modern age.

Of course, in optimal circumstances early experiences enter into (i.e., they are not repressed or otherwise so strenuously defended against) the flow of new associations or new circumstances and there is a translation or retranscription of the early memories/fantasies so that archaic material is represented or symbolized by contemporary events.

Here is the movement from the concrete to the abstract, from thing presentations to secondary process word presentations that stand in symbolic relation to the raw primary process laden "things." And this is what Freud is talking about in this all important letter of December 6, 1896.

Of course in less than optimal circumstances we attempt to do this in psychoanalysis. We make the unconscious conscious so that we can gain insight into how these *fueros* are shaping current experience. In the early days of psychoanalysis the hope was that by making the unconscious conscious patients gain insight into the confabulation of past and present and this will lead to positive change. Unfortunately, as Schlesinger (1988) quipped a number of years ago, it is an untidy fact that insight does not always lead to change. Something more is needed: every translation needs a translator, an "other" (Ellman, 2015), to complete the process of movement from the concrete to the abstract, from thing presentations to secondary process word presentations, that allows for a creative participation between the old and the new.

In the next section I will present a case vignette that I hope will give life to some of the ideas I have just mentioned. In the final section I will talk about some of Freud's early and, I believe, essential ideas about technique and their retranscriptions over time.

## *Case Vignette*

Sarah is a petite 33-year-old Ivy League educated corporate lawyer who understands very well the rules and regulations of the modern world. Yet there is a province in her mind that is entirely governed by experiences organized around fantasies that operate according to the laws of the primary process. This so dominates Sarah's life that she has arranged her world so that she specializes in an aspect of the law where she, for all intents and purposes, requires no contact with others. Save for the occasional professional conference or visit to the offices of her law firm Sarah lives a very solitary and isolated existence. And she suffers. She cannot tolerate the emptiness of her life nor can she tolerate personal relationships—although she craves them. The session I will describe took place in the third year of Sarah's analysis.

Sarah begins the session in an agitated state and tells me I have a helluva nerve taking a three-day weekend when she feels so alone, downtrodden and treated with contempt and indifference by everyone. She smiles and says that she knows that Monday was a holiday: "I'm not crazy, just angry." Sarah's most intense rage, however, was directed toward a longtime friend—one of the few friends in her life—whom she had met the previous day for lunch. Sharon was also a lawyer and Sarah knew she was worried about some shake-ups at her firm that might affect her; and shortly after sitting down Sharon received a call from her office. She said that she had to take the call, and Sarah was furious. She felt that Sharon was treating her with utter contempt and she seriously considered telling her to "get the hell out of my life." Sarah knew how worried Sharon was about work but felt that this really wasn't an emergency. She understood Sharon's anxiety, but Sarah felt unable to contain her anger even, as she said, "it was crazy." Sarah understood all of this and still wanted to end the friendship right then and there. She had a fantasy of excusing herself to go to the ladies room and just not coming back: "leaving the restaurant and getting her out of my life."

Sarah spent the better part of her analytic session moving between her murderous rage—"I'd like to kill her and probably you as well"—and her recognition that there really was a legitimate reason for Sharon taking the call and that I was really not being unreasonable taking a three-day weekend.

In reporting on a case—even giving a verbatim account, which this is not—it is not possible to convey what actually is going on emotionally in the room. The emotionality of this session was at a fevered pitch. And I am not just talking about the patient. My own emotions were in a state, as well. I had worked with Sarah for a number of years and I knew that she was treated with indifference and sadism as a child. She was, as she put it many times, "dropped emotionally, they knew how to get rid of me without actually throwing me out of the house." Therefore her reactions to the situations I have mentioned were not surprising and I certainly saw the positive value of her bringing these versions of the past into the present moment of the analysis. Sarah, like so many abused and traumatized people (and this is how she saw herself—and I saw her this way, as well) needed to show the world just what really went on in her childhood. This is especially so when, as in Sarah's case, her family appeared to the world at large as normal and loving. Even though I felt I understood all of this very well, the intensity of Sarah's feelings and the potential for action worried me. Let me take a step back to clarify that a bit: I think my worry for Sarah was based on my own concerns for myself as an analyst. What was I doing and what could I say that might allow Sarah to "see" on an emotionally meaningful level that the link between past and present was not optimal. The past was overwhelming the present and the actual content was not the crucial variable to under-standing what was going on. In other words, the content of the moment—the three-day weekend and the phone call were less im-portant than the emotional discharge, the expression of anger and victimization. The present moment did not represent the past but was the past personified.

And to some extent, more than I might like to acknowledge, this was the case for me, as well. I felt that my worth as an analyst and as a person was on the line here. And it was not. Sarah had become an archaic object that I had to "get through to," or I would be seriously diminished. The present moment had lost its symbolic significance for me as it had for Sarah. I imagined that, like with Sharon, Sarah wanted to get rid of me before I got rid of her. And I think the same might have been true for me, as well. I did not consciously feel that I wanted to get rid of Sarah but I did want her to understand what was going on and not act this way—anymore. I wanted to intervene and tell Sarah something to change her experience. And when she/I/or both of us are in the throes of such intense emotion, telling Sarah, in effect, to "shape up" is tantamount to getting rid of her [or to my saying]: "What you are bringing in for our perusal is not good enough. You better see it my way."

Here is the wonderful dialectical tension that is an integral part of all our analytic work: How do we help to transform the primary process memories/fantasies—thing presentations—into mental representations that stand for or symbolize the past and how do we not do this—or, stated differently, how do we see the present moment totally from the patient's perspective so that we can "contain" it until there is an opportunity for translation leading to transformation? Or, alternatively, does the containment per se bring about a transformation? This tension between very different positions can lead to rigidity (overly interpreting or rarely interpreting) or creativity, an analytic third—a creative compromise. In this situation my patient opened the door to a creative path. She screamed: "What the hell am I going to do? Speak up Frosch it's your turn now. Tell me what to do."

Now let me mention that Sarah was an enormously competent woman. She felt she could do or figure out how to do nearly everything; and her "grandiosity" had a pretty good basis in reality. (Remember, she worked for a major law firm and rarely—very rarely—went to the office or had contact with any professional colleagues or clients.) This probably helped me not to take her question on a concrete level and, after a moment or two with absolutely no idea what to say, I responded by saying that I understood the gut-wrenching paradox that she was in. On the one hand she knew the "reality" with me and with Sharon (and here I focused on Sharon) but on an emotional level—the level that really counts for all of us—it felt that her parents were throwing dirty laundry at her and telling her she was a piece of shit—something Sarah's mother actually did on a number of occasions during Sarah's childhood; and something Sarah had been telling me about very recently. That was the emotional meaning of both situations. And then something quite extraordinary happened something, I would say, quite magical; Sarah began to cry with relief: "It's true . . . nothing new... I'm touched that you said that even though . . . we've talked about this before."

Sarah was absolutely right. We had talked about situations like this before and it was, as she put it, nothing new. But it was new right now. It had an emotional significance, a meaning structure, which it did not have before. A primary process fantasy had begun an incremental process of translation to a more secondary process representation. Let me talk about how I think this might have happened and why I use such a charged word as "magical."

## Passionate Transformations

Around the same time that Freud wrote the letter to Fleiss that I cited earlier he said in a series of papers (1905a, b, c) that if we could establish a certain kind of rapport with our patients and have a passionate interest in entering into their soul (Seele) (Freud, 1905a, p. 283n; see also Bettelheim, 1983, pp. 72–73) something truly magical can happen. We can potentiate a state of mind characterized by an expectation of hope and faith and this leads to the patient's experience of the analyst's words as having a magical quality. So indeed we can cure through the power of the word: *ipso facto* the talking cure. There is a great deal to be said about these papers but I will limit my discussion to Freud's idea of rapport which he likened to the intimate relationship between a mother and her infant (1905a).

It is this passionate, loving relationship with the other that is the key to the process of translation (see also Bach, 2006). From my perspective the viscerally charged quality of this conduit for the retranscription of the ancient laws, these *fueros*, evolved (i.e., were translated by Freud) into the more sanitized formulation of the unobjectionable positive transference which Freud (1912, pp. 105–106; see also Schlesinger, 1988, p. 16) always saw as a necessary condition for interpretive work.

Again, the interpretive work that I am referring to in this paper is the translation from the concrete to the abstract, from unconscious raw experience imbued with fantasy to ideas that stand for these things. By 1915 the intimacy and passion were no longer much in evidence as Freud moved to what he later called "witch metapsychology" (1937) in the very abstract energy concept of a hypercathexis of thing and word that was now seen as the conduit for translation from the primary to the secondary process (Freud, 1915a).

In psychoanalysis we know on a clinical level that the past is always embedded in the present. And so it is on a theoretical level as well. We see early concepts embedded in more current ones. It is the evolutionary (perhaps revolutionary) aspect of psychoanalysis that enriches the pluralistic nature of our field. And it was Loewald (1970) who translated Freud's metapsychology—his hypercathexis—back into the intimacy of a mother child relationship.

Loewald's work addresses the question of how we understand the transformation of a patient's desymbolized or unsymbolized experience (i.e., experience/mentation that is regressed, or has always been repressed and never attained secondary status). Loewald's answer to this is the same as Freud's: there must be a "hypercathexis" (1970, pp. 64–65) of word and thing presentation to "bring about a higher psychical organization and make it possible for the primary process to be succeeded by the secondary process" (Freud, 1915a, p. 202). But Loewald translates Freud's hypercathexis from a purely energic term to a transformational concept that takes place in a libidinized reciprocal psychic field (1970, pp. 64–65). "The hypercathexis of word and thing presentations" becomes an emotionally charged relationship between analyst and patient where each is affected by the other. And all of this occurs in the context of love. For Loewald the analytic relationship is based on love and respect for the patient and the patient's love for the analyst. Just as it is impossible to have an analysis without loving the patient (1970, p. 65), it is impossible to have an analysis without the patient's love for the analyst. And like Freud, Loewald likens the analytic relationship to the emotionally intense intimacy of the mother-infant relationship. And Loewald makes it clear that in order to immerse oneself in the patient's world (i.e., to love his/her patient), the analyst "must be able to regress within himself to the level of organization on which the patient is stuck... (1960, p. 26)." The analyst, like the good-enough parent, must also be able to return to a more secondary process mode of functioning. When we can do this—and we certainly cannot do this all of the time—something magical does happen. In the words of the poet: the universe seems different . . . it becomes, as Proust (1913) put it, a "stirring arena" (p. 334). It is in this stirring arena of the analytic situation, this hypercathexis of self and other, that Freud was talking about when he said that the words of the analyst become magical and have the power to create "miraculous cures" (1905a, p. 289).

Whatever we may think of miracle cures let me very quickly disabuse you of the notion that this analysis was a smooth linear process characterized by my exquisite rapport with Sarah's suffering. It was not. Consider the following vignette:

Sarah went to a professional conference for the better part of a week. She made a presentation that was very well received but she felt that no one wanted to be around her; and this of course was a feeling she had all of her life. She wondered what she was doing to contribute to this. Again, the emotional tone was intense and anguished. I said to her that before she left for the conference she had mentioned a number of people who had been "less than respectful, downright condescending to me... just like my family and so called friends." Perhaps, I said, her expectations led her to feel that people at the conference would treat her this way as well.

And Sarah told me what a total jerk I was. It was about time I told her something she didn't already know; and it seemed that I was unable to tolerate the gravity of her life and, after all isn't this what she is constantly telling me about everyone. "But I pay you to hear it and it seems you can't or just don't care about me."

I thought she was right. My failure to contain, to metabolize Sarah's pain—to bear my own emotional pain, my own uncertainty about the value of our work in the face of her suffering led to a distortion of my interest in Sarah. Rather than having an interest in entering into Sarah's tortured soul I was more interested in protecting myself from her pain. My interest then was geared to "explaining" to Sarah what was going on and, consciously or unconsciously, dismissing her suffering. Where was my hope and faith? Where was the rapport that is necessary to work through and transform concrete things to representations that stand for them?

Working through here is clearly a two-person process. It is a process that the analyst as well as the patient must struggle with. As Freud said, no one who does this work comes out unscathed (1905d); and he was clearly referring to the analyst. The kind of emotional rupture I have just described is part and parcel of our work. It is the attunement and lack of attunement, the coming together and driving apart, that is the essential dialectic of the analytic process. And in the finer structure of these analytic moments we can see the repetition of the past. It is the way we bring the past, these primary process things, into the consultation room so that they can be known and translated in the context of current experience and knowledge. And this is what distinguishes psychoanalysis from all other treatments. It is as Loewald put it, the "blood of recognition" in the here and now (1960, p. 249) that awakens the ghosts from the past and a reworking (or retranscription) in the present allows for new links to be formed and new meanings to be created. To my way of thinking this is the psychoanalytic equivalent of time travel. Unlike the science fiction version of time travel where we are forbidden to modify the past we can, in psychoanalysis, modify our experiences from the past as they get reworked in the present. A necessary condition for this extraordinary process to occur is the analyst's capacity to experience the intensity of her own feelings, his own infantile primary process construction of the moment, and struggle to return to a more secondary process symbolized position.

But ghosts are scary things and while Freud (1914) argued that all the analyst has to do is be patient while the patient struggles to work through the wishes and defenses that make life so difficult, he also cautioned us not to send the spirits we have called up back to the underworld (1915b). In other words, for Freud, and everyone else, the emotional upheavals, the ghosts, spirits or demons that enter our consulting rooms are not so easy for us to bear.

The moments of attunement and lack of attunement are joint creations—the intersubjective dimension of compromise formations (Rothstein, 2005)—that allow us to bring the ghosts of the past into the room so that they can be exposed to the light of day. A translation takes place that brings these *fueros*, these primary process things into contact with new circumstances in the person of the analyst. And it is always a joint venture. There must be the "thing" to be translated in relation to the receptive or unreceptive other to provide the translation.

## All the World's a Stage

In the vignette just presented my countertransference, in the form of a poorly timed and somewhat formulaic intervention, is most noticeable. But if we leave it at that level we are missing the finer structure of the moment. Here is how Freud put it in "Analysis Terminable and Interminable":

> The adult's ego, with its increased strength, continues to defend itself against dangers which no longer exist in reality; indeed, it finds itself compelled to seek out those situations in reality which can serve as an approximate substitute for the original danger, so as to be able to justify, in relation to them, is maintaining its habitual modes of reaction. (Freud, 1937, p. 238)

The danger in Sarah's mind, in her unconscious primary process fantasy-laden experience is that of being treated with complete disdain—as an object to be used and discarded—like dirty laundry that has to be thrown away. At the same time the involvement with this fantasy laden other represents a relationship that is life sustaining—certainly in the context of what she experienced as complete indifference from her parents when she was not being tortured. Her mother (in particular) loved her, albeit with a negative sign. She hounded Sarah, tortured her and eventually Sarah did the same to her. We cannot kill the enemy in absentia. We need to bring the ghosts, spirits or demons right into the room and infuse them with the blood of our transference and countertransference. Analyst and patient unconsciously collude to create an opportunity to translate and transform the past into a different present and a better future. Both the analyst and the patient must be the receptive and unreceptive other to each other in order to experience the life changing potential of psychoanalysis. Sarah reproduces prototypical memories from the past using the materials of the present; and I am a key piece of material—but certainly not a passive piece. She is the author, lead actor and director of this drama. I am, if you will, a featured player who plays an active role in the creative process. And if all goes well we are both warmed by the fires of the unconscious but not before we go through the more intense heat of the transference/countertransference scenario.

## Acknowledgements

My thanks to Ruth Oscharoff for her helpful suggestions during the preparation of this paper. My thanks also to the members of my Writers Group for their input.

## References

Bach, S. (2006). *Getting from here to there: Analytic love, analytic process.* Hillsdale, NJ: The Analytic Press.

Bettelheim, B. (1983). *Freud and man's soul.* London: Chatto and Windus.

Eliot, T. S. (1919). Tradition and the individual talent. In *Selected essays* (pp. 3-11). New York: Harcourt, Brace and World, 1960.

Ellman, S. (2015). The importance of translations. *Caliban: The Latin American Journal of Psychoanalysis,* 13:158-160.

Freud, S. (1905a). Psychical (or mental) treatment. *Standard Edition,* 7:283-302

———(1905b). On psychotherapy. *Standard Edition,* 7:257-268).

———(1905c). Freud's psycho-analytic procedure. *Standard Edition,* 7:249-254.

———(1905d). Fragment of an analysis of a case of hysteria. *Standard Edition,* 7:1-122.

———(1912). The dynamics of transference. Standard Edition, 12:97-108.

Freud, S. (1914). Remembering, repeating and working-through. *Standard Edition,* 12:147-156.

———(1915a). The unconscious. *Standard Edition,* 14:159-215.

———(1915b). Observations on transference-love. *Standard Edition,* 12:159-171.

———(1937). Analysis terminable and interminable. *Standard Edition,* 23:209-254.

Frosch, A. (2012). (Ed.), *Absolute truth and unbearable psychic pain: Psychoanalytic perspectives on concrete experience.* London: Karnac Books.

———(2014). Psychoanalysis: The sacred and profane. *American Journal of Psychoanalysis,* 74:133-146.

Loewald, H. (1960). On the therapeutic action of psychoanalysis. *International Journal of Psychoanalysis,* 41:16-33.

———(1970). Psychoanalytic theory and the psychoanalytic process. *Psychoanalytic Study of the Child,* 25:45-68.

———(1978). Primary process, secondary process, and language. In *Papers on psychoanalysis* (pp. 178-206). New Haven, CT: Yale University Press, 1980.

Masson, J. (1985). *The complete letters of Sigmund Freud to Wilhelm Fliess 1887–1904.* Cambridge, MA: Belknap Press of Harvard University Press.

Proust, M. (1913). *In search of lost time, Vol. 1, Swann's way.* New York: The Modern Library, 2003.

Rothstein, A. (2005). Compromise formation theory: An intersubjective dimension. *Psychoanalytic Dialogues,* 15:415-431.

Schlesinger, H. (1988). A historical overview of conceptions of the mode of therapeutic action of psychoanalytic psychotherapy. In A. Rothstein (Ed.), *How does treatment help? On the modes of action of psychoanalytic psychotherapy* (pp. 7-27). Madison, CT: International Universities Press.

# CHAPTER 13

# Psychoanalysis: The Sacred and the Profane

### Reflections on "Psychoanalysis: The Sacred and the Profane"

*Elizabeth Cutter Evert*

"Psychoanalysis: The Sacred and the Profane" is part of Allan Frosch's and his intellectual cohort's generative "both/and" reformation of psychoanalytic orthodoxy. Reality is both constructed and immaculately perceived. Cure comes through insight and through the experience of participating in the analytic relationship. Analyst and analysand are separate individuals, and they are entangled in ways that continue to transform both members of the dyad long after they have ceased to meet. The paper is beautifully written—as such, it is expressive of the way Allan carried himself both personally and as a member of the analytic community in which he moved. That it now seems there is little to argue with belies the courage it took over decades to stand up to theoretical rigidity from a range of schools.

Frosch starts the paper by arguing that when psychoanalytic theory becomes dogmatic, it gets to be constricting, ossified, and ultimately anti-therapeutic:

"Colleagues from a variety of perspectives have written about the propensity to enshrine psychoanalytic theory...to cherish as sacred an idea or philosophy and protect it from change. Our theories of mind become holy writ....This is the kiss of death for theory, which must constantly evolve and change, but comforting for the analyst who believes he is on the side of the right."

He says that in our attempt to be accepted by the medical establishment, we have often lost the creativity inherent in Freud's nonlinear embrace of contradictory positions. I agree, but in preparing to write this introduction, I found myself subtly uncomfortable, as if aspersions were being cast not only on theoretical rigidity, but on the notion of sacrality itself. In 2017, when the world is reeling—in part—from a backlash by those who feel marginalized by global secularists, we are more sensitive to this issue than we were in 2014 when the article was published.

Oversensitivity is a possibility, but as analysts, we know not to discount the details—particularly those that seem not quite to fit. Allan was not dismissive, and some of my last conversations with him were about our shared interest in the relationship between psychoanalysis and the spiritual endeavor. I remember his speaking of analysis as a secular form of prayer. In my discomfort, I reached out to his friends in the hope of finding further articles that would elucidate the issue. Ruth Oscharoff, his wife, told me that in addition to his having always read voraciously about psychoanalysis, he had a lifelong, though somewhat private, interest in Jewish mysticism.

But no one could lead me to further articles. We are left with a deeper awareness of our loss. In the tone of the title was he looking askance at something he loved conflictually?

Was he speaking of a kinship between psychoanalytic and religious striving, where something starts off opening a window into what is deeply alive and mysterious, but can harden into dogma and hollow practice? Perhaps this is related to the problem of idolatry. My favorite take is that in his theory of psychic entanglement between analyst and patient, where both parties are transformed through the ongoing encounter, he was quietly recognizing and elucidating the sacrality of Martin Buber's *I and Thou*.

# Psychoanalysis: The Sacred and the Profane

*Allan Frosch*

*Colleagues from a variety of perspectives have written about the propensity to enshrine psychoanalytic theory. The meaning of the word "enshrine" is to cherish as sacred an idea or philosophy and protect it from change. In other words, the way we view psychoanalysis, our theories of mind and technique, become holy writ and we have divided the world of theory into the sacred and the profane. This is the kiss of death for theory, which must constantly evolve and change, but comforting for the analyst who believes he is on the side of the right, the sacred. In this paper I will discuss how our propensity to enshrine theory has had a debilitating effect on the development of psychoanalysis and, in particular, as a treatment for the most vulnerable people who seek our help. I also address the idea that movement away from enshrined positions allows us to construct different versions of reality. In this context, the notion of "action at a distance" is presented along with the attendant idea of psychoanalytic entanglement.*

## Introduction

Bion (1970) said that he tried to go into every session without memory or desire. He also said that he was frightened whenever he went into a session. This is not surprising. If we have some clear idea about what we are doing or what we think we should be doing, we can feel less anxious. It helps to have a plan. Whether any of us can actually do this work without some organizing principle is questionable. What is not questionable, however, is the idea that what the analyst can and should strive for in his or her self-reflective efforts is an awareness of his or her own personal organizing principles (his plan)—including those enshrined, as Stolorow (1990) put it, in his or her theories—and of how these principles are unconsciously shaping his or her analytic understandings and interventions (p. 122). In other words, the way we view the world, the organization of our wishes and defenses, our subjectivity, becomes holy writ, and we have divided the world of psychoanalysis into the sacred and the profane. This is the meaning of "enshrine"—to cherish as sacred an idea or philosophy and protect it from change. This is the kiss of death for theory, which must constantly evolve and change, but comforting for the analyst, who believes he is on the side of the sacred: God rewards the sacred and punishes the profane.

In this paper I will highlight Freud's rhetorical dialectical mode of thought where he passionately engaged the paradoxical unity and conflict of opposites (cf. Richards, 2013). If a dialectical position is characterized by a search for truth, rhetoric makes truth effective; it attempts to persuade (cf. Jacobs, 2000).

The richness and complexity of Freud's thinking cannot be reduced to linear concrete positions that do not allow for multiple perspectives. Freud could speak in a very authoritative way that was in marked contrast to his ability to play with ideas so that he did not get pulled into one way of seeing things. The complexity of this way of thinking stands in marked contrast to 20th-century psychoanalysis in this country where, under the pressure of striving for acceptance into the world of medicine, and later under the "threat" of burgeoning complexity, that is, psychoanalytic pluralism, psychoanalysis "hunkered down," so to speak, and adopted a certain kind of ideological absolutism. In the first part of this paper I will examine Freud's ideas about perception, which are a very clear example of his ability to move between diametrically different positions. On the one hand, Freud had a very clear active/constructive theory of perception. He also had a passive theory with philosophical roots in the principle of immaculate perception. He was passionate about both positions, and his rhetoric was always convincing. In the second half of the paper I will try to show how the enshrinement of certain ways of looking at things, sometimes in support of Freud and sometimes in opposition to him, continues to have deleterious effects on the developmental psychoanalysis, including, and for my purposes most especially, in its clinical application. I add to this a belief that my use of the phrase "in support of or in opposition to" Freud is misleading since it represents an interpretation of what Freud said—or did not say. It has been said that one can find support for nearly anything in Freud's writing. To the extent that this is true it represents not fuzzy thinking, but the product of Freud's creative mind.

## Freud's Theories of Perception

Dating back to the time of Aristotle, the principle of immaculate perception refers to the belief that our mental representation of reality is an accurate reflection of the external world. By the 1880s, however, Hermann von Helmholtz, the great German physiologist, proposed a theory of perception based on (what he called) "unconscious inference" such that an object (i.e., reality) was influenced or subjectified by the observer. Helmholtz had a projective theory of perception wherein, as the French psychologist philosopher Hippolyte Taine put it, "we have found objects are illusions, fragments of the Ego" (cited by Makari, 1994, p. 565). All of these ideas have been presented in a scholarly article by Makari (1994), who argued that Freud was certainly a part of this scientific-philosophical zeitgeist. Freud was undoubtedly very familiar with Helmholtz's work and Hippolyte Taine was one of his favorite authors. Makari argued that a passive model of mind that was integral to the idea of immaculate perception was untenable for someone like Freud who had already postulated psychic defenses in the neuropsychoses of defense in 1894 (Makari, 1994, p. 551).

In contemporary terms, Freud embraced a constructive theory of perception where the observer actively selects and organizes the data of perception based on mental representations, that is, memories organized around phantasies (wishes and defenses). From a psychoanalytic perspective, we are not talking about (at least not primarily) the actual physical perception *per se* but the quality of the perception. The quality of our perceptions falls along a continuum of pleasure-unpleasure such that reality can be hopeful, indifferent, despairing, or joyous depending on our subjective construction of an event or the meaning we attribute to it. Therefore, Makari argues that the notion of immaculate perception is wholly refuted by Freud's subjectively organized view of reality.

Not so, said Schimek (1975), a Freudian scholar par excellence, who argued that Freud's theory of perception is essentially the passive, temporary registration of an object, that is, reality. In this model, the perceptual apparatus functions like the lens of a camera. In order to keep its unlimited receptive capacity for new registrations, it retains no permanent traces of them; it is "without the capacity to retain modifications and thus without memory" (Freud, 1900, p. 539). This means that perception is uninfluenced by past experience, and in point of fact Freud often equates the two terms "perception" and "external reality" and uses them interchangeably (Schimek, 1975, p. 172). According to Schimek, Freud embraced a view sometimes labeled a "copy" theory of knowledge or the principle of "immaculate perception." And this, said Schimek, implies an innate capacity for veridical objective registration of external events, and a direct and intrinsic correspondence between the "real" external object and the perception of it (p. 172).

If, following this line of thought, perceptions are an accurate reflection of reality, then it follows that the lasting impressions of such perceptions—memories—are the more permanent accurate record of reality. But where do phantasies (wishes/defenses) come into the picture? Schimek argued that from Freud's model wishes and defenses distort the content of memories so that these inner copies (what Schimek called "immaculate perceptions") of external reality acquire a personal subjective meaning. In schematic terms, these immaculate perceptions are infused with earlier memories organized around phantasies.

A question that needs to be addressed is how two such eminent scholars came up with very different renderings of Freud's theory of perception. The answer to this question has important implications for how we think of psychoanalysis and who we think can profit from being in psychoanalysis, and, of course, our very ideas about the nature of our relationship with reality.

## Our Evolving Views of Reality

In 1933, the Nobel Prize-winning physicist Erwin Schrodinger said that different histories of a subatomic particle are "not alternatives but are really happening simultaneously" (cited by Deutsch and Ekert, 2013, p. 107). Schrodinger was concerned that people might think he was crazy for saying this. In 2013, the physicists David Deutsch and Artur Ekert wondered "how such an apparently innocuous claim could ever have been considered outlandish" (p. 107). Our understanding of reality has, to put it mildly, changed. Something can be here and there at the same time, at least on a quantum level. The world is not linear, and Freud's active and passive theories of perception are not alternatives but are best understood as happening simultaneously. They are here and there at the same time. They are Freud's way of trying to come to terms with the complexities of clinical material that he encountered daily. Therefore, Makari and Schimek are both correct. It was a sign of Freud's genius that he was able to embrace opposites. Here is how Freud (1915a) put it in 1915: "It is important to . . . reckon with the fact that mental life is the arena and battleground for mutually opposing purposes or, to put it non-dynamically, that it consists of contradictions and pairs of contraries. Proof of the existence of a particular purpose is no argument against the existence of an opposite one; there is room for both . . ." (pp. 76-77). This quotation is in the context of parapraxes, but the very same argument can be made about Freud the theoretician as he describes a situation in which we can look at one and the same event through two different frames of reference. These two frames mutually exclude each other, but they also complement each other, and only the juxtaposition of these contradictory frames provides a more exhaustive view of the appearance of the phenomena. This way of thinking was codified 5 years later by Neils Bohr and Werner Heisenberg in their concept of complementarity such that an electron is a wave and a particle simultaneously. This is a mode of thinking that is quintessential Freud. And it is always infused with passionate rhetoric. Freud is always intent on using rhetoric, argumentation, to persuade us, and himself, of the truthfulness of a particular point of view, and then another point of view about the same topic. We see it in his ideas about transference, about which patients are suitable for psychoanalysis, the role (or non-role) of the analyst's personality in the treatment process, and very clearly in his ideas about perception. Freud's (1924, 1927) paper in 1894 was an entrée into a series of papers that led to important ideas about disavowal and the withdrawal of a psychological investment in an object and its effect on the construction of reality. These ideas were elaborated in Freud's (1925a) paper on "Negation" where he argues for an active construction of the world and adds, perhaps wistfully, that perception is not such a passive process (p. 238). I say wistfully because in the model of immaculate perception the analyst remains outside the system and interprets the confabulation of past and present. It is, in this sense, quite safe and quite elegant. Insight reveals a reality that is there for our taking; all we need to do is be patient. It is no surprise, therefore, that less than 10 years after the publication of the paper on "Negation" Freud (1933, p. 75) reverses himself (again) and declares in fact that the ego must lay down an accurate picture of the external world in the memory traces of its perceptions.

The passive model of perception, or what Green (2011) referred to as "virginal receptors," provided a good fit for the pathological memory retrieval model (cf. Ellman, 2010) that played such a central role in Freud's professional life. Beginning with hypnosis and extending into the final years of his life, the idea of clearing away the phantasmagorical memories from the past so that we can invest in reality—a reality that was accurately recorded and therefore available to us—was seen as a form of insight that could transform one's life. Here the insight is about the shadow of psychic reality on the accurate registration of material reality, the external world. Or the insight, switching to the active model of perception, can be about the patient's contribution to the immediate construction of reality. From a contemporary perspective, the construction of reality in the analytic situation prominently includes the analyst's contribution. And in some forms of contemporary theory the ongoing contribution of the analyst is a central topic for mutual discussion (Fiscalini, 2004).

Many contemporary theories of psychoanalysis clearly place more emphasis on the immediacy of the transference/countertransference scenario, and are less inclined to believe that a recapturing of the past is necessary to demonstrate and diminish the persistent influence of the past in the present, and to meaningfully connect past and present (Blum, 2005). In short, the idea that current symptoms and behavior including, and especially as played out in the transference, are derived from the past, pales in comparison to the desire, as Gill (1984) put it, to ferret out the transference in the here and now so the patient can see his or her role in its construction. An enshrined version of this model has

302

its own form of immaculate perception in the analyst's countertransference that is seen by many as having a one-to-one relationship with what the patient is experiencing (cf. Heimann, 1950; see Wilson, 2013 for a critical discussion of this issue).

I believe that an appreciation of the complexities of reality argues for the simultaneity of both of Freud's models of perception. As analysts we live, or should live, in an intermediate zone such that movement between material reality and psychic reality is not impeded by the enshrinement of theory whereby all meaning is obliterated except that which satisfies our belief in the absolute. In the best case scenario, this intermediate zone is the area of creativity such that novel ways of constructing the reality of the psychoanalytic situation can be forthcoming. An enshrinement of either model must, by definition, rule out many patients for psychoanalysis. The religious fervor of absolute anonymity associated with the passive model is anti-therapeutic, just as the insistence on focusing on the construction of the transference from the outset of treatment sometimes, as Gill (1984, p. 510) put it, without regard for tact, can also rule out many patients for psychoanalysis.

But there is a striking similarity, a common thread that has been enshrined across analytic theories that can be lost in the "noise" of an either-or view of reality. I am referring to the belief that a conscious understanding mediated by language (ergo "the talking cure") as to how our mind works—self-knowledge—is the key to a better life. Insight leads to change. Not so, says Schlesinger (1988): "It's an untidy fact that insight does not always lead to change" (p. 19). And, we can add, when it does lead to a change in how we function it is not always equivalent to a change in how we experience ourselves (Freedman et al., 1999; Eagle, 2003). Something more is needed. And the something more has always been associated with the experience of being in analysis. This experience was virtually invented by Freud but, as Mitchell (1996) has argued, not fully appreciated by him. I think Freud did appreciate the experiential part of treatment, but it was overshadowed by the rhetoric of the positive transference being the means to an end—the end being interpretation leading to insight. In either case, the enshrinement of insight led the experiential factor into becoming a profanity that went by the name of a corrective emotional experience or transference cure. So if a person has the requisite ego strength to work in the transference from the beginning of treatment (Gill, 1984; Gray, 1988), and to profit from the insights that the analyst's interpretations provide (Eissler, 1953), that person is suitable for psychoanalysis. People who cannot do this are better served, said Gray (1988), by psychoanalytic psychotherapy where the corrective emotional experience of the benign transference has pride of place. Psychoanalysis is for healthy people. Not so, says Bach (1985), who argues that psychoanalysis is the treatment of choice for the more vulnerable patient.

## A Wave and Particle Approach to Psychoanalytic Technique

Bach (1985) argues that "more disturbed patients can only be helped permanently by psychoanalysis, although a period of 'holding,' ' introduction,' or 'preparation' may be necessary" (p. 236). During this period, the analytic work is geared toward the establishment of a context of safety and trust that provides the emotional milieu for interpretive work. And this introductory phase of the work, which may last months or years, "*is* the analysis *conducted in another way*" (p. 224, italics added). During this period, it is crucial that the analyst avoids making mistakes such as premature interpretations, particularly in the transference, since the more vulnerable, disturbed, or narcissistic patient may experience a point of view other than his or her own as a violent attack. The goal, however, is to work toward the development of interpretive work leading to conscious insight: "because insight oriented psychoanalysis offers these people the best hope for substantial improvement" (p. 222). Bach's observation that this introductory stage may recur repeatedly throughout the analysis (p. 228) argues against a reductive linearity that would diminish the complexity of the analytic endeavor.

Bach's ideas resonate with the research from cognitive neuroscience suggesting two memory systems. Declarative or explicit memory refers to memories as we typically think of them—images organized around phantasies. When these memories/phantasies are unconscious they have the potential to become conscious through analytic work. Procedural memories, on the other hand, are sensory motor emotional schemas that are nonverbal and unconscious ways of regulating the world emotionally that some would argue cannot be made conscious (see Ellman and Moskowitz, 2008 for a different point of view). These pre-verbal and pre-ideational memories, what Segal (2003) called basic hypotheses about the world encoded in the body, and Ellman and Moskowitz (2008) liken to thing representations, are presented (i.e., elaborated) through verbal and imagistic phantasies to which they become attached. In other words, procedural memories are an organizing influence in how the person experiences the world through their embodiment in unconscious phantasies of self and object representations (cf. Schimek, 1975).

In a truly seminal paper, Clyman (1991) argued that the modification of these procedural memories (implicit relational memories or implicit relational knowing) was the central task of psychoanalysis that could be accomplished indirectly, via our traditional approach of making these developmentally later imagistically organized memories conscious and subjecting them to analysis and eventual insight. The emotional procedures can also be reworked more directly through a genuine emotional experience in an empathic analytic relationship without conscious insight mediating the process. In this latter formulation, the analyst's behavior is central to therapeutic action. It is only because the analyst does not behave in accordance with the patient's procedurally encoded role relationship models that the patient can change during treatment (Clyman, 1991, p. 377). Schlesinger (1988) would put this as the patient waiting for the other shoe to drop, and the analyst not dropping it, and Bach (2006) might put it as the other shoe drops when the analyst does not really know his or her patient such that we treat him or her as if he or she were capable of a mutually cooperative endeavor before he or she actually is. Along these lines, Clyman argues that what patients learn from the analyst's actions does not always need to be stated explicitly for it to be efficacious. Indeed, discussing the patient's experience of our actions too early may vitiate the intervention, sapping it of its emotional strength (p. 374).

From Clyman's perspective (and Bach's as well) both conscious insight and a corrective emotional experience without conscious insight are essential to psychotherapeutic change. They are the metaphoric wave and particle of psychoanalytic technique leading to a change in how we experience ourselves in the world, and, in my opinion, are best understood as simultaneously embodied aspects of the therapeutic endeavor. They are part and parcel of each other and have a fluidic figure—ground relationship—contradictions that complement each other and can become polarized and mutually exclusive when either side of the dialectic is enshrined.

## Concluding Comments

When Freud argued that perception was a passive process he was going against the accumulation of experimental data that pointed in the opposite direction. Freud, the logical positivist, was, apropos of 21st-century thinking, saying that numbers, predictions, do not tell the whole story. Around the same time that he argued for his passive theory Freud (1905a) also said that there was something truly magical and miraculous about this procedure called psychoanalysis that he was in the process of inventing. Freud (1925b) the scientist, the godless Jew, had no trouble talking about miracles and magic. And these ideas are contained in his later work just as his contradictory ideas about perception persisted throughout his life. Freud wanted to change the world and he did, and in order to do this he took bold, often counterintuitive steps. He changed our view of psychological reality just as other scientists have changed our views of physical reality. In this concluding section, I would like to suggest, or perhaps more accurately speculate about, a possible link between how we think about these momentous changes in psychological and physical reality.

## A Nonlocal View of Reality

As we experience it, the world of reality is a local world. That is to say, if I want a piece of paper to move, I touch it, or blow a puff of air on it, or ask someone to move it. In the world of theoretical physics—quantum theory to be exact—there is an idea that some objects can affect other objects at a distance without any intervening variable—not gravity or movement of molecules in the air or anything smacking of reality as we know it. This is called nonlocality. A preposterous idea said many of our leading scientists in the early part of the 20th century: "spooky action at a distance" said Einstein derisively. Neils Bohr, the great Danish physicist, said that nonlocality (action at a distance) simply could not be: "There can be no question [he said] of a genuine physical nonlocality" (cited by Albert and Galchen, 2013, p. 98). In a recent issue of *Scientific American*, Albert and Galchen (2013) argue that Bohr's response became enshrined as the official gospel of theoretical physics and any consideration of nonlocality was considered "apostasy." Nonlocality became a profanity and was ignored for the next 30 years. That which threatens our view of reality becomes *persona non grata,* a heretic entering the sacred temple. In order to achieve ideological absolution we must purge it from consideration. In 2013 we can say that on an experiential level we live in a local world but, as Albert and Galchen (2013) put it, ". . . the actual physical world is non-local. Period" (p. 98). The idea of action at a distance or nonlocality is dependent on a special relationship between objects—a link that physicists refer to as entanglement. Entanglement speaks to a kind of, as some physicists put it, intimacy amid matter previously undreamt of (Albert and Galchen, 2013, p. 96). What this means is that when two objects interact or, if you will, are intimate, and then separate, they can continue to influence each other even after the separation (cf. Schrodinger, 1935). Of course, when talking about objects in the world of quantum physics we are talking about subatomic particles. At this point, I will turn to a discussion of objects in the psychoanalytic sense.

## Psychoanalytic Entanglement

When Freud (1915b) said that the unconscious of one person can read the unconscious of another he was talking about a special kind of link in the analytic relationship. And this is also the case when he talked about our interest in the other or, as I think Freud (1905b) used the term "interest," our passionate desire to enter into the mind or soul (Seele) of the other. Does this kind of intimate relationship have an effect on the other? Freud certainly thought it did. Freud (1905a,b) said that the analyst's investment in his or her patient potentiated a state of mind in the patient characterized by hope and faith that was essential for successful analytic work. Johnson (1949) took this idea and applied it to the parent-child relationship and argued that parents can shape or construct their children through unconscious communication such that a parent can "provide the child with an unconscious impetus to the neurosis" (p. 246). Of course, she continued, a parent's unconscious image of the child as someone who is loved and valued (p. 249) potentiates a very different outcome in the child. Along these lines, Bach (2006) highlights how important it is to let the patient enter into the analyst's mind so the analyst would have to be thinking about the patient a lot, not only during his or her sessions but also at other times throughout the day so that, in an ongoing way, the patient would become a constant living presence in the analyst's life (p. 132). Bach's ideas are placed squarely in the context of the analyst's love for his or her patient. If someone loves you the world feels different. And anyone who has experienced the love of another knows this. It is the kind of libidinal connection that Johnson is talking about when a parent loves his or her child; or that Freud is talking about when we can touch a patient's soul with our interest. It is the strength of the libidinal connection, the intimacy, not the physical proximity, that is of primary importance.

Freud, Johnson, and Bach are all talking about a special link or entanglement between objects, that is, people. In the psychoanalytic situation, and in life, it is a therapeutic agent of great import. At some point in the development of psychoanalysis, the kind of involvement that Bach talks about with a patient would have been considered a form of countertransference in need of immediate self-analysis. Things have changed in how we think.

And if we think about action at a distance, does it matter if such action occurs in close proximity such as in a family or an analyst's office? Bach, of course, has extended the distance (see also Bass, 2001). In the world of quantum theory the distance can also vary. I think this is true in the world of psychoanalysis as well. In psychoanalysis it is easy enough to increase the distance by looking at post-termination reports. When, for example, a patient writes us a note or calls many years after treatment to say he or she has been thinking of our work, or when a patient feels shaky and recalls (many years after we stopped meeting) how the consultation room looked, or our tone of voice and how this sometimes calms him or her down (cf. Falkenstrom et al., 2007), is this a form of action at a distance? In her book *The Analyst's Analyst Within,* Tessman (2003) reports that patients who felt their analyses were successful made post-termination statements such as "He's with me every day . . . . My analysis continues to grow"(p. 41); "I know I am important to him; and I will continue to be important to him and he will continue to be important to me" (p. 233). In successful analyses, the patient believed he or she would "maintain some intrapsychic residence in the analyst" (p. 33). In other words, there is an intrapsychic continuation of the analysis for both the analyst and the patient following the actual/physical termination. Or, to put it in more visceral terms, the continuation of the analytic relationship is "embodied" as Tessman puts it (p. 12) in the analyst and the patient. It becomes part of them.

In a long-term study comparing the effectiveness of psychoanalysis and psychotherapy, Sandell et al. (2000) showed that psychoanalytic and psychotherapy patients profited equally well from treatment. The two groups began to diverge significantly, however, 3 years after treatment had stopped. The psychoanalytic group continued to improve while the psychotherapy group did not. Shall we think of Tessman's and Sandell's findings as action at a distance? In a study by Freedman et al. (1999), a patient said in a post-termination interview that she never thought about her analyst but her analyst was with her all the time. Clearly, we can think of these findings in many different ways. The most obvious, of course, is that the analytic relationship became internalized and we can use evocative or embodied memory to bring back, reestablish, or continue a link with an important person in our life. And this would hold true for the analyst as well as the patient. Patient and analyst continue to influence each other. These ideas make a compelling argument for the continuation of the analysis after the analytic couple stops meeting. In reference to action at a distance, however, to ask how it works may be putting the cart before the horse. In other words, a first step might be to see whether we can even imagine that the idea of nonlocality is applicable to psychoanalysis. Is it at all plausible to consider action at a distance as an integral part of psychoanalysis? Can we let our imaginations have free rein and not be bound by enshrined ways of looking at things and consider using the metaphor of action at a distance? After all, the metaphors we use shape and define how we construct reality.

It may be that on a psychoanalytic level these ideas, as Neils Bohr argued on a physical level, do not make sense; they are "spooky." There was another famous Dane, however, a rather well-known neurotic, who said to his friend, "There are more things in heaven and earth, Horatio, than are dreamt of in your philosophy." I tend to side with Hamlet on this one. In this paper I have argued for a more broadened view of the reality of the psychoanalytic situation than we usually dream of. In order to do this we must extricate ourselves from the enshrinement of our sacred beliefs.

## Acknowledgements

Some of the initial ideas for this paper came out of a series of discussions with the late Norbert Freedman. My thanks to Richard Lasky, Hattie B. Myers, and Ruth Oscharoff for their comments and suggestions. I would also like to thank the members of my Writers Group for their input: Carolyn Ellman, Steven Ellman, Peter Kauffman, Michael Moskowitz, Douglas Van Der Heide, and Lissa Weinstein.

## References

Albert, D. Z. & Galchen, R. (2013). A quantum threat to special relativity. In M. Dichristina (Ed.), *Scientific American: Special Edition—Extreme Physics,* 22(2):94–101. New York: Scientific American.

Bach, S. (1985). Classical technique and the unclassical patient. In *Narcissistic states and the therapeutic process* (pp. 219–336). Northvale, NJ: Jason Aronson.

————(2006). Psychoanalysis and love. In *Getting from here to there: Analytic love, analytic process* (pp. 125-136). Hillsdale, NJ: Analytic Press.

Bass, A. (2001). It takes one to know one; or, whose unconscious is it anyway? *Psychoanalytic Dialogues,* 11:683–702.

Bion, W. R. (1970). *Attention and interpretation: A scientific approach to insight in psychoanalysis and groups.* London: Tavistock.

Blum, H. P. (2005). Psychoanalytic reconstruction and reintegration. In R. A. King, P. B. Neubauer, S. Abrams & A. S. Dowling (Eds.), *Psychoanalytic Study of the Child,* 60:295-311. New Haven, CT: Yale University Press.

Clyman, R. B. (1991). The procedural organization of emotions: A contribution from cognitive science to the psychoanalytic theory of therapeutic action. *Journal of the American Psychoanalytic Association,* 39 (Supplement):349–382.

Deutsch, D. & Ekert, A. (2013). Beyond the quantum horizon. In M. Dichristina (Ed.), *Scientific American: Special Edition—Extreme Physics,* 22(2):102-107. New York: Scientific American.

Eagle, M. (2003). Clinical implications of attachment theory. *Psychoanalytic Inquiry,* 23:27–53.

Eissler, K. R. (1953). The effect of the structure of the ego on psychoanalytic technique. *Journal of the American Psychoanalytic Association,* 1:104–143.

Ellman, S. (2010). *When theories touch: A historical and theoretical integration of psychoanalysis.* London: Karnac.

————& Moskowitz, M. (2008). A study of the Boston change process study group. *Psychoanalytic Dialogues,* 18:812–837.

Falkenstrom, F., Grant, J., Broberg, J. & Sandell, R. (2007). Self-analysis and post termination improvement after psychoanalysis and long-term psychotherapy .*Journal of the American Psychoanalytic Association,* 55:629–674.

Fiscalini, J. (2004). *Coparticipant psychoanalysis: Toward a new theory of clinical inquiry.* New York: Columbia University Press.

Freedman, N., Hoffenberg, J. D., Vorus, N. & Frosch, A. (1999). The effectiveness of psychoanalytic psychotherapy: The role of treatment duration, frequency of sessions, and the therapeutic relationship. *Journal of the American Psychoanalytic Association,* 47(3), 741–772.

Freud, S. (1894). The neuropsychoses of defence. *Standard Edition*, 3:45–61.

———(1900). The interpretation of dreams. *Standard Edition*, 4/5:1–626.

———(1905a). Psychical (or mental) treatment. *Standard Edition*, 7:283–302.

———(1905b). On psychotherapy. *Standard Edition* ,7:257–268.

———(1915a). Introductory lectures on psychoanalysis. *Standard Edition*, 15:15–239.

———(1915b). The unconscious. *Standard Edition*, 14:159–215.

———(1924). The loss of reality in neurosis and psychosis. *Standard Edition*, 9:183–187.

———(1925a). Negation. *Standard Edition*, 19:235–239.

———(1925b). The question of lay analysis. *Standard Edition*, 20:179–258.

———(1927). Fetishism. *Standard Edition*, 21:152–157.

———(1933). New introductory lectures on psychoanalysis. *Standard Edition*, 21:5–186.

Gill, M. M. (1984). Transference: A change in conception or only in emphasis? *Psychoanalytic Inquiry*, 4:489–523.

Gray, P. (1988). On the significance of influence and insight in the spectrum of psychoanalytic psychotherapies. In A. Rothstein (Ed.), *How does treatment help? On the modes of action of psychoanalytic psychotherapy* (pp. 41–50). Madison, CT: International Universities Press.

Green, A. (2011). The work of the negative and hallucinatory activity (negative hallucination). In M. K. O'Neill & S. Akhtar (Eds.), *On Freud's negation* (pp. 75–144). London: Karnac.

Heimann, P. (1950). On countertransference. *International Journal of Psychoanalysis*, 31:81–84.

Jacobs, S. (2000). *Rhetoric and dialectic from the standpoint of normative pragmatics*. Department of Communication, University of Arizona (Wikipedia).

Johnson, A. (1949). Sanctions for superego lacunae of adolescents. In K. R. Eissler (Ed.), *Searchlights on delinquency* (pp. 245–265). Madison, CT: International Universities Press.

Makari, G. J. (1994). In the eye of the beholder: Helmholtzian perception and the origins of Freud's 1900 theory of transference. *Journal of the American Psychoanalytic Association*, 42:549–580.

Mitchell, S. (1996). When interpretations fail: A new look at the therapeutic action of psychoanalysis. In L. Lifson (Ed.), *Understanding therapeutic action: Psycho-dynamic concepts of cure* (pp. 165–186). Hillsdale, NJ: The Analytic Press.

Richards, A. (2013). *Psychoanalysts of the far left: Marxist ideology and the development of American psychoanalysis.* 48th Annual Freud Lecture. PANY.

Sandell, R., Blomberg, J., Lazar, A., Carlsson, J., Broberg, J. & Schubert, J. (2000). Varieties of long-term outcome among patients in psychoanalysis and long-term psychotherapy: A review of findings in the Stockholm outcome of psychoanalysis and psychotherapy project (Stoppp). *International Journal of Psychoanalysis,* 82:921–942..

Schlesinger, H. (1988). A historical overview of conceptions of the mode of therapeutic action of psychoanalytic psychotherapy. In A. Rothstein (Ed.), *How does treatment help? On the modes of action of psychoanalytic psychotherapy* (pp. 7–27). Madison, CT: International Universities Press.

Schimek, J. G. (1975). A critical reexamination of Freud's concept of unconscious mental representation. *International Review of Psychoanalysis,* 2:171–187.

Schrodinger, E. (1935). Discussion of probability relations between separated systems. Proceedings of the Cambridge Philosophical Society. (31):555-563; (1936) (32):446-451. Cited in Wikipedia (2001): Quantum Entanglement and Information.

Segal, H. (2003). Phantasy and reality. In R. Steiner (Ed.), *Unconscious phantasy* (pp.199–209). London: Karnac.

Stolorow, R. D. (1990). Converting psychotherapy to psychoanalysis: A critique of the underlying assumptions. *Psychoanalytic Inquiry,* 10:119–130.

Tessman, L. (2003). *The analyst's analyst within.* Hillsdale, NJ: The Analytic Press.

Wilson, M. (2013). Desire and responsibility: The ethics of countertransference experience. *Psychoanalytic Quarterly,* 82:435-476.

# CHAPTER 14

# Absolute Truth and Unbearable Psychic Pain:
## Psychoanalytic Perspectives and Concrete Experience

## Reflections on "Absolute Truth and Unbearable Psychic Pain: Psychoanalytic Perspectives and Concrete Experience"

*Nancy R. Goodman*

Allan Frosch tells us that our basic way of communicating intimately with other human beings involves immersing ourselves in affect and the remarkable capacity to create meaning and understanding. He honors the heart of psychoanalytic clinical work and intellectual conceptualizing. Passion and theory are brought together as he explicates what it means to have concrete experience in the mind and how the music of symbolizing gets turned on.

Concrete experience is painful and lonely; thinking is impossible as is linking—linking to ideas, past and future, and to others. By defining concrete experience in relation to compromise formation processes and failures in contact, Allan brings hope to patients and to analytic process itself. The main route for bringing about the contact of communication in which different perspectives can be recognized, both within one's own mind and within a dialectic with another, is the willingness to know pain and to enter the unconscious mind, a journey best taken with another. By so doing one comes out of the imprisonment of unwavering beliefs and gains capacity for reflection upon oneself and others with the deepest of feeling. This is how "thing presentations" become "word presentations." This is how the baby and mother look at each other and intertwine; and this is how analytic progress ensues.

Through Allan's thinking the process of making symbolization is held within affective language. He uses words like miraculous, love, discovery, emotional field, passion and special meaning. Clearly Allan Frosch loves what takes place in the consulting room in psychoanalytic process with patients. We are brought into the mind of a truly available psychoanalyst who shows how listening intently means delving deeply into one's own psychic life with each encounter. Here is one example of how we find the spirit of Allan Frosch's belief in psychoanalysis when he turns to Freud's description of rapport between analyst and analysand as being similar to that between mother and infant, adding that " . . . he begins to tell us about the bidirectional passion and intensity of the analytic relationship" (p. xxvii). The analytic setting brings about "hypercathexis" in which the world of primary process and misguided certainty open to the making of an expansive mind and to new relating.

In his "Introduction," we also find the interconnectedness of writer/colleagues as Allan Frosch refers to Sigmund Freud, Sheldon Bach, Alan Bass, Norbert Freedman, Hans Loewald, Harold Searles, and Irving Steingart. Each has circled around how to expand knowing the concrete mind in order to bring about creativity, play, dreaming and most of all the freeing of the mind from unbearable psychic pain. I feel so fortunate to be part of this community as well. It is good to have a psychoanalytic home that generates belief in analytic work and expands reception to patients with extreme trauma and constriction in their psychic make-up. Allan Frosch believes that the rigidity and isolation of concrete mental experience can be invited into a meaningful analytic therapeutic process opening metaphor and symbolic capacity. This is a true gift to all.

In finding so much essential truth in this chapter, I miss the future that death deprives us of. I miss what would have been Allan Frosch's writing and thinking and just living that I would have been sure to learn from and to feel understood as a psychoanalytic colleague and as a person. As one of the writers in Frosch's volume about "unbearable psychic pain" and "the concrete," my co-editor, Paula Ellman and I (Chapter Four: "Enactment: Opportunity for Symbolizing Trauma") received Allan's respect and ability to establish a dialogue through which our work became more creative and better articulated. Grieving is a privilege of being able to have word representation, meaning, and love.

*       *       *

## Absolute Truth and Unbearable Psychic Pain

*Allan Frosch*

### Introduction

Abstract or conceptual thought is so much a part of our daily lives that, more often than not, we become acutely aware of it in its absence. Harold Searles (1962) brings this to our attention when he says to one of his patients, "It's just not in the cards for you, is it?" The patient responds to the metaphor by saying "I'm not playing cards," (p. 27). The literalness of the response can take us aback. This breakdown in metaphorical thinking is one form of what we call "concrete."

Concreteness, or what many refer to as desymbolised thinking/experience (Freedman, 1997, 1998; Freedman & Lavender, 2002; Searles, 1962) or thing-presentations (Freud, 1915), reduces complexity. Things are what they are! There are no other possibilities. Concreteness takes many forms, can be intermittent or persistent and, depending on our theoretical orientation, has different aetiological contexts that predispose analysts to take diverse technical positions in their clinical work. The contributors to this volume come from a variety of theoretical/clinical perspectives and their work highlights the protean nature of our subject.

In this introduction I try to articulate what I think may be a common thread in the diverse approaches whereby we attempt to help people transform the world of the concrete to the world of abstraction. In my effort to do this, I will use different terms or theory-based constructs to refer to the same thing. In using theoretically different but functionally equivalent concepts, I am responding to the richness of psychoanalytic pluralism that encourages us to look at things from multiple perspectives.

In this paper the term "symbolisation" (or abstraction) refers to a process whereby we can meaningfully understand that an event can be looked at from a variety of perspectives. Symbolisation makes it possible to look at things in an "as if" way rather than as "true" or absolute. It is a process where we can view our thoughts as objects of our thoughts (Flavell, 1963). We self-reflect. Furthermore, it is a term that always includes its counterpart: desymbolisation (concreteness), where things are what they appear to be (Frosch, 2006). In the language of metapsychology, the abstract and concrete correspond to "word . . . presentations" and "thing-presentations" (Freud, 1915). Thing-presentations operate according to the laws of the primary process. They are unconscious, absolute, driven, and have a "perceptual identity" like the hallucination of the breast for a hungry baby. Word presentation, or thought identity, is a secondary process activity that stands for/symbolises the unconscious thing-presentations. Here language is seen as a necessary part of a process of transforming primary process to secondary process organisation so that people can play with ideas, i.e., follow different paths between ideas without being led astray by the intensity of those ideas (Freud, 1900, p. 602; Laplanche & Pontalis, 1973, pp. 305–306). With this transformation we are no longer in the grip of compulsive adherence to the unconscious fantasies, i.e., thing-presentations. Words, however, while necessary, are not sufficient. The words of the analyst must take place in a particular emotional context.

I believe the analyst's capacity to regress to more primary process levels of organisation and then to re-establish his/her own level of symbolisation or secondary process activity is the central organising theme of our clinical work with all patients but, in particular, with those patients whose worlds are split into discrete bits of "reality" defined by the immediacy of experience. That is to say, those patients organised on a primary process "thing-presentation" or desymbolised level. This movement between primary and secondary process, between the concrete and the abstract, must take place in a libidinally charged emotional atmosphere in order for thing-presentations to be connected to word-presentations in a meaningful way. The libidinal investment, like the movement along the continuum of desymbolisation and symbolisation must be bidirectional. Although I believe each member of the analytic dyad helps the other in this fluidic process (Frosch, 2006), it is the analyst who must take the lead in the initiation and maintenance of this analytic milieu.

## Psychoanalysis and Concreteness

If the capacity for symbolisation is a basic requirement for social discourse (Searles, 1962) we can easily understand why the "concrete patient " is often considered *persona non grata* as a candidate for psychoanalysis. This exclusionary attitude is not limited to people who have difficulty with abstract (or conceptual) thinking and experience. It seems to be a tradition in our profession—although one best honoured by its breach—to exclude from analytic work people who make us uncomfortable. In this volume, however, we are focused on psychoanalytic perspectives of concrete experience and, in my opinion, it was Harold Searles as much, or more than anyone, who extricated the concrete patient from exclusion from the human race and from analytic treatment. He did this by making it crystal clear that the concrete thinking and experience we encounter in psychoanalysis is part of a dynamic process that he called "desymbolisation." Desymbolisation refers to a process where conceptual or abstract thought, secondary process thought, is now very literal or concrete so that once-attained metaphorical meanings have become "desymbolised" (Searles, 1962, p. 43). The impact of Searles's paper cannot be overestimated. He laid out the conceptual terrain for future generations of analysts to explore (see Lasky, 2002).

## Concreteness and Complexity

Concreteness is a topic that has been denigrated because it is both poorly understood and, most importantly, because it makes us as people and analysts so uncomfortable. As Searles says, we tend to look at the concrete person as alien, not part of the human race. The very title of this volume, *Absolute Truth and Unbearable Psychic Pain: Psychoanalytic Perspectives on Concrete Experience,* includes a variety of perspectives on how we view desymbolisation as a way of coping with psychic pain; but I think it is most likely the defensive function that we think about. And this has been a major emphasis in the literature but not an exclusive one at all (see Frosch, 1998; Grand, 2002; Schimek, 2002).

My own approach to this subject is to view concrete or desymbolised experience as a compromise formation driven by psychic pain. Like all compromise formations it has a defensive function as well as expressing libidinal and aggressive wishes. As analysts we tend to highlight its maladaptive aspect although a more even-handed approach that also highlights certain adaptive aspects is necessary for a more complete understanding of the concept. Consider the following vignette presented by Dr. Stefano Bolognini ( IPTAR, 16 January 2011):

> In her first analytic session a woman in her mid-twenties presents a dream rich in religious and sexual imagery. As she begins to associate to the dream, she stops and asks the analyst whether he would prefer to be paid in cash or by cheque.

In the context of this volume, this is a very clear example of the movement from the metaphorical to the concrete serving a defensive function. The patient seems to move away from the passionate imagery of the dream to the more prosaic topic of the business arrangements of the relationship. As analysts we know, however, that money is rarely, if ever, a passionless issue; and Dr. Bolognini tells us that the issue of money came to play a significant role in the transference. The patient wanted to be the analyst's special child and be treated free of charge. So her movement from the abstract to the concrete also allows this patient to express an inchoate transference wish; and it provides the analyst with an opportunity to have some sense of the unconscious fantasies as they present in early derivative form.

When we embrace the notion that the "the concrete" is another piece of complex analytic material, we can bring our psychoanalytic exploration of concrete experience into a more encompassing domain that allows us to look at things from multiple perspectives; but not all the time. When we are riddled with unpleasure (e.g., anxiety or some form of depressive affect) we can all narrow things down to one point of view. It is a point of view that reduces our emotional discomfort; and it is a point of view that stands alone. That is to say, it is not part of a world of ideas.

Searles (1962) puts it as follows: concrete thinking has a static, fatalistic quality, associated with severe psychopathology that sets the person "hopelessly apart from his fellow human beings" (p. 23). What Searles is referring to here is the schizophrenic patient being stuck in a world where things are what they seem—absolute truth. In the world of the concrete, there is no differentiation between inside and outside, between thought and actuality, between self and other. Thoughts and emotions have a "thing" quality that is absolute. There is no *other*, no *other* perspective. "Rarely indeed, in these writings, is there any intimation that the therapist can have the rewarding, and even exciting, experience of seeing a schizophrenic patient become free from the chains of concrete—that is undifferentiated—thinking, able now to converse with his fellow human beings" (1962, p. 27). In this scenario, of course, Searles brings in the clinician's countertransference. In other words, the therapist/analyst may also be stuck in a static, fatalistic world vis-a-vis the patient: "I found him [the same patient as above] maddeningly and discouragingly unable to deal with any comments which I couched in figurative terms. When, for example, antagonised by his self-righteous demandingness, I told him abruptly, you can't have your cake and eat it too!, I felt completely helpless when he responded to this at a literal, concrete level, by saying, I don't want to eat any cake in this hospital! You can eat cake here if you want to; I don't want to eat any cake here" (1962, p. 26).

In this vignette Searles shows us how the analyst's emotional state (antagonised by his self-righteous demandingness...told him abruptly) is a trigger to the patient's "failure" to understand the metaphor. While this kind of concreteness is not typically seen in an outpatient practice of most analysts, nor do most analysts treat schizophrenic patients, Searles makes it clear "that there is an essential continuity in all symbolic functions, the psychodynamics to be described here possess relevance to other kinds of symbolization than metaphorical thinking alone" (1962, p. 23). I would add to this that the ideas contained in Searles's paper need not be confined to the schizophrenic patient. For example, a non-schizophrenic patient said to me: "My life has always been this way and will always be this way; and there is nothing you can tell me that I haven't thought of already." In other words, "There is no inner world that I can understand so that my life can be better; and there is no difference between us." I think this example is probably fairly common and easily identifiable by most analysts. What is also identifiable, but not necessarily in the clinical moment, is the analyst's input into an enactment. Clearly, this is not peculiar to Searles or to work with a particular kind of patient. My own experience (Frosch, 2002, esp. pp. 622-629) is that the analyst's discomfort is an important catalyst for these enactments; and concrete patients often make us very uncomfortable.

The pre-Oedipal world of concrete patients is a world of great intensity. It is alive in a very particular way. It certainly may not be pleasurable in the ways that we ordinarily think of pleasure. But it is passionate and action-oriented. More often than not the passion does not have a libidinal quality but is more organised around aggression. This link to the perversions (Bass, 1997) highlights a world of part objects, driven by the immediacy of the moment. The consensual world of "reality" pales in comparison to this fantasy world (see Steingart, 1983), driven by sensation and infused with wishes that reign supreme. What we ordinarily call "emotion" is qualitatively different in this anal/paranoid-schizoid world. Emotions have a primary process "thing" quality, feel all powerful, and are inexorably linked to action (Frosch, 1995, p. 432).

The world that I am describing exists to a greater or lesser extent for everyone. We can all think of myriad examples in our own lives—just consider the battles and attendant feelings on an organisational level in the world of psychoanalysis, or at your own institute. We can certainly identify such feeling states in the patients we work with. For some, this world is intermittent and represents a regressive alteration in ego functioning; for others it has, as Searles put it, more of a static quality. And on the world's stage, assassinations are done by people who unequivocally believe that only through a direct expression of aggression to another can their own lives have any meaning. The "rightness" of their cause is absolute. And when as analysts we feel that the rightness of our cause (our interpretation) is clear and we are passionate in our conviction, we might consider that we can be setting the stage for an enactment. It is customary to say that certain kinds of patients "induce" us into an enactment. Cause and effect become organised from our subjective perspective, and we label as accurate and absolute what, in retrospect, may be our countertransference. Arnold Rothstein talks about the analyst's love for his patient as the analyst trying to work through his/her countertransference (1999); and Hans Loewald (1960) talks about the analyst's resistance in a similar way.

## Thing-presentations and Word-presentations

In this section of the paper I will outline some of Loewald's (1960, 1970, 1980) thinking that allowed him to bring the metapsychology of psychoanalysis—"the hypercathexis of word and thing-presentations" (Freud,1915)—into the world of an emotionally charged relationship between analyst and patient where each is affected by the other. Loewald's work addresses the question of how we understand the transformation of a patient's desymbolised or unsymbolised experience, i.e., experience/mentation that is regressed, or has never attained secondary status. Loewald's answer to this is the same as Freud's: there must be a "hypercathexis" of word and thing presentation to "bring about a higher psychical organisation and make it possible for the primary process to be succeeded by the secondary process" (Freud, 1915, p. 202). In his discussion Loewald moves hypercathexis from a purely energic term to a transformational concept that takes place in a libidinised reciprocal psychic field (1970, pp. 64–65). Loewald is very much aware of the impact of his words: "While this may sound unfamiliar and perhaps too fanciful, it is only an elaboration, in nontechnical terms, of Freud's deepest thoughts ... " (1970, p. 65).

For Loewald defence—and here he is talking about repression—is "understood as an unlinking" (1980, p. 188) between thing and word presentations. The link between symbol and that which is symbolised (word and thing presentations) is repressed, i.e., severed or loosened; and the act of hypercathexis re-establishes the link (1980, pp. 183, 188). The analytic task involves (and here we can say this in a number of ways), e.g., 1) making the unconscious conscious, 2) transforming experience-bound and action-oriented, unconscious things to "mental representations that stand for the experience" (Lasky, 1993, p. 260n.), or 3) bringing the primary process under the domain of secondary process organisation. The language we use to describe this process differs depending on our theoretical orientation. Whatever terminology we use, however, the process of transforming things to words is life-altering. It is a new way of ordering the world and allows the person to make inferences about an event that go beyond the immediately observable experience (Bruner, Goodnow & Austin, 1956). And the analyst does this through the use of words, i.e., interpretation. Even if we leave aside what we mean by "interpretation," there are a number of points to be made about this statement that bear directly on our understanding of the analytic process in general and, in particular, on how we understand the notion of concreteness.

## *Love and Miracles*

The interpretive work that links primary process things and secondary process words represents a link between analyst and patient. And this is Loewald's "novel" (1970, p. 68) approach to the concept of hypercathexis. "Hypercathexis, I believe, cannot be adequately understood if we fail to take into account that it originates within a supraindividual psychic field. Expressed in traditional psychoanalytic terms, the essential factor is that cathected objects are themselves cathecting agents. The subject which cathects objects is at the same time being cathected by those objects ..." (1970, p. 63). The mother-infant/child relationship and the analyst-analysand relationship:

> Are relations between mutually cathecting agents, and the cathecting of each partner is a function of the other's cathecting ... The higher-order cathecting activity of his libidinal objects ( parents) constitutes, as it

were, the first hypercathexis. In so far as the objects' cathecting operations are on secondary process levels (although they are by no means
exclusively so), they have the potential of hypercathexes in terms of the
subject's psychic processes. (1970, p. 63)

In the therapeutic situation it is the analyst "[who] helps to bring this
about ... the analyst, mediates this union . . . a new version of the way in
which transformation of primary into secondary processes opened up in
childhood, through mediation of higher organisation by way of early
object-relations (1960, p. 31)." And Loewald makes it clear that in order
to immerse himself in the patient's world, the analyst "must be able to
regress within himself to the level of organization on which the patient
is stuck .. ." (1960, p. 26). The analyst, like the good-enough parent, must
also be able to return to a more secondary process mode of functioning.

And all of this occurs in the context of love. For Loewald the analytic
relationship is based on love and respect for the patient and the patient's
love for the analyst. Just as it is impossible to have an analysis without
loving the patient (1970, p. 65), it is impossible to have an analysis
without the patient's love for the analyst. We can put all of this into the
language of libidinal investments or transference/countertransference.
In doing this we communicate to our colleagues and ourselves that the
love we are talking about falls within the "scientific," the "analytic,"
domain. We do not want to be misunderstood, and Loewald is acutely
aware of the potential impact of his words: "In many quarters there still
seems to be a tendency to put up a 'no admittance' sign when
metapsychological considerations point to object relations as being not
merely regulative *but essential constitutive factors in psychic structure
formation*" (1970, p. 66, my emphasis). In the words of the poet, when
we make an emotional (i.e., libidinal) investment in another person,
"that person seems at once to belong to a different universe, is sur-
rounded with poetry, (and) makes of one's life a sort of stirring arena .. ."
( Proust; 1913, p. 334). It is in this stirring arena of the analytic situation
that the words of the analyst can take on a special meaning, a meaning
that leads to an internalisation of a differentiated relationship that
increases "the hypercathectic resources of the individual" (1970, p. 63).

It is this emotional atmosphere, this hypercathexis of self and other, that Freud was talking about when he said that the words of the analyst have the power to create "miraculous cures" (1905a, p. 289). It is easy enough to write off Freud's comments as hyperbole, as the overly optimistic words of someone embarking on a path of great discovery. While this may well be the case consider for a moment the patient that Searles discussed who was so concrete. This patient, Searles tells us, "after five years of work ... can communicate confidently, with rare exceptions, in metaphorical as well as literal terms, seeing both levels of meanings in his own comments and in mine" (1962, p. 30). This seems like quite a miraculous accomplishment.

## *Passionate Abstractions*

Although Freud's language in the 1905 paper is very far from the metapsychology of energy transformations, his ideas in this paper are consistent with his own metapsychological abstractions in 1915 as well as Loewald's use of metapsychology. In the 1905 paper Freud presents, in the concrete immediacy of experience, the underpinnings of his energic abstractions. When Freud talks about the rapport between analyst and patient and likens it to the relationship between a mother and her infant (1905a, p. 295), he begins to tell us about the bidirectional passion and intensity of the analytic relationship.

Freud says quite directly that the analyst helps to create an expectation of faith and hope in his patient that lends a certain magic to the analyst's words (1905a, p. 291). And it is the analyst's interest that potentiates this "propitious state" of mind in the patient (p. 293). And, I would add, it is not an interest that can be understood in purely intellectual or cerebral terms. In English the word "interest" refers to the relation of being objectively concerned in something. In the German *(Interesse)*, there is more of a sense of personal involvement. It is related to a very common phrase *(im stiche lassen)*, "to leave in the lurch" (cf. Freud, 1910, p. 12); thus "one's interest or personal involvement with a patient allows us to enter most profoundly into the core of the patient's life—or soul" (Seele, 1905a, p. 283n.; 1905b, p. 254). Without this interest/involvement we are left out in the lurch.

Freud's language conveys a very personal connection and repulsion that speaks directly to the passions of the analytic relationship. In the complex and highly charged analytic situation the reciprocal relationship between expectations based on hope and faith and the analyst's interest argues against linear statements of cause and effect, so that interest and expectation are co-constructed or subject and object are hypercathected. This kind of process has been described by Bach (2006) who likens the analyst's attention to his patient as a kind of secular prayer with curative value in its own right.

## Concluding Comments

It is in this emotional context that we can best understand Loewald's thinking that the analyst's interpretive activity gives rise to a new mental representation: "an intrapsychic perception induced by the words of the analyst that may be conscious but in *all likelihood may occur outside of consciousness*" (1980, p. 183). I emphasise the latter part of Loewald's statement because it resonates so well with much of our current psycho-analytic outcome research that highlights the central importance of the internalisation (largely unconscious—see Falkenstrom, Grant, Broberg & Sandell, 2007, p. 666) of the differentiated relationship with the analyst for long-term therapeutic gain (Frosch, 2011). I believe this is what Loewald means when he talks about increasing the patient's resources for hypercathexis. I understand this as an increased capacity to [re]-establish a link between the thing and the word so that the concrete can enter into the world of abstraction.

But Loewald has more to say about interpretation and the transformation of the concrete to the abstract. It is not simply establishing or re-establishing a connection between the unconscious fantasy (thing-presentation) and the consciously (Loewald refers to it as preconscious) perceived object (word-presentation). There must be an optimal linking. Mental functioning is seen as a compromise between a too intimate and intense closeness to the unconscious (with its "creative and destructive aspects," 1980, p. 189) and a less than adequate libidinal link between word and thing so that language has a "hollow quality . . . no longer vibrant and warmed by the 'fire' of the unconscious" (p. 189). In the first instance the unconscious fantasy replaces reality and we are in the world of things—the concrete. In the second instance language is meaningless and the consensual world of reality loses any significance. These are two aspects of the same multidimensional continuum differentially emphasised by the authors in this volume depending on their theoretical orientation and clinical technique. In the chapters that follow, the abstractions of thing presentations and word presentations in a hypercathected psychic field are replaced with the concrete immediacy of the relationship between analyst and patient as they work to transform absolute beliefs into ideas that stand in relation to other ideas.

## Acknowledgements

My thanks to Dr William Fried, Batya Monder, and Ruth Oscharoff for their input during the preparation of this paper.

## References

Bach, S. (2006). *Getting from here to there: Analytic love, analytic process.* Hillsdale, NJ: The Analytic Press.

Bass, A. (1997). The problem of "concreteness." *Psychoanalytic Quarterly,* 66:642–682.

Bolognini , S. (2011). A session with Antonia. Presentation at IPTAR.

Bruner, J. S., Goodnow, J. L. & Austin, G. A. (1956). *A study of thinking.* New York: Wiley.

Flavell, J. H. (1963). *The developmental psychology of Jean Piaget.* Princeton, NJ: Van Nostrand.

Freedman, N. (1997). On receiving the patient's transference: The symbolizing and desymbolizing countertransference. *Journal of the American Psychoanalytic Association, 45:* 79–103.

———(1998). Psychoanalysis and symbolization: Legacy or heresy? In C. Ellman, S. Grand, M. Silvan & S. Ellman (Eds.), *The Modern Freudians: Contemporary psychoanalytic technique* (pp. 79–97). Northvale, NJ: Jason Aronson.

————& Lavender, J. (2002). On desymbolization: The concept and observations on anorexia and bulimia. *Psychoanalysis and Contemporary Thought,* 25:165–199.

————Lasky, R. & Ward, R. (2009). The upward slope: A study of psychoanalytic transformations. *Psychoanalytic Quarterly, 78:* 201–231.

Freud, S. (1900). The Interpretation of Dreams. *Standard Edition, 5.*

————(1905a). Psychical (or mental) treatment. *Standard Edition, 7.*

————(1905b). Freud's psycho-analytic procedure. *Standard Edition, 7.*

————(1910). Five lectures on psycho-analysis. *Standard Edition 11.*

————(1915). The unconscious. *Standard Edition, 14.*

Frosch, A. (1995). The preconceptual organization of emotion. *Journal of the American Psychoanalytic Association,* 43:423–447.

————(1998). Narcissistic injury and sadomasochistic compensation in a latency-age boy. In P. Beren (Ed.), *Narcissistic disorders in children and adolescents: Diagnosis and treatment* (pp. 263–280). Northvale, NJ: Jason Aronson.

————(2002). Transference: Psychic reality and material reality. *Psychoanalytic Psychology,* 19:603–633.

————(2006). Analyzability. *Psychoanalytic Review,* 93:835–843.

————(2011). The effect of frequency and duration on psychoanalytic outcome: A moment in time. *Psychoanalytic Review,* 98:11–38.

Laplanche, J. & Pontalis, J. B. (1973). *The language of psychoanalysis.* New York: W. W. Norton.

Lasky, R. (1993). *Dynamics of development and the therapeutic process.* Northvale, NJ: Jason Aronson.

————(Ed.) (2002). *Symbolization and desymbolization: Essays in honor of Norbert Freedman.* New York: Other Press.

Loewald, H. W. (1960). On the therapeutic action of psycho-analysis. *International Journal of Psychoanalysis,* 41:16–33.

————(1970). Psychoanalytic theory and the psychoanalytic process. *Psychoanalytic Study of the Child,* 25:45–68.

————(1980). Primary process, secondary process, and language (1978). In *Papers on Psychoanalysis* (pp. 178–206). New Haven, CT: Yale University Press.

Proust, M. (1913). *In search of lost time, Volume 1, Swann's way.* New York: The Modern Library, 2003.

Rothstein, A. (1999). Some implications of the analyst feeling disturbed while working with disturbed patients. *Psychoanalytic Quarterly,* 68:541–558.

Searles, H. F. (1962). The differentiation between concrete and metaphorical thinking in the recovering schizophrenic patient. *Journal of the American Psychoanalytic Association,* 10:22–49.

Steingart, I. (1983). *Pathological play in borderline and narcissistic personalities.* Jamaica, NY: Spectrum.

## Reflections on "Silent Interpretations, the Creation of New Meaning and the Transformation of Facts into Information"

*Ruth Oscharoff*

Allan and I met when we were in analytic training, and it was my good fortune to be married to him for 30 years. We shared not only our personal and family lives, but also much in our psychoanalytic worlds. He had an unwavering belief in psychoanalysis and a deep interest in theoretical understandings, clinical process, and the complexities of the relationship between analyst and patient. As this collection shows, his papers reflect the progression of his thinking over his career.

Until shortly before his death, he was drafting a paper that, unfortunately, was not completed, and therefore is not included in this book. The working title he crafted for it was "Silent Interpretations, the Creation of New Meaning, and the Transformation of Facts into Information." The theme continues and clarifies his thinking about the intertwining and relative influence of explicit and implicit processes in determining the mutative effects of psychoanalytic treatment. Along with this, the paper reflects his interest in the unconscious processes in the minds of both analyst and patient and how one affects the other consciously and unconsciously, verbally or silently. Clinical observations led him to believe that there are times of silence in sessions where there is unconscious communication between patient and analyst resulting in the transformation of facts into analytic information that is mutative. He considered such moments "silent interpretations."

It is interesting and poignant that Allan was writing about this theme when there were more silent times for him; he was coming to terms with the waning of his life as he gradually succumbed to cancer. These were often moments, I know, when words could not express his own experience although powerful connections were felt within himself and between himself and others. Emanating from a realm of the unknown and unknowable, such silences were filled with meaning for Allan and those around him.

He had hoped that this paper could be completed, but it will have to remain as a silent expression of his evolving psychoanalytic thinking and his deep feelings for all of those who were part of his life.

# *Allan Frosch*

Allan Frosch, PhD, FIPA, was a Fellow (Training and Supervising Analyst) and Faculty at the Institute for Psychoanalytic Training and Research (IPTAR). He served as IPTAR President for two terms, and prior to that was co-director of the IPTAR Clinical Center (ICC) and Dean of Training. He was also on the Faculty at the Institute for Psychoanalytic Education of the NYU Medical Center. Dr. Frosch maintained a psychoanalytic practice with adults, adolescents and children in New York City.

# THE ALLAN FROSCH LEGACY FUND

In the decades since Allan helped found IPTAR's Clinical Center, the ICC has provided treatment to thousands of adults and children in the New York metropolitan area in eight different languages. It has sponsored research projects, professional conferences, new community models of psychoanalytic treatment, internship and externship programs in six New York City elementary and high schools, and programs to provide pro-bono treatment to asylum seekers; and in conjunction with the International Rescue Committee and Sanctuary for Families, it has also sponsored group treatment for refugees. The IPTAR Clinical Center has won national awards from the American Psychoanalytic Association for bringing psychoanalytic treatment to the community.

The Frosch Legacy Fund was established in the last weeks of Allan's life. Its sole purpose is to strengthen and preserve the infrastructure of the ICC which has been supported by a vast volunteer network of administrators, program coordinators and clinical supervisors.

When Allan was told of IPTAR's decision to create this fund, he wrote to us:

> I am touched and honored. The ICC is IPTAR's legacy, and it has meant a great deal to me to have been involved in its growth. I've always believed that psychoanalysis is for all people and I'm proud to have played a role in providing clinical help to those adults and children who could not afford it without the services of the ICC. I'm grateful that you are thinking of continuing that legacy in my name.
>
> My love, Allan.

All profits from this book will be donated to the Frosch Legacy Fund. The Editors would like to thank IP Press for making this possible

If you would like to donate to the Fund, please go to the website: iptar.org/icc-frosch-legacy-fund.

CPSIA information can be obtained
at www.ICGtesting.com
Printed in the USA
FSHW021616090519
57978FS